THE SPEECH OF THE GRAIL

To Liron —
who did so
much to welcome
my coming to Oregon
And who models the
strong individuality that
people born on June 13
seem to embody. You were
A birthday gift for Grandma
And you also have been for
me. I want to know
you better!
wherever you're ready!
Love,
Linda

STUDIES IN IMAGINATION

A series edited in collaboration with
THE INSTITUTE FOR THE STUDY OF IMAGINATION

THE SPEECH OF THE GRAIL

A Journey toward Speaking that Heals and Transforms

Linda Sussman

LINDISFARNE PRESS

Published in the United States by Lindisfarne Press
RR 4, Box 94-A1
Hudson, N.Y. 12534

Library of Congress Cataloging-in-Publication Data
Sussman, Linda, 1945–
    The speech of the grail : a journey toward speaking that heals and
transforms / Linda Sussman.
        p. cm. — (Studies in imagination)
    Includes bibliographical references.
    ISBN 0-940262-69-X
    1. Wolfram, von Eschenbach, 12th cent. Parzival   2. Perceval
(Legendary character) — Romances — History and criticism.
3. Arthurian romances — 4. Grail — Romances — History and
criticism. I. Title. II. Series.
    PT1688.S87   1995
    831'.21 — dc20   95–1146
                                                                   CIP

Cover art: Grosse Heidelberger Liederhandschrift "Codex Manesse,"
courtesy of University of Heidelberg Library

Book design by Studio 31

10 9 8 7 6 5 4 3 2 1

Printed in the United States of America

Permission has been granted for the following. Rumi, "Answers from the Elements"
from *Open Secret: Versions of Rumi,* translated by John Moyne and Coleman Barks,
published by Threshold Books, Brattleboro, Vermont. Reprinted by permission.
Rainer Maria Rilke, "Sonnets to Orpheus" #7 from *Selected Poems of Rainer Maria
Rilke,* edited and translated by Robert Bly. Copyright 1981 by Robert Bly. Reprinted
by permission of HarperCollins Publishers, Inc. William Stafford, "When I Met My
Muse" from *An Oregon Message* by William Stafford. Copyright 1987 by William
Stafford. Reprinted by permission of HarperCollins Publishers, Inc. Lewis Hyde's
version of "Taittiriya Upanishad" from *The Gift* by Lewis Hyde. Copyright 1979,
1980, 1983 by Vintage Books. Reprinted by permission of Random House. Mary
Oliver, "The Swan" from *The House of Light,* published by Beacon Press. Reprinted
by permission.

*This book is dedicated to the
marriage of heart and mind in speaking
and to all who strive in service of this union.*

Why does one write,
if not to put one's pieces together.
From the moment we enter school or church,
education chops us into pieces; it teaches us to divorce
soul from body and mind from heart. The fishermen of the
Colombian coast must be learned doctors of ethics and
morality, for they invented the word *sentipensante,*
feeling-thinking, to define language
that speaks the truth.

EDUARDO GALLEANO
The Book of Embraces

Table of Contents

Foreword
by Robert Sardello

The Grail story forming the substance of this wonderful interpretive study by Linda Sussman was set down in writing around A.D. 1208. *Parzival* differs considerably from other epics because it is a story, not about what happened in humanity's past, but about what can happen in its future. Moreover, this great work does not belong as much to literary tradition as to the body of initiation practices; that is to say, it forms a practical guide by which any individual can find the way to the spiritual worlds. Linda Sussman's book helps us along this way by suggesting a healthy approach to spiritual practice. This begins by developing the capacity of attention and a strong, reproductive imagination. Her close, descriptive approach to the text of *Parzival* also provides a basis for developing further capacities.

The value of what this author contributes cannot be overestimated. It is a beginning, which nonetheless is carried through to the deepest and highest levels to which one might aspire. Until one can make, hold, and sustain inner pictures in consciousness, further inner work falls apart into abstractions or self-constructed egoistic fantasies. An additional merit of Sussman's approach is its indication that strengthening imagination does not have the purpose of merely expanding consciousness beyond ordinary perception and thought. Rather, such strengthening is always intimately concerned with our earthly world, with becoming ever more vividly alive, which for our author shows forth most clearly in human speaking.

Sussman's detailed recounting of each of the sixteen books of *Parzival* is far more than a summary intended to simplify the work of encountering a complex text. In retelling the story, she is demonstrating the necessity of developing the ability to reproduce inner pictures of something given first through the senses. Practicing the art of the storyteller, she is, at the same time, practicing the art of transforming a text that is read into a story that is heard. Her readers will immediately recognize an inner experience that is quite revealing. When we read something that is in the nature of an explanation, it makes us tired; it is as if our life forces were expended in giving body to something that, by its nature, is abstract. Abstractions suck the life out of us. Sometimes such a sacrifice is well worthwhile. But, if it is carried out prematurely, that is, without a living imagination, the result is that we feel we have been depleted to provide life for a sclerotic world that left on its own would run its rightful course of withering away and dying. Hearing the story of Parzival, on the other hand, and recreating it in the inner word, does something quite different. We are refreshed rather than exhausted. A work of the imagination gives life rather than sucks it away. We know that Sussman is a storyteller rather than a summarizer because, hearing the story as she tells it, we feel more alive, more awake, more vital.

An alchemical picture may help us to understand the artistry involved. Alchemy is concerned with transforming soul life in such a way that one gradually comes to perceive the world not as a collection of objects but as a living, metamorphosing, creating activity. Such alchemical work begins with the process known as putrefaction. A well-known alchemical emblem of the twelfth century, for example, was the alchemical Tree of Knowledge. This tree had twelve branches, each containing a picture to be contemplated. The first picture — the first branch — depicted a black bird, with wings outstreched, standing on the earth. Beneath this, under the earth, lay a human skull.

This bird, flexing its wings, is an image of our ordinary consciousness, ready to take flight and take in whatever the world offers for perception and thinking. It is an image of the way we take in the contents of the manifest world, while the skull beneath the earth depicts the dying away of immediate perception into the dark recesses of the skull. The whole tableau thus indicates what typically happens in our ordinary way of being receptive to the world. We take in the world and it recedes into the tomb of the skull. An immediate presence to something living is deadened when we try to know about things by separating them from us rather than by finding the way to let them live within us, which would lead to a new kind of thinking, a thinking with the world rather than about it. Putrefaction takes place because what we take in recedes into us and lies there rotting, like stinking refuse. This refuse becomes the habits of our soul life — all the opinions, half-formed ideas taken from others, prejudices, reactions — with which we navigate in the world. The alchemists recognized that putrefaction must be met with the development of inner forces, primarily the force of imagination. The first step toward true imagination involves developing the capacity to make accurate inner pictures that mirror what we encounter from outside. This first step develops the ability to concentrate the soul. Linda Sussman's retelling the story of Parzival teaches this art of concentration. Nevertheless, it is up to the reader to form the inner images of the story, gradually building them up to the point that he or she can live within the story as a whole, and not seek quick results.

One can work a very long time with the tale of Parzival, the first thread composing the tapestry of this book. However, the retelling of each episode of the story is followed by two commentaries. The first addresses the reader as a person working with the process of initiation. The second addresses the reader's gradual development toward a deepened experience and practice of the mystery of the word, of speech. The first commentaries can be seen as a way of intensifying the images of the story. They are not so much interpretations of the story as aids in hearing the story more vividly. It is extremely helpful, following a reading of a commentary, to go back and re-read the episode of the story that it deals with. Sussman's work, I believe, is best approached as a process to work with, rather than a text to read through from beginning to end.

The second commentary following the retelling of each part of the story is more on the order of interpretation. This interpretive work constitutes one of the ways of approaching the question of the meaning of *Parzival*. Linda Sussman, who has a particular interest in the act of human speech, has discovered that Parzival's path of development corresponds to what is involved in working to transform our use of words from a mere utilitarian mode of communication into an imaginative language that simultaneously embodies thinking, feeling, and action. This interpretation of *Parzival,* of course, is only one of the many possible ways of understanding this work. Other interpretations include cultural, psychological, spiritual, literary, historical, and even educational ones. That Wolfram's text can simultaneously make itself available to such a variety of approaches verifies its worth as a true world view. As a further orientation toward Ms. Sussman's work, therefore, I would now like to say something more about the world view inherent in the Grail quest. This will perhaps show why her truly new understanding of this quest as having to do with living speech perhaps comes closer to its essence than previous interpretations.

The Grail is said to be the chalice of the Last Supper which Joseph of Arimathea used to received Christ's blood on the cross at the moment the spear of Longinus pierced His side. Such a legendary origin has led to many quests for the literal object, the chalice, known as the Grail. A broader, more comprehensive view, however, shows that we have to do not with a literal object, but with the mysteries surrounding the possible connection between the earthly world and the spiritual worlds. Stories of a mysterious concave object surround this connection.

Over six thousand years ago, at a particular time of the year, shamans would go into a dark cave or carefully constructed mound built at a geomantically selected site aligned with particular star movements and the yearly course of the sun. This cavernous hollow was completely dark except for the light admitted by a single slit. At a particular moment, a beam of light from the starry world would enter the opening and fall upon two cups carved into a rock receptacle. A polished rock crystal was placed in each cup and, at the moment the beam of light entered, it was split by the crystals, striking the shaman who was in deep meditation and transforming him or her into the lightbeam itself. At that moment, the shaman experienced a vision of his or her own creation. This vision consisted of seeing that the human being was the microcosmic form of the whole of the macrocosm. The macrocosm, in this vision, was seen to be the working of angelic beings, and the forming of the cosmos was seen to be at the same time the forming of the Cosmic Human. The shaman then carried this vision of the birth of the Human to the community by carrying some of the water from the hollowed stone in a cup and distributing it. For the community, this ritual was a constant reminder of the necessity of harmonizing the human being with the cosmos, of maintaining the ongoing relationship of the human and the spiritual worlds as an actual reality. The site of the ritual I have described still exists at Newgrange, in Ireland, and its use for this purpose has been carefully verified.[1] The content of the vision, of course, is not available as physical evidence, but was given to us through the clairvoyant research of Rudolf Steiner, who also spoke of the work of Anthroposophy, the investigation of the human being as a being of the cosmos, as a Grail science.[2]

The shaman saw an intimate correlation between the dome of the heavens and the inverted dome of the receptacle which received the light; that is to say, all of earthly creation is in the image of the divine spiritual worlds. Further, the spiritual worlds need the earthly world to complete their purpose, and the earthly world needs the spiritual worlds to complete its purpose. Virtually all sacred traditions acknowledge this relationship by giving special significance to a sacred vessel. The Buddhist focuses on the rice bowl as a sacred object of meditation; the Taoist sees the three-legged bronze cauldron, the I-Ching, as reflecting the divine world; the Jew passes the Seder cup, which contains knowledge of the Cabala; the Christian takes communion from the chalice, uniting the recipient with Christ.

In many myths, the ongoing relation between the spiritual worlds and this world is depicted as a miraculous vessel that gives abundant life. Irish legend tells of Dagda's Cauldron, which could feed an entire army without becoming empty. Nordic myth speaks of the vessel of Sinnreger containing a beverage of wisdom and inspiration. Welsh legend speaks of the basket of Gwyddno Gahanhir. Although food for only one person was placed in this basket, it was found on opening to contain sustenance for a hundred. Similarly, Joseph of Arimathea, who was imprisoned for forty years without food, was sustained by the chalice in which he had caught Christ's blood.

This Grail chalice, the chalice of the blood of Christ, which became the focus of the thirteenth-century stories of Parzival, is of particular importance, because it has to do with the transformation of the individual human being into a chalice. The responsibility for maintaining the connection with the spiritual worlds now falls upon each and every individual and must be carried out in completely individual ways. The many stories, myths, and sacred practices surrounding a holy vessel all prefigure and prepare the way for transferring cosmic responsibility to the individual. Further, the mystery of true individuality lies in the fact that the Christ lives within each of us, making the way to the Grail a Christ initiation. Wolfram von Eschenbach's *Parzival* is the story of such an initiation.

As Linda Sussman points out in the very beginning of her work, Parzival's quest is a path not to perfection, but rather to forming a right relationship to our imperfections. Parzival makes all kinds of errors and mistakes, and, indeed, commits murderous deeds. This path through the middle, through the veil of the world, requires learning through earthly misery and guilt, rather than trying to maintain innocence and purity of soul. Further, it requires moving beyond the self-absorption that can come about through suffering. It demands sensing a possible future, rather than feeling endlessly trapped by the past. The spiritual path of the middle is the path through the world. This means coming into a right relationship with evil, neither rejecting it, trying to stay away from it, projecting it onto others, or fighting it only from the outside; rather one must become conscious of it, which is a gradual process. Because it directly confronts the mystery of evil, a mystery that we are just now entering into in ways never encountered before, Parzival is a picturing of the future rather than of the past.

In the far distant past, evil was imagined primarily in cosmological images and myths as a cosmic struggle between the creating angels and the fallen angels. Thus, evil was imagined as a struggle that was of concern mainly to the gods, the results of this concern filtering down into the human world. Later, among the Greeks, evil was felt to be closer to this world; but its resolution was primarily an aesthetic work. Then, in the Middle Ages, evil became a soul problem, and the task was to maintain purity of soul in the face of clear temptations. Today, however, and this has been coming for a long time, evil is pervasive in the human world; and it is no longer possible to delineate clearly where good and evil separate. Here, the importance of speech comes to the center. In the future, as is already clear in the way that cold, institutional evil now permeates the world, it will be impossible to tell in any outer way what is good and what is evil. Good and evil will use the same language — as is already happening. Navigating through this mixture will require an inner sense of truth for how one speaks rather than for the content spoken. Now, this inner sense of truth in speaking concerns a living connection with the Christ as Logos — the divine Word made human — living within the heart of each individual.

The path of initiation into the Christ as Logos has nothing to do with institutionalized religion. The Church, as an institution, can no longer serve as an adequate outer guide into the inner mysteries of human evolution because it too, of necessity, is pervaded by evil. This is not to say that the Church is evil. It is no longer possible to say that some things are evil and others are good. Evil is like death; everyone takes part; it is unavoidable. But that does not give everything over to it. However, it does mean that navigation becomes infinitely more difficult, primarily because everything on the outside that looks evil must be located by each one of us within, as part of who we are. We must find the forces within to gradually transform evil through a self-transformation that never takes its eye off the wider world. Such transformation, as shown in *Parzival,* begins with the steps toward self-knowledge, beginning in Soul Wisdom, whose intricacies in *Parzival* revolve around the women of the Grail.

Linda Sussman works in a wonderful way to bring to the fore of our imaginations the central importance of the women of the Grail. She carefully avoids casting this epic into a male initiation experience or falling into the traps that could cast the whole story into an anti-feminist tale, of interest only as new fodder for the Men's movement. She also avoids quick categorization of the figures of this story into the now standard Jungian abstractions of Anima and Animus. Indeed, all of the actions of *Parzival* can be said to originate from, be sustained by, and revolve around the feminine characters. The women of the Grail are representatives of the soul qualities necessary for transforming the self, for realizing that true individuality lies in coming to know ourselves as human spiritual beings. None, absolutely none, of the women figures of the Grail are passive; they are all receptive, and a totally new, active sense of the quality of radical receptivity slowly dawns on the attentive reader.

Attention to the women figures in this story leads to the great temptation of interpreting the story in terms of depth psychology. A new and enlarged sense of soul is needed not to commit another reductionistic psychological explanation. Soul is first and foremost the Wisdom of the Cosmos, known in the Egyptian Mysteries as Isis and, later in earth evolution, as the Sophia. There is Soul, and then again, there is soul. Soul as Sophia, as described in the Gnostic myths, refers to the Intelligence of the Cosmos, She through whom everything in the Cosmos works with the right rhythm, the right timing, and in the right relationship. At the same time, Sophia is the Intelligence of the Earth, She through whom everything of the natural world reflects Cosmic Wisdom. But, Sophia, again as told in the Gnostic myths, is also fallen. In Her desire to be united with the Creator, she becomes disoriented and is cast into the realm of Chaos at the center of the Earth. Here She suffers torments instigated by other fallen beings — the demiurge and a lion-faced being filled with pride. Her torments are grief, fear, bewilderment, and ignorance, from which the elements of earth, air, fire, and water are formed, condensing into fallen nature. In *Parzival,* we must gain a feeling for the women or Soul figures as depicting Sophia intertwined with individual soul life. Sussman does not make this distinction, but it is crucial. Four of the Sophia representatives — Herzeloyde, Belacane, Jeschute, and Sigune — express the quality of grieving. Only when there is a redemption of the Sophia, which occurs in various ways for each of these Sophia representatives, does a harmonious individual soul life become possible.

The difference between Isis and the Sophia concerns the fact, made available to us through the spiritual research of Rudolf Steiner, that Sophia has united herself completely with the human being in such a manner that the whole of the Cosmos exists within each individual; every individual human is an expression of the whole of the spiritual Cosmos, the macrocosm in the microcosm of individuality. But, because Sophia is fallen, soul life is pervaded with an intractable ground of grieving, fear, ignorance, and bewilderment. Individual soul life is separate from, but not independent of, these passions. Individual soul life consists of all our sympathies and antipathies; it is filled with all our desires, needs, wants, and, most importantly, with all that needs to be worked through from past lives, namely karma. What modern depth psychology has yet to see, but what is already contained in *Parzival,* is that soul work must be simultaneously oriented both toward becoming free in the individual soul realm — which does not mean clearing all desire, but rather becoming fully conscious of desire — and toward a soul conversion, a turning around of soul life in the larger sense of Soul that is fully receptive to the world and reaches toward the spirit. This is necessary to bring about the restoration of Nature from the effects of the fall. If modern psychologies of soul were completely successful in finally getting every person in the world to care for individual soul life, the primary passions of fallen Sophia would still exist; in fact, we would be more present than ever to grieving, fear, ignorance, and bewilderment. Until it becomes apparent that soul work is not for our benefit alone, but for the sake of the world, care of soul is doomed to becoming trapped forever in one egotism after another. Now, the nexus uniting individual soul with World Soul lies in the realm of the heart, which involves the adventures surrounding Gawan.

Some of the best work done by Ms. Sussman is to be found in the chapters relating to Gawan. As she points out, many literary critics over the years have been unable to make sense of the Gawan books, and thus leave them out of consideration, feeling they are not a part of the original text and must have been added later. Building on the work of Walter Johannes Stein, Sussman sees that Gawan concerns the heart aspect of Parzival. The conversion of soul life from individual matters alone to a concern for the Soul of the World takes place through uniting cognitive capacities that are spiritually-oriented with the life of feeling, centered in the heart. The heart is also the center of the commingling of the individual soul with the Soul of the World. From Gawan's first appearance, we learn that he is a healer. The capacity of healing depends on the ability, demonstrated by Gawan, of individual soul perception coupled with perception of the soul qualities of the world. Gawan heals a wounded knight with herbs and is also instrumental in the more subtle healing of his beloved, Orgeluse. He loves her from the moment he sees her, and in spite of her constant and vociferous rejections, he never wavers from his love. He sees deeply into her soul, sees that something is blocked, but does not seek to make her reveal it so he can gain power over her; rather he acts in the world on her behalf in such a way that healing follows. Psychotherapists and counselors would do well to carefully study these books for insights into the way soul healing comes about and, in particular, into the delicate balance needed between individual soul and World Soul.

Through Gawan's actions, we are also led to insight into how evil may be healed through soul. Here, even Gawan has much to learn. The marvelous scene of Gawan's trials in the Castle of Wonders, the domain of the black magician, Clinschor — his encounter with the Wonder Bed, being tossed to and fro, warding off the arrows from all sides, fighting to the death with the lion — are all pictures of coming face to face with the interior of the heart, the center able to work in the right way with evil.

First, we have a picture of evil in the very construction of the Castle of Wonders. Upon entering the castle, Gawan sees a great domed entrance hall painted the colors of a peacock. The peacock signifies a level of spiritual initiation. In alchemy, this stage of initiation has to do with attaining a first level of connection with the spiritual worlds. But what is attained at this level must be sacrificed. That is, one must give up what one learns of the spiritual worlds at this stage. If it is not given up, and instead, the knowledge is used to bring about effects in the physical world, the result is destructive to the world, even though it might initially look helpful. For example, contemporary scientists, the truly creative ones, sometimes come to this level of consciousness, mostly without knowing it. Discoveries are made and then immediately put into practical use, without an understanding of the whole picture. Thus, some invention, some technology, some scientific discovery is put into use prematurely. Only much later, often generations later, do we see that what looked helpful is actually harmful. The Castle of Wonders is a citadel for this kind of bringing of evil into the world, which, remember, is not to be fought against, but balanced with soul capacities.

In a way, the Castle of Wonders is a technological marvel. The centerpiece of this technology is the magical pillar in the tower. Looking into this pillar, one is able to see what is happening for a distance of six miles. Such a marvel is somewhat analogous to the present electronic technology, which allows us to make phone calls anywhere in the world, but works also to make us forgetful of far more important connections to be made — connections with the spiritual worlds — that can never come about through materialistic technology.

Another most important aspect of the magical powers of the Castle is connected with the fact that four hundred women are imprisoned here. And, while there are men in the castle, no relationship takes place between the men and the women. Coupled with this, Clinschor's magical powers stem from the damming up of his desires because of his being castrated. Clinschor, master of the Castle of Wonders, apprenticed himself to black magic, transforming sexual energy into power. Here, we have another, most helpful image related to the present technological world. The kind of technology now promoted is not only excessively masculine, it is also a deviated masculine, lacking a healthy relationship to the feminine or soul element, which it nevertheless relies upon, and indeed feeds upon. It is as if a great deal of modern technology replaces what is supposed to be going on in healthy relationships between men and women with materialistic comfort. As soul activity is in the process of being replaced by comfort, it requires deliberate, attentive work to make and keep it conscious.

Gawan shows the way through the imprisonment of the feminine soul element. The way through is to enter into the realm of the heart, which, as the story shows, is no easy matter. Gawan's turbulent, dizzying, disorienting, life-threatening encounters in the room containing the Wonder Bed, the attacks of arrows from unknown sources, his fight with the pure instinctual passion of the lion, all picture what is involved in coming to be conscious of desire rather than simply acting out of desire. The closest we come to such an experience in ordinary life are obsessions of the heart. Obsessions take us into the heart of desire, but usually we think that we are obsessed, in love, with another person; the intensity is such that all other capacities are totally disrupted. As obsession, however, the object of such a symptom is an opening of the heart. This demands not that we kill or control desire but that we come into a right relationship with it: that we recognize desire as the living movement of soul life itself and accept the attendant responsibility of coming to experience the inner and outer worlds through the heart in a fully conscious way. Through initiation into the realm of the heart as the nexus of soul life, love is enlarged in such manner that love for another is never separated from love for the world.

This introduction would be incomplete without giving attention to the third aspect of *Parzival,* pictured in the mysterious figure of Feirefiz, the offspring of Gahmuret and Belacane. We do not hear anything of this half-brother of Parzival until the closing books. If Parzival has to do with the quest for spiritual knowledge through development of soul capacities, and Gawan has to do with the quest of soul to find heart through the right relationship with the feeling life, then Feirefiz has to do with the quest for a right relationship with the will. In this regard, note well Ms. Sussman's careful attention to Feirefiz's appearance. He is truly a magnificent sight. His armor is bedecked with every imaginable precious jewel. His shield is made of asbestos, which can neither burn nor decay. On top of his helmet, he wears the strange emblem of a being known as the Ecidemon. Feirefiz is a picture of pure human nobility, of all that a human being can develop into solely out of purely human, earthly forces. That he belongs to the earthly element is shown by the jewels he proudly displays; it is as if he has reached down into the earth, finding there precious material to be shaped, formed, forged into works of beauty. He leads vast armies consisting of every race, an image indicating that his work concerns the earthly world and the transformations of that world possible through the forces of the will. Feirefiz is a representative of humanity, of all of those individuals who strive and work in the world with great nobility, carrying out what they have to do, making important contributions — but having little inkling of the spiritual worlds.

The Ecidemon, a dragonlike being, is the source of Feirefiz's inspiration and action for noble work. The Grail scholar Walter J. Stein says that the Ecidemon is one's angel united with the human being. The description we are given certainly does not look like an angel, but is a description of what others see. When we first get a glimpse of another person's true being, we do not see the individual spirit in the other person. Instead, what is felt is hostility. That is the real paradox; when we see the true individuality of another person, it is as if we fear that we will be robbed of our own strength. When we see someone accomplish something in the world, we feel as if we have been robbed of what we might have done. Moreover, and even more paradoxically, the further one develops spiritually, the more hostility toward others becomes a possibility. After all that Parzival has been through, after all he has suffered and learned, when he sees Feirefiz, he does not see the guiding star of this individual, but rather the Ecidemon, and he meets Feirefiz with hostility.

When Feirefiz and Parzival meet in a duel, Feirefiz wins. Parzival's sword breaks. But the noble brother will not kill an unarmed person, and instead they sit down and talk, discovering that they are brothers. Here, again, we find a hint intimating why Ms. Sussman pursues the importance of speech in her interpretation. But, what is most important in this picture is that it is Feirefiz who stops short at the moment when he could have destroyed his brother. What an amazing picture! It is a picture that says no matter how far one goes in spiritual development, no matter how far one develops the interior life of the heart, what must not be forgotten is the central fact of being an earthly human being. In the image given earlier of the alchemical Tree of Knowledge, the final stage of spiritual work, of concentration, contemplation, and meditation, is the picture of the

sparrow. The final aim of spiritual initiation is to be able to see ourselves as a sparrow, an ordinary bird, out in the world, the beautiful
earthly world, making our way just like everyone else.

Of course, the speaking encounter between Parzival and Feirefiz
changes them both. After Parzival discovers his human brother, a
self-discovery of his own humanity, and Feirefiz discovers his
brother, his own aspects of spirit and soul being, significant events
follow. Parzival is now able to return to the wounded Anfortas and
speak in an entirely new way — as a human being, from the heart,
with spiritual knowledge. He is also able to lead his brother to the
place of the Grail; that is to say, initiation into the path of love is not
for one's own sake, for one's own salvation, but for the sake of others.

The question that Parzival is now able to speak to Anfortas, which
previously he was unable to speak because of ignorance, is "What ails
thee?" Other legends of the Grail indicate that there are two further
questions: "How can I help?", and "Whom does the Grail serve?" By
this time, in working carefully, meditatively, with the text, there can
be no doubt whatsoever that these questions are not spoken merely
out of curiosity, but from the very depth and core of Parzival's full
being. The first question expresses the capacity of true compassion.
Only because Parzival has suffered all he has, only because he knows
error and guilt, and has come to know love, is he able to ask this
question. There is no need for Anfortas to answer the question, to
describe the nature of his ailment. The questioning itself suffices
because it is the speaking, the true soul gesture of an act of compassion, that heals.

The second question, "How can I help?", speaks the action of
love. Often, asking "How can I help?" means "How can I help myself
in helping you?" Here, the questioning issues from a transformed
heart. Again, this is not a question seeking an answer, a sure sign of
egotism, but contains its own answer; love is not for one's own sake,
but for the sake of others, for the sake of the world. These first two
questions are asked not out of duty, not out of obligation, not out of
the stance of a professional helper of others, but out of true freedom,
fully respectful of the freedom of the other. These questions are not
general, abstract questions; we must not look at their content but
rather at the way they are spoken from an individual who has come,
through an initiation experience, into the mystery of love. Indeed, we
have to say that when Parzival asks these questions the whole of the

spiritual worlds are focused, through the individual, in compassion and love.

Then there is the third question, "Whom does the Grail serve?" The Grail serves the servers of the Grail. Still, we have not satisfactorily answered the question of what the Grail is in the first place. On the one hand, the Grail is the Christ at the center of the whole vessel of the Cosmos, the Christ at the center of the spiritual worlds, the spiritual Sun. On the other hand, the Grail is the Grail server, the individual as vessel with Christ as the center and light of spirit, body, and soul life. And the Grail is also the whole Earth, the Earth as vessel containing Christ's blood, open to the streaming spiritual forces of the Cosmos. But, this is no definitive answer to the question. Each reader, in taking up this marvelous book is brought into the region where it becomes possible to live with the question and mystery of the Grail.

I am aware that still more esoteric understandings of Parzival are possible. The aim of this introduction has been to try to orient the reader toward the importance of what Linda Sussman has created. I am also aware of much that I have bypassed in order to say something briefly. Readers of this book will be led into the contemplation of many more things than I have addressed. For example, one may contemplate how entering into this quest involves leaving behind all that we have been given from the past. Here we find a basis for truly encountering what comes to meet the soul, rather than endlessly analyzing how we are formed out of influences from the past. One may meditate, too, on the peculiar, important figure of Cundrie, the sorceress. Doing so, we experience that what is most vile and uncomfortable is actually our most precious source of guidance and our protection from trying to meet our destiny too hastily. One may reflect, further, on the full significance of a path through the middle between longing, which if followed leads to literalizing the forces of spirit, and sorrow, which if followed leads not only into the depths of the soul, but also to self-absorption. And, finally, one may also meditate on the significance and the true reality of community — for, after all, the Grail also refers to the Grail kingdom, to the renewal of the whole Earth through the renewal of community.

A great deal of praise is due Linda Sussman for what she offers in this book. While she draws adeptly from many sources, we are never led into a single view, a reductionistic way of looking. Rather, the reader is taken into a complete, if unfamiliar world, the world of the possible future. Praise be, that we are not given yet another interpretation, either from psychology or from the results of someone else's spiritual investigations! We are left free to enter into Parzival's world — aided to be sure, by a great deal of study and inner work carried out by the author, but none of this is imposed. Nor do we find in this book an abstract, removed, intellectual, scholarly approach to the subject. The reader is able to be fully engaged because the author was fully engaged, not only in the text of *Parzival,* but in the deepest questions of her life, which are also the deepest questions of everyone's life. The result is a book that is alive and can be worked with again and again. One is led from reading into meditation and then from meditation back again to this book. And one is led from this book back to the original, and from that text itself again into further meditation. And most important, all of this inner activity does not take us away from the world, but rather much deeper into a capacity to see the world anew, to begin to act differently, from a different center, from love.

NOTES

1 See, for example, H. Harrison, *The Cauldron and the Grail* (San Francisco, The Archives Press, 1992).

2 R. Steiner, *An Outline of Occult Science* (Spring Valley, NY: Anthroposophic Press, 1950).

Illustrations

The following labyrinths have been used: title page, diagram of the labyrinth in the nave of Chartres Cathedral; page 13 (Prelude), diagram of Julian's Bower, turf labyrinth at Alkborough, Lincolnshire, England; page 21 (Chapter One), labyrinth at Rheims Cathedral; page 35 (Chapter Two), paleolithic talisman from a ritual cave burial in Siberia; page 65 (Chapter Three), pattern of a hedge maze; page 89 (Chapter Four), labyrinth in Amiens Cathedral; page 117 (Chapter Five), labyrinth of large pebbles found on the uninhabited Island of Wier; page 147 (Chapter Six), labyrinth known as the "Virgin's Ring" in Sweden; page 181 (Chapter Seven), spiral labyrinth known as "Shepherd's Race," formerly at Boughton Green, England; page 211 (Chapter Eight), Dharma Wheel; page 249 (Epilogue), diagram of the labyrinth in the nave of Chartres Cathedral.

Introduction

The Grail! The word stirs a deep response in the Western imagination. Joseph Campbell called the medieval stories where it is first mentioned "the founding myth of Western civilization" because "according to this mythology, there is no fixed law, no established knowledge of God, set up by prophets or priests, that can stand against the revelation of a life lived with integrity in the spirit of its own brave truth."[1] Campbell and many other scholars, artists and seekers have seen the Western wisdom path disclosed in the image of each knight entering the forest where no one else has made a path. The quest is to recover the elusive Grail, thereby returning its sustenance to the world. The presence of the Grail nurtures an invisible web of relationships that connect individual destiny to service of others and to the earth, thereby granting meaning.

But when one asks, "What is the Grail?," no definitive reply is possible. In the various versions of the story, it appears as a vessel, a cup or chalice, a dish, a jewel, a stone. The stories of its origin, even the source of the word "Grail," differ, sometimes conflict. Do the roots stretch back to ancient Celtic, goddess-centered culture where Ceridwen's magic cauldron brewed all-embracing world wisdom? Or was the Grail formed from the heavenly jewel loosened from Lucifer's crown when he plunged to earth? Or is it the cup in which Joseph of Arimathea collected the precious blood of Christ?

All these possibilities prompt fruitful contemplation, but the overall impression remains that the physical manifestation of the Grail and its history are not as pertinent as the ability to recognize its significance, to know its mission. The Grail can be known only through its *activity* which, as depicted in the stories, is the nourishing of each person according to his or her needs and capacity. The stories clearly illustrate that one can know the Grail only by becoming like it.

The various medieval versions agree that the Grail cannot be owned or possessed. Instead, it must be served. It calls to itself those who are worthy to serve it. And worthiness for this service shines through the person's speaking. The central heroic deed upon which the resolution of the story depends, in all the versions, is the protagonist's asking a certain question at the right time. Thereby, the questing knight heals the wounded Grail king, succeeds him in office and restores order and felicity to the community and countryside.

Rulership of the Grail castle passes to the person who, after much searching and many trials, has so matured in self-knowledge, spiritual understanding *and* compassionate perception of others that she or he can speak just what the moment calls for. This quality of speaking not only heals and transforms individuals and groups but also ends the long divorce between word and world that began, as Biblical and other sacred stories portray, when speech was put in service of fear and greed rather than of communion and praise. The possibility of this kind of speaking, and the question of whether an initiatory path toward it could be found in our times, inspired my own engagement with the Grail story, particularly the twelfth-century epic *Parzival* by Wolfram von Eschenbach.

Wolfram von Eschenbach was born in southern Germany in the last third of the twelfth century and died, most likely, by 1220. He was a knight — and proud of it — who also had a calling as a poet, a combination not too unusual for that time. He probably began Parzival around 1197 and completed it by 1212.[2] The poem is so skillfully crafted that, scholars find hard to believe Wolfram's assertion in the text that he was illiterate.[3] Nonetheless, he claims to have learned the story from a troubadour, Kyot, who swore Wolfram to secrecy until just the right time for the story to be told.

Kyot had unearthed the story in an ancient book by Flegetanis, a Middle Eastern scholar and astrologer, who had read about the Grail in the starry script of the night sky. The book described a race of noble people who served and guarded the Grail, and Kyot researched in many lands to discover this lineage, finding it at last in "Anjou" (which may exist only in Wolfram's poetic geography). Since no historical record confirms the existence of either Kyot or Flegetanis, scholars tend to doubt Wolfram's account and point to other sources. Volumes of scholarship have attempted to uncover the sources of the various Grail stories, and different scholars give preference to Celtic, Middle Eastern, Indo-European, Christian or alchemical sources, or to some combination thereof. The most obvious progenitor for Wolfram's version is the French romance by Chrétien de Troyes entitled *Perceval: or, The Story of the Grail*, composed somewhere close to 1180. Chrétien, a cleric whose values and priorities were quite different than Wolfram's, died before his story was completed, so his hero never fulfills his quest. Furthermore, Chrétien's work does not account for Wolfram's first two or last three chapters, and Chrétien's many continuators wrote nothing comparable to Wolfram's finished epic. Scholars recognize that Chrétien himself must have worked from previous orally transmitted tales, and his debt to Welsh sources in particular is clear.

Scholars have investigated many other dimensions of the Grail stories and particularly Wolfram's. Numerous works discuss the relationship between Grail legends and Arthurian lore; the structure of the narratives; interpretations of the symbolic images and themes; analyses of the characters; the psychological significance of the story; its historical or anthropological underpinnings; its Christian connotations; its esoteric, spiritual basis; and its initiatory power for spiritual seekers.

Informed by all these perspectives, I have yet been intrigued that no scholar I have read has shown much interest in the theme of speech. Many give consideration to the Grail question itself in its various forms in different versions, debating what the content of the question may mean. However, none of the commentators devotes much attention to the fact that all of Parzival's initiatory trials, as well as those of other Grail heroes, prepare him to speak — in a certain way, in a certain context, at a certain time. I know of no other story of such length, complexity and historical importance in which the essential heroic deed is an act of speech.

However, I am aware that some may question the authority I claim for this exploration of *Parzival* as an initiation for speaking. Following Wolfram's example, when he states in his opening paragraphs that "Never have I meet a man so wise but that he would have liked to find out what authority this story claims,"[4] I will not claim any. I will just say, as he does, that, if my story about this story is of any value, it is not because it claims authority as final truth but only because the individual reader has found something useful herein. I do not contend that Wolfram intended his story to reflect an initiatory preparation for attuned speech. I *do* assume that he considered the story very important, not solely for entertainment. It is vitally worth remembering, I think he would say, because it presents a journey toward balance — wrought in the course of living daily life — between the earthly and spiritual requirements of being human. That the epic can still seem relevant to us eight centuries after it was composed evidences its enduring value and its worthiness to be rendered correctly and completely for the sake of future generations.

I chose Wolfram's version of the Grail story because of its completeness. Other versions stress the Celtic or Christian elements while muting or omitting entirely the Middle Eastern (Judaic/Islamic) and alchemical images. Some versions exclude Gawan or portray him as the Grail knight, omitting Parzival. Yet others leave both of them out, instead giving the Grail adventure to such heroes as the mystically pagan Welsh Peredur or the idealized Galahad. No other versions contain the range and depth of characters, old and young, or the key roles played by a colorful variety of strong female characters.

Wolfram's poem consists of sixteen "books," divided into sub-sections of thirty lines each, a total of 24,810 complex, elliptical lines of Middle High German which differs enough from modern German to be almost another language. Scholars have compared these mathematical relationships in the external structure of the poem to the mirroring rhythms in the internal structure, where images and characters dance. To retell the story in this study required summarizing, which, I feared at times, risked being disrespectful. However, I did not want to assume the reader's prior acquaintance with the detailed story, and I hope as well that the retelling will allow the reader to think along with me more easily and thereby be more actively engaged. I have striven to show how Wolfram endearingly inserts himself into the narrative and also to tell in each episode only what Wolfram included, trusting his choice of when to explain or reveal things. I encourage the reader to do likewise and not be discomfited if something is not immediately clarified.

The structure of this study is as follows: A "Prelude" discusses Wolfram's opening paragraphs in detail. In Chapter 1, I explore the first two books of *Parzival* as background for the quest and for the speech of the Grail. The next seven chapters each examine two of Wolfram's books. Each retelling of an episode from *Parzival* is followed by two commentaries: "Initiatory Themes" draws directly upon the text for general initiatory steps relevant to the speech of the

Grail; then in "Toward Speech of the Grail" I improvise on these themes as they might suggest specific practices for a person who feels called to the speech of the Grail. The "Epilogue" elucidates the overall labyrinthine pattern that represents the journey.

A conundrum present at the outset was how to write about speaking in a way that would inspire greater attention to the practice of speaking rather than just generating more ideas *about* speaking. In writing, particularly nonfiction writing, it is difficult to retain the nuance and multisensual experience of speech between persons. The written words might reinforce a reader's tendency to regard the speech of the Grail as a "thing," a category of behavior, subject, therefore, to clear definition and delineation. This is not at all the case. The path to the speech of the Grail is circuitous and indirect, not a linear movement from A to Z. The speech of the Grail, likewise, darts and flashes like a trout, now leaping above the surface to partake of celestial airs, now diving into murky depths, stirring up the mud, now swimming swiftly, now poised, silent, stationary, before the next movement. Such speech can be tricky as well as true, ambiguous as often as clear.

I am not convinced that I resolved these dilemmas, but as a gesture in that direction I have preceded each chapter with an illustration of a labyrinth and a verse-speech from the "Grail King." These verses, mostly my own, are epigrams, alluding to the central themes in the episodes and commentaries that follow. I aim to engage the reader's auditory sense to augment the visual sense that predominates in reading. The labyrinth images invite the reader to participate kinesthetically as well, acting as reminders that the movement pattern of the Grail journey is not straight lines but spirals. My hope is that these adornments encourage the reader to journey through the study with the alertness and ceremonial sensibility one has on a pilgrimage rather than the more one-dimensional awareness one has in reading a "how to" book.

Describing a journey in the Grail story, like the Grail itself, defies easy articulation. The journey is not a "thing" outside oneself, and thus, for instance, my life and my study have not been separate over these years. They have unfolded in tandem, with Wolfram's epic providing images and a narrative context to orient me as the journey ensued. I became acquainted with the characters through "living" them; they were evoked in me through the events and experiences of my life. I would be responding to a certain experience and suddenly recognize that one of Wolfram's characters was speaking not only *to* me but *in* me and *out of* me. I learned, in this way, how different and more distant a character on a page is from a character one has found in oneself.

The multilayered meanings of the story and its characters posed a challenge for me to write clearly about them. As I experience the story, each character or major image is a metaphorical complex, a hieroglyphic. A character like Gawan, for example, is not only a character in the story but also a psychological attribute of Parzival (who is himself a character but also the whole, as the title indicates) *and* an aspect of the consciousness of the modern person called to the speech of the Grail. The actions of a character like Gawan, then, are effected both as inner activities within Parzival and within the modern seeker, and also as outer actions or practices. Meanwhile, we can assess the significance of characters only by holding them in mind against the backdrop of the whole to which they belong, just as we can understand the significance of branches only if we can see the whole tree — and even the ecosystem to which it belongs. Viewed this way, Wolfram's narrative becomes a prism, refracting through each of its characters a wholeness to which the entire story refers. That all the main characters are actually related to one another is Wolfram's literary device for representing this wholeness.

The reader is thus challenged to keep in mind that the characters are resonances of all these various levels and that the boundaries — between literary and psychological, inner and outer, symbolic and actual, part and whole, microcosm and macrocosm — become very fluid and porous. The quality of consciousness generated by such multilayered attentiveness resembles that of artists creating their work, of tribal shamans presiding at healing ceremonies, or of alchemists blending their elixirs. The craft of all these endeavors is to transpose inner visions, perceptions and dreams outward into physical mediums, words and enactments to form a coherent, aesthetic whole. The same can be said of the journey toward the speech of the Grail. It instructs one in becoming an artist in each moment of life. Life lived as hermetic, shamanistic art is life lived in speaking.

In this sense, "speaking" refers to what can appear not only in verbalizations but also (though not necessarily so) in sounds, inflections, facial expressions, tears, laughter, gestures and eloquent silences. Speaking underlies all art forms because it emanates from the intention to express, name and communicate something. Speaking is the particular gift, the special form of nourishment, that human beings alone can give to each other and to the earth. In the Biblical story God brings the earth's creatures to be named by the first human being. In some way we are still trying to discover, speaking allows human beings to participate in creation.

I do not imagine the speech of the Grail as a particular style or content of speech. In the many forms in which it can appear, the speech of the Grail is speaking that transmits meaning and inspires change or movement by opening a space in which its recipients experience the freedom to choose, the freedom to create. No intentions of coercion, manipulation or persuasion — overt or subtle — cloud this speaking. The speech of the Grail is fully embodied speaking, possessing all the energy, exactness and expressiveness of physical gesture. However, in keeping with the invisible mystery of meaning, the speech of the Grail calls attention neither to itself nor to the speaker. Like art and the Grail itself, such speech is something and nothing at the same time.

The speech of the Grail depends largely upon the qualities of awareness and presence developed in the speaker. Wolfram's story portrays Parzival's transformation from insensitive, blabbering fool to wise, compassionate speaker and King of the Grail. Some commentators have gone so far as to suggest that the story can effect a like transformation in those who hear or read it and allow its images to live in and expand their awareness. Walter Johannes Stein declared in 1928, "The Temple of the Grail is not a medieval Saga. It is still continuously in the course of construction, and the Grail-Saga, far from being finished, is in continuous living development."[5]

Still, the use of "initiation" as a synonym for that transformation may require justification, even though Parzival's journey follows the general pattern closely enough to be archetypal. The work of anthropologists and mythologists has clarified the underlying form of initiations, whether in tribal puberty rites, mystery cults, or the more individual quests of shamans and culture heroes and heroines. The first phase involves a separation; the initiate must leave all that is familiar and comfortable — people, things, habits, even thought patterns. The second phase is a metamorphosis, usually accomplished

gh an ordeal of some kind — physical, psychological and spir-
— and then an intensive learning experience whereby the initiate develops a new way of perceiving and experiencing self and
world. In the final phase, the initiate returns to the tribal or cultic
group, sometimes bearing a new name, new status, new privileges
and responsibilities. The community receives the initiate's new identity as a gift which strengthens its continuity with both the past and
the future. Through initiation, not only the individual but also the
community is revitalized and renewed.[6]

However, most of us in the late twentieth century no longer live
in the relative containment of a tribal world, and modern cults seem
either lost in guru-adulation or desperately clutching some fundamentalism that inevitably denies individual freedom. There are those
who claim to be shamans or medicine people, and they will perform
an initiation if you sign up and pay enough. However, their adver-
tisements do not inspire much confidence. What impact a medieval
epic can have in these circumstances could be dismissed as negligi-
ble. Some may wonder whether the word "initiation" can apply at
all in such secular, materialistically oriented times.

Others, recognizing the crucial role of initiation in the lives of
individuals and cultures, have sought to understand how the fundamental initiatory pattern can be experienced by persons living in
these times. Rudolf Steiner and C.G. Jung (in quite different ways)
were among the first to apprehend and articulate a new vision of initiation for the twentieth century. Joseph Campbell and Mircea Eliade elaborated it, and many commentators since have advanced the
idea. It is the conception that each human life is an unfolding story
or myth, which, if viewed that way (and that part seems critical),
becomes an individual initiation that confers a sense of membership
in an emerging global "tribe."

One can perceive one's life as a story, unfolding in a spiraling
series of experiences each having the three-phase form of separa-
tion/ordeal-learning process/return. This is precisely Parzival's path,
and, like him, the modern seeker comes to know his or her calling
only by undergoing these initiatory trials with increasing consciousness, courage and faith. As in Parzival's story, there will be many
characters and subplots to sort through before a sense of an overall,
framing story grows more secure. In the process, one has quite often
to give up a favorite storyline to gain access to a larger context. Yet,

over time, almost imperceptibly, one develops a more certain sense of the calling which constitutes one's connection to the greater whole — all of the earth and humanity.

The person seeking initiation at the end of the twentieth century is called not just to connect with the tribe(s) of the past but also to prepare the way for the "tribe" of the future. Obviously, this tribe will be very different from the ones our ancestors knew. Most of us today are living between the tribes of the past and whatever the tribe of the future will be. We live between paradigms: between the old science and the new science, the old religion and the new religion, the old education and the new education, the old ways of healing and the new ones, and so on. Many, if not all, of the discomforts, diseases, depressions, depravities, addictions, and social pathologies we see everywhere in Western culture are symptomatic of the disorientation and doubt endemic to our era. We are the tribe of the "between." We are like Parzival who, once he has seen the Grail, no longer quite fits in the welcoming company of the Round Table yet does not know the way back to his future, which is the Grail company. Going backward to go forward? A probe like that must delve beyond tribal roots to the mother lode, the very source of our humanness, which has to be our language and speaking.

This raises the question whether there is really any distinction between initiation in general and initiation toward the speech of the Grail. The distinction may be artificial or at least somewhat so. Initiation transforms the speech of any initiate just as it transforms all other aspects — physical, emotional, mental, spiritual. However, a given individual may have an especially strong interest in or aptitude for speaking, and specific awarenesses and practices might help develop this aptitude. This study concentrates only upon those facets of the more overall initiation that support the appearance of the speech of the Grail, but it must be remembered that the journey toward the speech of the Grail cannot be separated from the more general initiatory path.

Two areas of study and practice relevant to speaking are, regrettably, beyond the scope of this study. The subject of sound, particularly the sound of the speaker's voice, its meaning and what it reveals, receives scant attention. This utterly individual sound, as unique as a fingerprint, is always heard by the listener(s), along with the words, phrasings and inflections. The journey toward the speech of the Grail will change not only how the person speaks but also how the speech sounds; that is to say, voice quality will change. Working directly with the voice can assist in expanding and deepening the resonances in the speaker's voice because certain voice work promotes interconnectedness of body, emotions, mind, soul and spirit, but these practices will not be dealt with here.[7]

A second subject that will not receive sufficient attention is "context": the readiness of the listener and what creates and supports such readiness. This would also be a far-ranging exploration, including the process of listening as well as that of timing and environmental circumstances. In Wolfram's story, the wounded Anfortas has endured a long time of suffering and begs for relief, even if it be death. He certainly is ready to hear the healing words. We can wonder if the words would have had any effect if Parzival had arrived at the castle earlier, prepared to ask the question, while Anfortas was still healthy and hell-bent on serving his passion rather than the Grail. That seems unlikely. So not only speakers, but also listeners, must be ripe for the speech of the Grail. Parzival must become a listener before he can become a speaker, so listening will be discussed, but a thorough exploration of the listener's readiness for the speech of the Grail and the role of context in furthering or obstructing such speech will not be attempted here.

The speech of the Grail is not the sort of speaking that attracts much interest in these times, and it might seem, at most, a quaint anachronism. We live in an era when words are manipulated mostly for power and profit, when lying has been almost institutionalized by politicians and corporate executives, when great poetry and literature are neglected in education, when there is more curiosity about how computers can meaningfully "speak" to each other than about how human beings can, when speech is flattened continually by catch phrases, professional jargon, disembodied abstractions, fundamentalist literalism, and the predigested verbiage of advertising, pop culture and television journalism. I was quite aware when I began to write this study that the speech of the Grail does not now exist to any great degree, nor do we know to what degree it ever existed in the past — although we have legends about bards, shamans and many wise teachers whose speaking changed people's lives. Therefore, this book has the nature of a dream or fantasy about a speech which might exist or could exist. It imagines a speech of the future —

always; for every speaker, the next utterance and not the one past is the focus of attention.

I salute and follow those who regard the current cultural conditions as a summons to inhabit more fully — more consciously and conscientiously — the language and speech that we human beings alone can offer this earth. Might it be that speaking is the natural "habitat" of human beings and that we can be crowned and revealed in our nobility only when we have made the Grail journey to find and make ourselves a home there? Is this the path toward a more inclusive healing, in which the wounded, lost human individual is restored to his or her rightful place, thereby no longer desperately pursuing a sense of belonging through accumulation of property, power and prestige which inevitably leads to oppression of others and destruction of the environment?

If the end of the Grail journey is to become like the Grail, then the crowning achievement is to stand with humble dignity upon the threshold between the earthly and spiritual worlds. Like the Grail, human beings who inhabit their speaking are the connection, the common boundary, between visible and invisible realms. The Grail journey brings Parzival and each seeker to realize that, as Robert Sardello says, "the new temple of initiation is the world itself."[8] With that insight, the re-sacralization of the earth becomes possible through renewal of the individual and collective understanding of the significance of human speech.

NOTES

[1] Joseph Campbell, *The Masks of God*, 565.

[2] Most of the background information is taken from the Introduction by Helen Mustard and Charles Passage in their translation of *Parzival* by Wolfram von Eschenbach, vii–lvi.

[3] Wolfram von Eschenbach, *Parzival*, trans. Helen M. Mustard and Charles E. Passage, Book II, 115. (*Parzival* has sixteen books, each divided into sections of thirty lines each. Notes in this study will give the book and section number(s) for reference.)Wolfram repeats his claim in his later unfinished story *Willehelm*.

[4] Wolfram, Book I–2.

[5] Walter Johannes Stein, *The Ninth Century and the Holy Grail*, 148.

[6] Mircea Eliade describes the significance of initiation in *Rites and Symbols of Initiation:*

> Initiation represents one of the most significant spiritual phenomena in the history of humanity. It is an act that involves not only the religious life of the individual, in the modern meaning of the word "religion"; it involves his entire life. It is through initiation that, in primitive and archaic societies, man becomes what he is and what he should be — a being open to the life of the spirit, hence one who participates in the culture into which he was born.... From a certain point of view it could almost be said that, for the primitive world, it is through initiation that men attain the status of human beings; before initiation, they do not fully share in the human condition precisely because they do not yet have access to the religious life. This is why initiation represents a decisive experience for any individual who is a member of a premodern society; it is a fundamental existential experience because through it a man becomes able to assume his mode of being in its entirety.

[7] Examples of such voice training are that developed by Alfred Wolfsohn and Roy Hart (which continues today at the Roy Hart Theater School in southern France), the work of Richard Armstrong (founding member of the Roy Hart Theater and international teacher), and the voice and speech training developed from the original work of Rudolf and Marie Steiner and now taught at anthroposophical centers around the world.

[8] Robert Sardello, *Facing the World with Soul,* 182.

Wolfram's Beginning

We shall not cease from exploration
And the end of all our exploring
Will be to arrive where we started
And know the place for the first time.[1]

"The end is in the beginning," as T.S. Eliot artfully observed. Beginnings are full of lasting significance, echoing throughout the evolution of whatever it is that has begun — a narrative, an organization, a community, a marriage, a work, a journey — living within it as a ghostly shadow, often barely remembered and yet continually present. Therefore, it is important to be alert at any beginning; to be aware of what is being said, what is happening among the people present and in the environment. The beginning of a story as comprehensive and carefully crafted as *Parzival* tells much about where we are going and where we will be at the end.

The five opening paragraphs of *Parzival,* where Wolfram seems to address the reader, could be dismissed as obscure, construed as a reference to personal conflicts Wolfram was having with his critics. (Indeed translators Helen Mustard and Charles Passage suggest as much.[2]) An equally legitimate choice is to regard these paragraphs as the beginning of the narrative.[3] As such, they deserve our wakeful attention. Here are the opening lines:

> If inconstancy is the heart's neighbor, the soul will not fail to find it bitter. Blame and praise alike befall when a dauntless man's spirit is black-and-white mixed like the magpie's plumage. Yet he may see blessedness after all, for both colors have a share in him, the color of heaven and the color of hell. Inconstancy's companion is all black and takes on the hue of darkness, while he of steadfast thoughts clings to white.[4]

These first lines do not imagine, or prepare the reader to imagine, a perfect hero. Wolfram posits his view that the fundamental nature of every human being is "black-and-white mixed like the magpie's plumage." Perhaps he is suggesting, therefore, that the Grail journey describes the evolution in consciousness not only of an individual but of all humanity. Certainly Parzival's adventure takes him toward awareness of his own black-and-whiteness. This inner awakening will receive its complement when Parzival can accept the black-and-whiteness of his fellow human beings, represented by one approaching him from the future, his half-brother from the East. Wolfram will then use the same words to describe the wondrous Feirefiz, who does not appear until the next-to-the-last book. Only after embracing Feirefiz — whose skin is black and white — can Parzival return to the Grail castle and complete his task.

"A brave man slowly wise — thus I hail my hero"[5] says Wolfram in the closing lines of this prelude, just before the tale begins in earnest. He obviously admires Parzival, going to the trouble of transcribing an epic about him, so he seems to be saying that it is not imperfection itself that limits us, but rather lack of awareness of it — and its true nature. We can gather, here at the beginning, that this story is not about achieving perfection, but about more wisely relating to imperfection. And, even at this early juncture, Wolfram gives a clue that his central theme is the imperfection that manifests in our use, and misuse, of speech.

Wolfram's evocation of the magpie supplies the hint. This flashy black-and-white bird has a tainted reputation in the West. Remarkably, as Beryl Rowland reports, the predominant trait which contributed to the bird's evil reputation appears to have been its ability to talk. Not that it was thought to talk well. Oliver Goldsmith declared that "its songs were too thin and sharp to be an exact imitation of the human voice" and that sometimes its tongue was cut in an effort to improve its speech. It was said to have been the only bird which refused to enter the Ark, preferring instead to perch on the roof and gabble over the drowning world. In ancient Rome its vocal reputation was perpetuated in the legend of the nine sisters called the Pierides who challenged the Muses to a singing contest. So objectionable were they when they were judged the losers that they were turned into magpies as punishment.[6]

Although magpies are viewed more charitably in the East, still in both East and West superstitions propose that it is unlucky to kill this bird and that a magpie's chattering near one's house signals the arrival of guests. Around the world, it has been noticed that the wily scavenger can be trained to imitate a few human words.

This black-and-white being only imitates speech. Since its speaking comes solely from training and habit, the magpie's speech cannot be "true." Its words are not a response to something listened to, nor does its speaking have the quality of address — a real wish to be heard. This is a picture, in the extreme, of inauthentic speaking. With the amazing economy of a specific image from the natural world, Wolfram captures and critiques essential attributes of unconscious, unrelational human speaking. Appearing in the first lines of the story, the image foreshadows much that will unfold later.

Next, Wolfram propels us with a series of rapid images connected to the hunt. Recalling the magpie in his first paragraph, he taunts that "this flying metaphor will be too much too swift for dullards. They will not be able to think it through because it will run from them like a startled rabbit."[7] Issuing a challenge, he advises that, unless someone undertakes the (successful?) pursuit of that "flying metaphor," the person will see only the surface of this story, which will be like a reflection in a "mirror coated on the back with tin, and blind men's dreams,"[8] though some "fleeting joy" will be gleaned.

Anyone who grabs the hair in the palm of my hand, where there isn't any, has indeed learned how to grab close. And if I cry "Ouch!," it will only show what kind of mind I have. Shall I look for loyalty precisely where it vanishes, as fire in running water, dew in the sun?[9]

Now it is not the flying metaphor the reader must hunt and pursue; it is Wolfram himself, or rather his kind of mind. He is not a magpie chattering aimlessly in the roof beams. If we enter into the metaphoric reality of this story, we will find he has, quite consciously, left us a trail to follow below the surface. If we are willing to suspend distance and disbelief and "grab the hair in the palm of [his] hand, where there isn't any," he will cry out. Grabbing closely at what seems invisible will be the task; that is, through amplifying and extrapolating from the themes, images and characters, the hidden route becomes clearer, like an animal trail submerged in forest undergrowth. Through the text, Wolfram will respond to our gesture, validate our understanding, and reveal the great depth of this story.

In the third paragraph, Wolfram enjoins the reader to hunt the story itself. He says he has never met a "man so wise" but that he "would have liked to find out what authority this story claims and what good lessons it provides."[10] However, to answer these questions, one must be prepared to follow the story closely, for it "never wants for courage, now to flee, now to charge, dodge and return, condemn and praise."[11] The story as a whole has now become that "startled rabbit" of the second paragraph.

In the rabbit, we perceive quite an opposite image from that of the magpie. Here is a long-eared listener, living life in very alert silence. If the reference is to a hare, we have, in addition, the reports that hares will stand courageously as decoy while a tiring comrade escapes to safety. To hunt such quarry successfully, ancestral hunting traditions tell us, it is necessary to find or develop these qualities in oneself. And Wolfram concludes the third paragraph with the encouragement that "whoever can make sense out of all these turns of chance has been well treated by Wisdom, or whoever does not SIT too tight, or WALK astray, but in general underSTANDS" (emphasis Wolfram's).[12] The thoughts of one who is false, however, will lead that person nowhere in this story.

We can conclude that a receptive attitude, though necessary, is not sufficient for following Wolfram and his story. A hunting stance is also required, a stance which is "under," leading therefore to understanding. To be under something feels quite different than being on top of it. To be under, means, in some respect, to take something into oneself and to be taken in, thereby allowing a "standing" which is straighter and stronger — just as the earth under a tree supports its sky-reaching arms. If we can stand being under, we may learn to stand in the world in a new way.

I imagine this "under" to be what the tribal hunter experiences under the mask, the skin, the feathers of the prey, in mimicking and dancing the animal before the hunt. The dance, possible only after thorough knowledge of the animal is achieved through hours of careful observing and listening, reveals that the hunter has become one with the animal — before the hunt ever begins. The actual stalking, killing, flaying, cooking and eating of the animal is a concretization of a preceding imaginal process. All these practices are required for a proper and successful hunt, and their purpose is to nourish the hunter (and the community) with the life-giving power of the animal — first in its metaphorical, spiritual meaning and only then as physical food.

Wolfram is suggesting that each person must bring something to this story, not just expect to take something away from it. But developing the awareness that intentionality must accompany receptivity may require repeated journeys through the story. The reader initially approaching this story resembles Parzival arriving at the Grail castle the first time: something is expected, although the reader, like Parzival, may not be aware of it. During that first visit, Parzival relies on virtues he has been taught: virtues that are quite fine in themselves, but not enough to meet what is expected of him. During his long journey of return to the Grail castle, these initial virtues are tempered and transformed, allowing him success upon his return.

In the next paragraphs of this beginning, Wolfram emphasizes four virtues that will qualify the reader to be a successful hunter of the story's flying metaphors and shy strategies. Two of the virtues seem to be required at the outset; the second two will mature — in Parzival and in the reader — during the unfolding of the story.

Wolfram says right away and definitively that his story is not for men only: "For women I will set up these same goals."[13] He then assigns one each of the first two virtues and one each of the second two to men and women, respectively. In so doing, Wolfram, long before Jung, begins to separate the physical sex of a person from qualities (here referred to as "virtues") which can, but not necessarily, characterize members of a sex. This would mean that each Grail seeker must come to embody all these virtues, although they may be somewhat differentiated depending on whether one is a man or a woman.

The first of the virtues assumed to be already present — and mentioned in the opening sentence — is constancy. For Wolfram, this virtue has a masculine quality. The translators, and I assume Wolfram himself, use this word almost interchangeably with "steadfastness" and "loyalty" — although the latter is often used as well in reference to female characters in the story. We can understand "constancy/steadfastness/loyalty" as perseverance. The person pursuing the flight of this story and, by extension, the speech of the Grail, must persevere. Success will not be immediate or perhaps even obvious.

A second virtue the reader must bring, says Wolfram, turning to one he regards as feminine in quality, is modesty. He carefully explains that this means not having a "counterfeit" heart:

> Anyone true to her womanhood I will not examine as to her complexion or the heart's external roof, for if she is well protected within her heart, her praise will not be paid amiss.[14]

Modesty, here, seems to be a scrupulous self-honesty. A person exemplifying such modesty need not parade made-up beauty, other superficial attributes or accomplishments nor need such a person shy away from deserved acknowledgment and praise. A person with this quality of modesty knows, and welcomes, what is due, but nothing more. A person with this kind of self-knowledge can truly know another — even if that "other" is a story running forth like a startled rabbit.

Given constancy and modesty in the reader, Wolfram says he can now tell his tale, "a story that speaks of great faithfulness, of the ways of womenly women and of a man's manhood so forthright that never against hardness was it broken."[15] In this way, he suggests that the pursuit of this tale will engender — in Parzival and in the reader — two additional virtues: "great faithfulness," associated with women and thereby feminine in quality; and "forthrightness," associated with men and masculine in quality. From a certain perspective, these two seem to be transmutations of the first two.

On the feminine side, the virtue of great faithfulness will evolve from modesty. Augmenting scrupulous self-honesty will develop the ability to trust. When one truly knows oneself and wears the knowledge lightly, then one also possesses patience — the ability to wait in courageous trust. Such trust actually creates the conditions for whatever is awaited to arrive, as Laurens van der Post poetically extols:

> The waiting of the feminine is there and was always there, born with the feminine, always alive in the feminine. It was the waiting of creation itself, the waiting which is at the heart of time where out of a longing the stars are made and the child is formed and born. How could one not have known that all the living and growing and all the light and shining things coming out of the darkness at the beginning were made out of this waiting?[16]

Parzival definitely must strengthen his ability to wait in trust, but the paragon of this virtue is Condwiramurs, his wife. We meet her first as a modest young girl in Book IV and only find her again in the last book when she, along with the twin sons she has raised alone for five years, reunites with Parzival. Yet, since Parzival constantly is thinking about her, her presence permeates the story. Wolfram thus portrays the presence of great faithfulness as both context for and result of the journey through the story.

On the masculine side, the virtue of forthrightness will develop out of constancy. Given the perseverance inherent in constancy, and despite the circuitous, seemingly endless wanderings, dead-end detours, and a frustrating sense of being lost, a quality of straightforward truthfulness will increasingly appear in Parzival and in the reader. One who embodies forthrightness is direct yet open, exposed, standing sovereign on a ground of values which one feels defined by, bound to live by. In the past, the defining ground was literal, geographical, *or* was an external cultural code of behavior. The Grail journey supports self-definition. Another word we might use now for this virtue is "integrity." When a person can say "Here I stand" and mean it, he or she exhibits a forthrightness strong enough that "never against hardness was it broken," as Wolfram says.

Wolfram's allusion cannot be accidental. In the natural world, the hardest substance is the diamond, a brilliant white crystal, transformed over time and under tremendous pressure from the blackness of crumbly coal. Here, in the last sentences of the beginning of the beginning, is another indication that this story accomplishes an initiatory transformation. Thus, from here on, I will refer to the "reader" as the "initiate-speaker."

NOTES

[1] T.S. Eliot, "Little Gidding," *Collected Poems, 1909–1962*, 208.

[2] Wolfram, Introduction by Mustard and Passage, 3.

[3] Throughout this study, my approach to Wolfram's story will be to "believe" it, rather than to "doubt" it. I drew inspiration for this from Peter Elbow's appendix essay, "The Doubting Game and the Believing Game — An Analysis of the Intellectual Enterprise," in his book *Writing Without Teachers*, 147–91.

[4] Wolfram, Book I, 1.

[5] Wolfram, Book I, 4.

[6] Beryl Rowland, *Birds with Human Souls*, 102.

[7] Wolfram, Book I, 1.

[8] Wolfram, Book I, 1.

[9] Wolfram, Book I, 1.

[10] Wolfram, Book I, 2.

[11] Wolfram, Book I, 2.

[12] Wolfram, Book I, 2.

[13] Wolfram, Book I, 2.

[14] Wolfram, Book I, 3.

[15] Wolfram, Book I, 5.

[16] Laurens van der Post, *About Blady*, 249.

"Oh, Where Is My Desire Driving Me?"

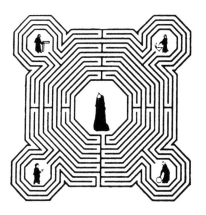

The Grail King Speaks

Be forewarned, Oh Speaker.
Behind the quest burns
Aspiration,
A yearning for the heights
So intense
That ultimate failure,
Even death itself,
Though risked,
Is no obstacle

And, as well,
You must come to know,
Indeed must embrace,
The deepest, moist sorrow
Of your heart.

Fire and water,
The marriage of yearning and sorrow,
Give birth to the quest.

Seed Sources of the Quest
BOOKS I AND II

Parzival is not born until the end of Book II. Before that, Wolfram tells about Parzival's father and mother. These parents give birth to the seeker and therefore to the quest; as such, they represent the motivating sources of the journey within Parzival and the initiate-speaker.

Gahmuret is the name Wolfram gives to the father-energy from which the quest is born. From the start, Gahmuret displays two characteristics that represent an essential foundation for this quest. Gahmuret's father, Gandin, has been killed in battle. As was customary at that time, the oldest son inherits all of the father's lands and wealth. If younger siblings receive anything, it is only at the dispensation of the eldest brother. It so happens that Gahmuret has a very generous brother who offers him more than sufficient lands and wealth to identify him properly as a son of Gandin.

Gahmuret declines the offer, however, saying he wants to earn whatever riches and fame he acquires in his life. He asks only to be properly outfitted for the journey. Thus we learn that Gahmuret is not content to settle for what is given, or what he has not earned for himself. The story refers to lands and wealth, but it also implies that Gahmuret is not satisfied by what is given him on any level — customs, ideas and ideals included. Although Gahmuret's brother invites him — as co-inheritor of Anjou — to share the title "Angevin" with him, Gahmuret does not adopt his father's emblem. He chooses instead a white anchor sewn on forest green silk.

Notice that this resistance to the given does not presuppose any particular ability to question. Gahmuret resists more out of the drive to "do it myself," such as parents can see in their toddlers. This step is as necessary in the background of a quest as it is in the childhood of any adult, but it is quite different than when one begins to question the given.

In the case of Gahmuret, however, there is a question surging within, though he only dimly feels it as a question. What he does experience is a great yearning, as he explains when his brother protests Gahmuret's decision to go off into the world to earn his fame:

My heart, however, yearns upward to the heights. I do not know why it is so full of life that the left side of my breast swells to bursting. O where is my desire driving me? That I shall find out if I can![1]

The yearning for the heights confessed by Gahmuret is not necessarily experienced as a spiritual yearning; indeed it is not for Gahmuret. Rather, it is experienced as a "drive," which is so strong, so demanding in its presence, that all else seems secondary to its satisfaction. The "heights" for which Gahmuret yearns are charged by volcanic depths. The yearning is a blazing forge, but just what will be shaped in its heat is not determined. Gahmuret and all those who experience such yearning associate it with their heart, with the very center of their being. If that yearning is not followed, they feel that they literally have lost their center.

Such a yearning is not the same as worldly ambition, though the two are sometimes confused. Gahmuret interprets his yearning to mean that he must offer his knightly service to the greatest king. Wolfram points out that Gahmuret is a man of great modesty, and yet he knows his worth. He will settle for nothing less than service to the most powerful earthly ruler, who, in this story, is the Baruch of Baghdad. The father-energy of the Grail-king-to-be will travel to the East, toward the fire of the rising sun. And there his own rising is as swift and hot as the sun's on a summer dawn; he does win fame and the fond favor of the Baruch he serves.

At the zenith of this achievement, he comes to Patelamunt, castle of the black queen Belacane, in her country of Zazamanc. As a result of a fatal misunderstanding, the castle is under siege by two armies, one black and the other white, who think Belacane has caused the death of their liege lord, Isenhart. Gahmuret agrees to fight for her, defeats both the black and the white armies, and in the process, falls in love with the queen, winning her love as well as her country.

Who is this black queen Belacane — woven briefly into the background of the quest? The text reveals little about her, with the exception of a wonderful moment when, while Gahmuret is simultaneously overcoming his hesitation regarding these people of dark hue, she wonders aloud if this pale-skinned knight is high enough born to be worthy of her kiss of welcome. (One of her courtiers, who knows Gahmuret from the army of the Baruch, assures her he is.) Certainly she appears very foreign to Gahmuret — an unbaptized "heathen" whom he nonetheless chooses to defend and to wed, following his heart's bidding. Furthermore, it is she who will bear Feirefiz, Parzival's half-brother. When Feirefiz has grown and earned fame and great wealth, he will travel west to find his father, finally encountering Parzival in Book XV. Thus, at the very least, Belacane is the birthing source of something (Feirefiz) in the far past which comes to Parzival, to the initiate-speaker, out of the future.

The strong emphasis on the sounds "A" and "Z" in the names of the kingdoms Gahmuret wins suggests again that beginning and end are intricately connected. "Azagouc," the country of Isenhart, and "Zazamanc," the country of Belacane, belong to Gahmuret after these battles at the beginning of the story, and Feirefiz, whom we do not meet until nearly the end, will inherit these lands. Walter Johannes Stein proposes that in Patelamunt, with its sixteen gates and its sixteen black and white armies, Wolfram quite consciously encapsulates his whole poem (of sixteen chapters):

> As we read Wolfram's *Parzival*, we have the feeling that the opening chapters were written last, and this has been noted by commentators. . . . We must picture the sixteen adventures arranged diagrammatically in a circle, so that when the circle is complete the first adventure seems to be a continuation of the last. This kind of architecture will be found in all medieval spiritual writings; beginning and ending seem to be connected in a peculiar way.[2]

Gahmuret, however, does not follow through on his glorious beginning. During the remainder of the first book and until he dies near the end of the second book, his actions are far less noble. He has risen swiftly in the story, and his descent is almost as sudden.

Despite his passionate love for Belacane and his reputed knightly nobility, Gahmuret deceives and deserts her. He sails away at night with a sea captain, leaving her a note that he has gone because she is not baptized. Of course, upon reading the note, she says that if he had just told her, she would have become a baptized woman. Since Gahmuret's departure is never more fully explained, Belacane and her relationship to the initiate-speaker remain mysterious. She is something or someone abandoned long before the quest begins who will yet be a source of new energy and animation at its end.

In his letter, Gahmuret tells Belacane his lineage so that she may tell their son growing in her womb. We thus learn two important things. First, Feirefiz and Parzival, through Gahmuret, are closely related to King Arthur. Second, Arthur's father, Utherpendragon, and Gahmuret's grandfather were sons of two brothers who themselves were the sons of Mazadan and a woman of the fairy world who had stolen him away. From a wealth of stories about fairies and their wells, we can assume that through this fairy ancestor Gahmuret inherits an otherworldly tendency and a penchant for the watery element.

Perhaps Belacane is abandoned because, for all her virtue, she lacks the relationship with the element of water that Gahmuret needs to fulfill his role in this story. His emblem is an anchor, he arrives in a storm, he sails away in an ocean ship, and he leaves Belacane because she has not undergone the initiation by holy water. Belacane, whose crown is a single fiery ruby, and her son Feirefiz are fire-radiant beings from the East. Fire is necessary energy for the quest, but it is from the water element that the Grail-king-to-be will be born — out of the tears that flow through his mother's name. Carried by the sea, Gahmuret now sails toward his union with Parzival's mother.

Book II begins with Gahmuret having arrived in Spain, where, in medieval times, East and West met and mingled, producing a verdant flowering of art and scholarship. Following the trail of his cousin Kaylet, the King of Spain, Gahmuret comes to Waleis, where the queen is offering herself and her two countries as the prize in a tournament she has arranged. This queen, "a maiden and not a wife," is Herzeloyde, whose name means "heart's sorrow."

Herzeloyde is no passive, pitiful, half-wilted wallflower, however. Her actions and words are those of a confident woman who, within this medieval, courtly context, actively chooses and tries to shape her destiny — and will try to do likewise with the destiny of her son, Parzival. She is not easily impressed by outward displays of wealth; she seeks a richness of character in the knight who will win her. When Gahmuret makes a grandiose entrance into the tournament, showing the great wealth he has won in the East, Herzeloyde's page marvels and says that her crown and country could be pawned for half the value of Gahmuret's riches. Her first words in the text are her reply: "You need not praise it so to me. My mouth will tell you this: it must belong to a distinguished man who knows nothing about poverty."[3]

The Queen of France, who once had a relationship with Gahmuret, has sent him a letter with her ring enclosed as token of her love and claims him for her champion. He honors her claim and agrees to represent her in the tournament. For practice before the tournament, Vespers games are held. They escalate, becoming such intense battles that everyone feels there is no need to hold the "real" tournament the next day. Gahmuret has clearly prevailed against all the great knights. Herzeloyde gladly pronounces him winner of the tournament, her hand, and her kingdom.

At first Gahmuret declines, saying he already has a wife. Representatives from the Queen of France also demand to have their lady's rights respected. Still, Herzeloyde does not back down. She insists they go before a magistrate to receive a judgment; otherwise, she will be shamed before all. Gahmuret tries to convince her that there is no shame because, after all, these Vespers games were not the "real" tournament, so his victory is not "real" either, but this argument falls on deaf ears.

Actually, in the company of this very determined woman, Gahmuret begins to "disappear" and, despite his warrior prowess, seems just to float along on the domestic tides. When the judge decides for Herzeloyde and against the French queen — Belacane being dismissed as a heathen who has no legitimate claim to Gahmuret — Gahmuret accedes. He sends a somewhat lame message to the French queen that he still serves her; then he proceeds to consummate his marriage with Herzeloyde.

The last time Gahmuret can be felt as a presence in the story is when he tells Herzeloyde that she must not constrain him from knightly combat. He claims that Belacane did this, and he left her because of it. Herzeloyde agrees to this condition, and he says that he will fight in one tournament a month. Meanwhile, Gahmuret has learned that his brother and mother are dead. Sorrowing for them, he decides to adopt the emblem of the panther, because, anyway, "my anchor has found its anchorage. The anchor suits a wanderer knight: let anyone who wants it take it and wear it."[4] Eighteen tournaments later, Gahmuret learns that his lord, the Baruch, is battling with the Babylonians and decides to go fight for him. He will meet his death during that adventure.

Herzeloyde's ascent to married bliss has been as meteoric as Gahmuret's to fame and fortune. She wins him, agrees to his terms, and commands him to "Yield to my tending,"[5] which she carries out with royal abandon. On the morning of each tournament he attends, she gives him the white silken shirt she has worn next to her skin all night, and he wears it over his chain mail. When he returns, she takes the shirt, nearly shredded with spear thrusts, and wears it to bed with her beloved. This is all her joy now, to live her passion for Gahmuret. She pays no attention to wins or losses on the battlefield; that is another world, far away from her own.

Her descent begins with a dream. Pregnant now with Parzival, Gahmuret having departed to serve the Baruch, Herzeloyde tosses and turns with a violent dream during an afternoon nap. Just as she awakes, news is brought to her of Gahmuret's death, and she faints.

The "fire" in the East has quite literally consumed Gahmuret. His squire describes how he died. He had removed his coif of mail, "forced to do so by the great heat." While so disarmed, an enemy knight poured he-goat's blood on Gahmuret's diamond helmet, "whereat the helmet became softer than a sponge."[6] (T.H. White's translation of the twelfth-century *Bestiary* explains that the he-goat's "nature" is so hot that a stone of adamant, which neither fire nor iron can alter, is dissolved by its blood.)[7]

A wise old man comes to revive Herzeloyde, whereupon she screams:

> What has become of my beloved? . . . My heart's full joy was Gahmuret's high worth, but his audacious aspiration has robbed me of him. I was much younger than he, and yet I am both his mother and his wife. I bear him here within me and also the seed of his life which our two loves gave and received.[8]

Quite suddenly, Herzeloyde is no longer an entranced young lover. She wants to die because of Gahmuret's loss, but realizes that the death of the child inside her would be "Gahmuret's second death." She calls on God to help her, and then, with passionate resolve, rips her dress to expose her breasts. She clasps them, kisses them, presses some milk out and, gaining strength from seeing "this nourishment lying above her heart," addresses the milk:

> You come from faithful love. If I had never received baptism, I would want you to be my baptismal water. I shall anoint myself with you and with my tears, both in public and in private — for I shall mourn for Gahmuret.[9]

Two weeks later, she gives birth to a son, a child "of such size that she hardly survived."[10] She joyfully nurses this beautiful boy, remembering that Mary, high Queen of Heaven, had so nursed the infant Jesus. Yet still, "The country's mistress bathed in the dew of her heart's affliction, and upon the boy rained down the tears of her eyes."[11]

Parzival's parentage is clear. The seeker and the quest are begotten from a "yearning for the heights" and birthed from the depths of "heart's sorrow." He will later learn that his name means "right through the middle," but it seems likely that the heights and depths must be known before the middle can be found. In acquainting us with Parzival's parents, Wolfram provides a picture of all that Parzival's journey will have to encompass before he has fulfilled his mission.

Initiatory Themes

All initiations require a separation phase: being pulled gently or violently away from the familiar — from family and community, and from behavioral habits and accustomed ways of thinking and feeling. Christ admonished his followers to leave their parents, and Parzival and the initiate-speaker, likewise, will have to leave theirs.

What does it mean to leave one's parents? Many young people misunderstand this inner urge, which, for ancestral, tribal adolescents, was codified in puberty rites. Too often now, leaving means "cutting off from," "ignoring," "becoming absent." This is an inadequate and incomplete interpretation, as Parzival's adventures will show. Parzival's father dies before he is born. Then, at a young age, Parzival rides away from his mother, never looking back. Thus divested of both mother and father, we might think, in accordance with the interpretation above, that Parzival is now "free" to meet his destiny. We would be only partially correct.

Physically leaving the childhood environment introduces Parzival and the initiate-speaker to new, challenging situations which force self-confrontation. They then discover and develop their own strengths and struggle with their shortcomings. However, as Parzival will soon demonstrate, what has been absorbed in the family matrix forms much of the basis for one's thoughts, feelings, actions. Uncovering these unexamined inner patterns incorporated during childhood and then starting to question their appropriateness and truth, this is the beginning of the "leaving" to which Christ and Wolfram refer.

Even then, the leaving is not complete. In the deepest sense, leaving one's parents means to surpass, perhaps by transforming, the central striving at the core of the parents' lives. One looks for themes and patterns underlying surface attitudes and actions, which means that one must know oneself and one's parents very well. In this way, one begins to reincorporate the parents at another level in one's being.

Parzival will discover that the yearning for knightly glory he inherited from his father and the determination he inherited from his mother quickly mire him in a circus of difficulties. Only as he begins to "leave" them — to transform raw yearning for the heights into a clear relationship to God and to temper dogged determination with a trust that he does not have to do everything himself — will his circuitous wanderings develop direction and lead to his goal.

The journey toward the Grail leads Parzival and the initiate-speaker to embody fully the Old Testament injunction to honor one's father and mother. The most conscientious way to honor one's father and mother is to "leave" them: to accept and understand, with gratitude, what has come through them and to take those motifs to their next level of expression.

But, before that happens, Parzival and the initiate-speaker will experience the extremes of various opposites. This journey will include portentous meetings, ordeals, exuberant successes and dismal failures. Such outer events, however, provide just the raw material for initiation; the transformation results from what is happening within. As alchemists realized, transformation cannot be observed directly; it is an inner experience long before anything observable appears. Some key questions that can help track the process are: How are these outer events experienced by the initiate-speaker? What "story" can the initiate-speaker tell about them? What inner growth or crumbling does the initiate-speaker notice that results from these experiences and interpretations?

The portrayals of Parzival's parents supply pictures of the inner readiness required to begin the journey. Gahmuret's two major knightly adventures are clues to two conditions. In the first, he fights the black and white armies besieging Belacane, and causes them to cease their war. He then overcomes his reluctance to embrace the people with dark skins, marries their queen, and becomes their king. As background and preparation for the quest, the black and white aspects of life and of oneself have been acknowledged and wrestled with to some degree.

For the second feat, Gahmuret joins an inner army in fighting an outer army in order to participate in Herzeloyde's tournament. Fortified with his prowess, the inner army overcomes the outer army. The analogue within the initiate-speaker occurs when the "inner army" — dream characters and events, conscience and inner promptings, fantasies, feelings, the need for meaning — gains ascendance over the clamor of the "outer army" — the events and people in one's external life.

Please note, however, that this is not a "real" contest. Gahmuret wins only the Vespers games, not the real tournament scheduled later. The story implies that this seeming stronger emphasis on the inner world is not "real." Only a very thin line separates the two worlds. Through the initiation journey, the initiate-speaker will come to realize this more fully. Indeed, Herzeloyde's violent dream just before she hears of Gahmuret's death clearly indicates that inner and outer are intimately connected.

Within the actual text, Gahmuret's life is very externally oriented. He has prepared the ground for his son, in his battles with the black and white, and inner and outer armies, but he himself never reflects or questions. This is Parzival's path, not his father's: to become one who *experiences* as well as acts. All of Parzival's battles will culminate in two poignant moments when he will realize that, for him, the most intense fighting is with *himself*.

From Herzeloyde, Parzival and the initiate-speaker receive another quality of inner readiness. Just as willful yearning drove Gahmuret to distant shores and sometimes to less-than-honorable actions, an equally strong will makes Herzeloyde passionately determined to have what she wants and to control her world so that she can keep it. It does not work. Herzeloyde wins Gahmuret, but loses him; she then tries to keep Parzival away from the world, and, when he leaves her anyway, dies of grief.

In the initiate-speaker, Herzeloyde represents striving for what one wants and doing everything possible to hold on to it, only to have all such efforts frustrated, seeming failures. The resulting sorrow is often what engenders willingness to undertake a journey of initiation. People who achieve lasting worldly success rarely choose to undertake the inner quest, the very first stage of which involves being stripped down, made to appear a "poor fool." This is perhaps why Christ says it is easier for a camel to pass through the eye of a needle than for a rich man to enter heaven. At the crossroads, where the tempting road of glamour, acclaim, worldly wealth and status intersects the road of lonely, tedious, ordinary struggle, and ego-death, the former will, invariably, seem the sweeter path. Until a person has experienced failure, brokenness, fear, emptiness and alienation, the rigors of the initiatory path will not appeal.

This road has few landmarks; this classroom gives no grades; this job offers no salary increases or bonuses; this effort accrues no applause or recognition. For the most part, traveling this path will feel like being lost, abandoned, alone, stretched beyond one's limits, left angry, frustrated, disappointed and ashamed. The goal will often seem not only unattainable but even non-existent. Great yearning and determination are mandatory for such a journey, and, though transmuted, they do not disappear. They are the enduring gifts the initiate-speaker and Parzival receive from their beginnings.

Toward Speech of the Grail

Parzival and the initiate-speaker, bearing within the preparatory conditions of yearning and determination, are about to enter the dark forest of initiation. But first we must ask just who are Parzival and the initiate-speaker in the context of the speech of the Grail, and how does this general background relate to their specific quest? As to who they are, the most general answer is the most true — anyone who is ever in a position to say something important to someone else. Yes, there are professions where speaking is the definitive activity — in helping, educational and pastoral professions as well as politics, public speaking and the spoken arts. However, these are but specializations of the speaking which happens daily and everywhere in human relationships: between spouses, parents and children, business associates, lovers, enemies, and friends.

Under normal circumstances, all human beings learn to talk. To speak requires something more. Like the young Parzival we shall soon meet, few initiate-speakers, professional or otherwise, recognize this dimension of their calling. But a yearning sometimes grows within, and they, like Gahmuret and later his son Parzival, feel called to leave the familiar, habitual ways of talking to find a place in the wider world of speaking.

To reiterate, this journey is not, primarily, an external one, nor is the aim to produce a "product" — some kind of unerringly profound speech. Rather, the initiation slowly transforms all aspects of the initiate-speaker so that person can more consciously inhabit language and speaking. If the word "inhabit" seems questionable, consider the meanings of the first two letters of the Greek alphabet. "Alpha" means "the one who experiences breath" (i.e., the human being), while "beta" refers to an enveloping, enclosing quality like that of a house. Alphabet would thus mean "human being in house."[12]

Inhabiting language entails more than vocal articulation. The initiate-speaker ventures toward an experienced sense of an eternal, unconditional "I," very different from the conditioned "I" of the worldly ego.[13] This means to become Word-like in oneself, and thereby in one's actions, including speaking. In Christianity, the incarnated Word, the Logos, is Christ, and thus it is not irrelevant to the initiate-speaker or merely a cultural nicety that Wolfram gives Herzeloyde the vision of Mary and Christ when Parzival is born.

A definitive yearning burns within all initiate-speakers, including those who feel authentically called to a profession where speaking is central. This yearning is to "communicate" — in the sense of "commune with." Though the initiate-speaker may not be aware of it at first, this yearning inaugurates a quest for knowledge and truth arising through dialogue. Such dialogue sharpens distinctions and even makes them delightful but, at the same time, dissolves artificial walls which exist within and between people. Christ promises that, when two or more are gathered in His name, He will be present. Communion in dialogue both requires and creates the willingness to relate to self and other as "thou." "Thou" is then felt to be inside and outside simultaneously. "Thou" is the "presence" or the "love" that manifests in communication which is communion.[14]

Immediately, a conundrum appears, for what accompanies this yearning is determination — the determination that communion will be established through words. The determination could seem ludicrous because it is precisely language and words that separate and distinguish. It is no coincidence that political boundaries have most often also been linguistic ones. Yet, for an initiate-speaker, the possible foolishness does not extinguish this determination to speak in such a way that language may become a medium of communion.

The force of this determination comes from the intuition that, as Georg Kühlewind articulates,

> language really exists so that man can exercise and realize his humanity through it. Without speaking, a human is not really

human, and this means that without an interlocutor a human is not really human. In earlier times this partner in conversation was the godhead — his first "thou" — and today it is the nearest godhead: his neighbor, another human being.[15]

Gestures, glances, mimicry, smiling, weeping, dance, music, pictorial arts and even "eloquent" silence can all "speak"; they have an expressive intention behind which is language. Those on the path toward the speech of the Grail, however, are called particularly to expression through the spoken word. For them, the spoken word is like the sonar soundings of whales and dolphins. Through speaking, they come to know themselves and others — and to feel known.

The songs of whales ring wistful, even melancholy, to the human ear. Perhaps this tone belongs to all those who plumb the depths. The initiate-speaker dimly recognizes that the audible, visible parts of language are its smaller aspect. No word has any significance outside the context of the whole of language. The sounds, the letters, the words and their combinations float upon the hidden side of language — the vast, generating, yet silent, unseen and unspeakable ocean of meaning. The journey, therefore, will not be toward definitions which delimit words, distinguishing them from each other. Rather, Parzival and the initiate-speaker must swim in the deep, wild waters of meaning — which connects all words. The sunken treasure to be found there is the speech of the Grail.

NOTES

[1] Wolfram, Book I, 9.

[2] Stein, *The Ninth Century and the Holy Grail*, 65–70.

[3] Wolfram, Book II, 62.

[4] Wolfram, Book II, 99.

[5] Wolfram, Book II, 99.

[6] Wolfram, Book II, 105.

[7] Wolfram, Book II, 105. Note regarding he-goat's blood is provided by translators Helen Mustard and Charles Passage, 59.

[8] Wolfram, Book II, 109.

[9] Wolfram, Book II, 111.

[10] Wolfram, Book II, 112.

[11] Wolfram, Book II, 113.

[12] Adapted from Roy Wilkinson, *The Origin and Development of Language,* 50. Remember also Martin Heidegger's famed phrase, "Language is the house of Being," elaborated in *On the Way to Language,* 63, and in the essay ". . . Poetically Man Dwells . . ." in Poetry, Language, Thought, 213–229.

[13] Georg Kühlewind, in *From Normal to Healthy* amplifies: "If someone *experiences* his own being with unshakable firmness, and also knows this being to be eternal and immortal because he experiences it independently of the body, and if he knows that nothing can touch or affect this essence unless this being allows it, then every turn of fate will be met differently than if all of this is only thought or if one is convinced that it is not true. In the latter case one experiences one's being as dependent on outer life, on other people's opinion, on external circumstances. . . . We can only give, only really help, only serve others, if we are. And man only is when he experiences this being in a living way. Tauler's maxim applies here: 'If I were a king and did not know it, then I would not be a king'" (62).

[14] Georg Kühlewind adds *(Becoming Aware of the Logos)*: "Since man is a Logos-being, he can radiate the light of the Word. But the Word requires at least two people. Only in this way does the human word, even the unspoken word, encounter the human understanding and shine back. That is the Logos-being's presence on earth. . . . The relation of the Logos-being to man is one of reciprocal indwelling — that is what makes a human being human — but the Logos-being can have its earthly realization only in humanity, in the common reality of *all* human beings. For the Logos is present in everyone, and man cannot find his own reality alone, but only in the totality of the Logos-Light. The Logos-nature cannot unfold in isolation, in single human beings" (115).

And regarding dialogue, please consult Martin Buber, *I and Thou.*

[15] Kühlewind, *From Normal to Healthy,* 99.

CHAPTER TWO

"A Fool Came Riding Along Here"

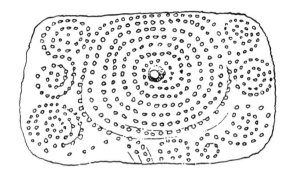

The Grail King Speaks

Oh, Speaker,
There is no place to hide,
And you will go directly
Toward what you most fear —

Awkward foolishness,
With innocence no excuse
For ignorant blunders,
And the world jeering in scorn.

Yet, in all innocence, comes first love,
And the union whose nourishment
Replenishes the world.

And, then, Oh gift of soul!
Arrives memory,
And, with memory
The threshold beckons

BOOK III

Her husband dead, Herzeloyde is determined that her son will live. She leaves her three kingdoms, exposing them to takeover by the sinister knight Lehelin, and takes Parzival into the forest of Soltane to hide him away, forever if possible, from the world of knighthood, battles and the inevitable sorrows that world causes a loving heart. Herzeloyde instructs her attendants in the forest clearing never to utter a word regarding knighthood, so Parzival grows up ignorant of his heritage. He doesn't even know his name.

As a young boy, he crafts a small bow and some arrows and begins to hunt birds. However, every time a bird he has killed falls from the sky, "he would weep and tear his hair,"[1] until his hair actually becomes thin. Herzeloyde asks why he is so distraught, but he cannot explain it.

> For a long time she kept pursuing the matter. One day she saw him gaping up at the trees toward the song of the birds, and then she realized that it was their voices that made her child's bosom swell. His heritage and his desire thus compelled him. Without knowing quite why, Lady Herzeloyde turned her anger against the birds and wanted to destroy their song. She bade her plowmen and her field hands make haste to snare the birds and twist their necks.[2]

Soon after, Parzival sees the men killing the birds and asks his mother: "What do they have against the birds?"[3] She kisses him and muses aloud that she really has no right to alter the supreme commandment of God against killing. His next question is, "O, what is God, Mother?"[4] Herzeloyde describes the deity as being "brighter than daylight, yet He took upon Himself the features of man."[5]

Parzival eventually has grown so large that, when he hunts game, he can carry whole carcasses home on his back. One day, while out hunting, he encounters a prince and three knights in gleaming armor, galloping across a meadow. Entranced by their shining brightness, he thinks they must be gods, as his mother described, and he immediately begins to interview them. His incessant, simple-minded questions amuse the prince who tells him that they are not gods but knights of Arthur's court and that, if he is interested, he must go there to be knighted by Arthur.

Straightaway, Parzival goes to his mother, tells her that he has seen "four men more shining than God,"[6] and that he wants a horse so he can go to Arthur's court and become a knight. She is horrified, of course, and, unable to dissuade him, thinks she can nonetheless insure he will not be accepted at court and will come back to her and the safety of Soltane. For his clothes, she makes a shirt and breeches of sackcloth, the normal garment of fools, and then mounts him on a nag barely fit for a bumpkin, let alone an aspiring knight.

Herzeloyde also supplies him with advice for navigating successfully in the world. She tells him to beware of crossing streams where the bottom is not clear and to find shallows; to be polite and greet people; to accept the teaching of older, grey-haired men; and, whenever possible, to win a good woman's ring by kissing and embracing her. She informs him as well that greedy Lehelin has wrested away two of her countries, and he swears to avenge this.

Oblivious of his clownish appearance, Parzival boldly rides away, unaware that behind him Herzeloyde has fallen to the ground, dead from grief. Through all that day and into the next, he follows her advice to cross streams only at the shallows until, in the heat of midday, he comes to a luxurious tent pitched in a broad meadow. He enters the tent of the knight Orilus whose beautiful, young wife, Jeschute, lies sleeping naked on the bed. Seeing the ring on her small, white hand, Parzival again faithfully follows what he understands to be his mother's instructions. He leaps onto the bed and, over the protests of the startled lady, forces his mouth to hers. Even as she struggles, he roughly snatches her ring and a brooch from her smock as well. Then he complains that he's hungry. Jeschute, who by now thinks him a boy who's lost his wits, points to the food on a side table. He quickly gobbles this down, gives her his blessing, and skips off to his next encounter.

Jeschute is then left to cope with her husband, Orilus, who, upon his return, sees the trodden ground and assumes she has betrayed him with another man. He punishes her, despite her protests of innocence, forcing her to ride behind him in rags, exposing her to shame. They will ride like this for a year before meeting up with Parzival again.

Parzival does not witness Jeschute's grief, but he meets it in another form. Beside a cliff, faithful Sigune sits, mourning, tearing her hair and wailing, with her dead lover in her lap. Parzival asks her who has killed this knight, saying that he will go to fight the offender, but Sigune declines, explaining that Schianatulander died in fair combat.[7] Much impressed with this young man's beauty, which is not obscured by his fool's garb, Sigune asks his name. Parzival admits he does not know it, that he was always called "sweet son," or "dear boy" or "beautiful son" by his mother. These pet names are familiar to Sigune, and she now recognizes her cousin, telling him his name is Parzival, "which means 'right through the middle'."[8] She also describes his lineage and his inheritance, part of which has been stolen by Lehelin. Indeed, Schianatulander was killed defending Parzival's lands. Parzival is ready there and then to find the perpetrators and avenge Schianatulander. However, fearing for his safety, Sigune sends him off in another direction.

Parzival seems to forget this encounter completely. He rides merrily along, greeting everyone he meets and informing them that his mother told him to do that. He spends the night in the home of a stingy fisherman, who refuses to offer lodging or food unless he is paid well for the service. Lady Jeschute's brooch satisfies him, and he even agrees the next day to conduct Parzival to Arthur's court. The two travel to the outskirts of Nantes, but there the fisherman leaves, claiming that all the highbred townspeople would take offense at a peasant coming into their midst.

As he approaches the castle, Parzival meets a knight dressed in magnificent red armor, bearing a red spear and shield, and riding a red horse with crimson trappings. The red knight has rushed from the castle, carrying a goblet of red gold that he grabbed from the Round Table after delivering a challenge to Arthur. The knight greets Parzival courteously and asks him to deliver his apology to Queen Ginover for inadvertently spilling some wine on her when he took the goblet. He tells Parzival to challenge Arthur's knights to come out and retrieve the goblet from him if they want to maintain their reputations.

Parzival rides into Arthur's court with the same naivete, insensitivity and ignorance of proper form that have previously characterized him. Even though he admits he does not know which of the men in the hall is Arthur, he delivers the red knight's messages. The members of the court notice his beauty, as well as his rough clothing and crude manners, and Arthur greets him. Parzival immediately asks to be made a knight, and Arthur says that can be done in the morning when a proper outfitting can be arranged. However, Parzival declares he wants only the armor, horse and outfitting of the red knight he has just met, adding "If I can't get his armor, I don't care who talks about kingly gifts. Those my mother can give me, for after all she is a queen."[9]

Arthur explains he cannot give that armor to Parzival because it belongs to Ither, whose homage he has lost through no fault of his own. Keie, the king's cantankerous seneschal, suggests that Arthur send this rash boy out to meet Ither on the field and retrieve the goblet. If he can do it, then he can get the armor too. Since Parzival is also eager for this, Arthur relents and allows him to go.

As this motley fool ambles forth, a strange thing happens. The Lady Cunneware laughs. This is strange because she has been under a constraint never to laugh until her eyes behold the knight who is to win the highest praise and honor. Also, just as she laughs, the fool Antanor speaks. Antanor was thought a fool because he did not speak, and he was never to speak until Cunneware laughed. What he speaks is a prophecy to Keie, who, enraged at Cunneware, has begun to beat her for honoring such a poor excuse for a knight as Parzival after so many knights of renown have come and gone at the court. Antanor predicts that, although Keie has not been prevented from thrashing Cunneware for smiling upon Parzival, pretty soon Parzival's hand will take away all Keie's joy. For these words, and the speaking itself, Antanor also receives a sound beating by Keie. Parzival observes all this and feels greatly distressed by the pain these two have suffered on his account.

Nonetheless he proceeds to the field to meet Ither. Once there, he accosts Ither with the announcement that none of the knights in the hall have chosen to fight him but that Arthur has given him, Parzival, the gift of Ither's armor. Ither feels dishonored by Arthur's decision and tells Parzival he will have to win the armor from him. Parzival responds, "I dare to earn whatever I deserve,"[10] and grabs Ither's bridle, wondering aloud if this knight might be Lehelin. Ither then reverses his spear and roughly knocks Parzival off his pony. Infuriated, Parzival aims and throws his javelot, which is for hunting and not at all a knightly weapon. It enters the opening of Ither's visor, penetrating his eye and head. Ither, one of the finest knights in the land, falls, dead from this unchivalrous blow. Parzival's only regret is that he does not know how to pull the armor off the dead man. He has to wait until a squire comes along to help him.

The squire, Iwanet, tries to advise Parzival that the garments he has on are not fit for a knight. Parzival refuses the suggestion that he should take them off. "Anything my mother gave me is not going to be cast off, whether for the better or for the worse,"[11] he says, and proceeds to pile on the armor over his sackcloth jersey. He does follow Iwanet's bidding to give up his javelot and thereafter uses the red knight's spear instead, but only after asking Iwanet how to use it.

Then he sends Iwanet back to the court with the goblet and with the report of the "great insult" done to him when Keie beat Cunneware. "The lady's undeserved suffering does not touch just the edge of my heart but lies at its very center."[12]

While Ither is being mourned at court for his untimely and shamefully accomplished death, Parzival rides away, dressed as a knight but still "ruled by simplicity." We are told that "He rode at a gallop, rarely a trot, because he did not know how to check the speed."[13] In the evening, he arrives at a castle in front of which sits an old knight. Parzival announces that his mother instructed him to accept advice from men with grey hair and offers his service to the old man. Gurnemanz de Graharz, who has lost three sons in knightly battles, replies that the young man must first guarantee his friendliness. Very soon, Gurnemanz welcomes Parzival as a foster son, teaching him the ways of knighthood. One of his first directions to Parzival is to "stop talking about your mother and think of other things."[14]

Soon after, Gurnemanz imparts a code of behavior that he deems necessary for any knight. These eleven rules of conduct include: valuing a sense of shame; showing compassion, modesty, politeness; being thoughtful, alert and trusting of the senses; being manly, cheerful and truthful, especially to women; and respecting the great worth of marriage. Also among these is the injunction that will be so fateful for Parzival: "Do not ask too many questions."[15]

Parzival advances rapidly in knightly skill under Gurnemanz's tutelage, and he even gives up talking about his mother — "in his speech, but not in his heart, as is still a true man's way."[16] Gurnemanz no doubt hopes that this foster son will become a son-in-law by marrying his daughter Liaze, but Parzival wants "to have fought better before enjoying the warmth of what they call 'a lady's arms'."[17] After two weeks at Gurnemanz's castle, he announces his departure, though his heart and his body have been stirred by Liaze.

Initiatory Themes

Within the initiate-speaker, something very large emerges. Wolfram introduces a Parzival who is so big that Herzeloyde barely survives his birth and so strong that, as a youth, he can carry whole stags home from the hunt. Everyone he meets, even early on, can see his beauty, radiating despite his odd clothes, ignorance and awkwardness. Parzival-within-the-initiate-speaker must likewise be very big, an imposing presence who can be denied only at the peril of whoever tries to obstruct him.

Parzival pursues first the birds, then the knights, then Ither's horse and armor. Whatever calls the initiate-speaker forth may seem equally capricious or mysterious, felt perhaps as a discomfiting yearning that will translate, eventually, into a guiding vision. This guiding vision, fashioned by each initiate-speaker from his or her life experiences, takes the place of the overarching myths that provide the framework for ancestral initiations. Meanwhile, the initial reaction may be resistance. Something in, or around, the seeker — in Parzival's case, Herzeloyde — senses this strong calling in the seeker's being. There can be a definite urge to run away and hide — particularly if one intuits what discomforts and changes the calling will precipitate.

Inevitably, however, we always move toward what we fear. In the attempt to protect Parzival — and herself — Herzeloyde actually gives impetus to what she fears most: his departure. True to his heritage, Parzival yearns determinedly to touch the heights by shooting birds with his bow and arrows. Trying to prevent his despair when he sees them plummet lifelessly to earth, Herzeloyde orders the birds killed. Her action soon leads Parzival to question her and to receive in her answers the shining image of God he will soon see in the knights and want to follow.

Once on the path, as Parzival demonstrates, there is no looking back. The process of initiation does not resemble a trip to Disneyland. One does not "visit" initiation, linger for a while, and then depart unchanged. Yet, when seeker and quest first emerge, they are hidden away from each other as tree is hidden in seed. Paradoxically, the tree, which cannot see the seed, calls from within the seed to grow, while the seed, which cannot know the tree, must abandon the protection of the fruit in order to sprout.

Vulnerable seedlings that they are, Parzival and the initiate-speaker may at first appear ill-prepared for the journey. Their fumbling efforts to find direction may prove to be not only graceless but even a source of pain for others. In fact, the first demon glaring at the initiate-speaker from the threshold of initiation will be the fear of appearing foolish. The fear is justified. One *will* be awkward, make mistakes, hurt others.

Crossing that threshold depends on the strength to endure one's own foolishness, failure, embarrassment and humiliation. Remember, Parzival and the initiate-speaker are not striving for perfection. They seek a new understanding of imperfection, thereby making imperfection an ally — the means by which the journey is made. Scholar of religions Northrup Frye concurs:

> . . . We follow a "way" or direction until we reach the state of innocence symbolized by the sheep in the twenty-third Psalm, where we are back to wandering but where wandering no longer means being lost. There are two senses in which the word "imperfect" is used: in one sense it is that which falls short of perfection; in another it is that which is not finished but continuously active, as in the tense system of verbs in most languages. It is in the latter sense that "the imperfect is our paradise," as Wallace Stevens says, . . .[18]

Poetically said, but Parzival and the initiate-speaker find thorns in that garden, pricking them with shame. These wounds can, however, become openings toward greater awareness and sensitivity. Parzival is shaken from his slumber of "simplicity" for a few moments when he observes Cunneware's beating. Stung by the pain he watches her suffer, he will never again be as insensitive and self-centered in regard to women as he was with Jeschute. (It takes longer for him to become more sensitive toward the men.) He has already been softened by seeing Sigune's grief, though he seems more focused on Schianatulander's undeserved death than on Sigune's anguish. But Cunneware's pain is, seemingly, on account of him, and the shame he feels will spur him to win many battles and to send the losers to give themselves to her service.

Neither imperfection nor shame much impedes Parzival's progress. He proceeds, albeit awkwardly, in pursuit of the beckoning vision of knighthood. Not to be intimidated by one's fear of appearing foolish requires either blithe innocence or plucky intrepidness. Parzival and the initiate-speaker probably possess both in good measure at the beginning of their journeys. They are mounted on a new momentum now, after a brief but heady success, but the horse does not really belong to them and they are carried at a gallop only because they do not know how to slow the pace.

Galloping fast and far from the hideout in the forest, Parzival arrives at the castle of Gurnemanz whose teachings will supersede those of his mother. Her advice, interestingly, was very externally-oriented, couched mostly in terms of actions. It was easy, therefore, for Parzival to take her words too literally. Gurnemanz's teachings are more internal in essence, more "moral" in content: (1) Know the value of the sense of shame. (2) Show compassion for the poor and needy. (3) "Be both poor and rich appropriately." (4) "Leave bad manners to their own quarrel." (5) Do not ask too many questions. (6) Give thoughtful answers to questions and let your senses — of sight, taste, and smell — guide you to wisdom. (7) "Let mercy go along with daring" and do not kill defeated opponents. (8) Wash well after removing armor so that your beauty can be seen. (9) "Be manly and cheerful of spirit." (10) "Let women be dear to you" and do not lie to them for that can never serve love. (11) "Husband and wife are as one, as are the sun that shone today and the thing called day itself. . . . Strive to understand this."[19]

Gurnemanz's very first counsel reminds Parzival to recognize the value of his sense of shame. The advice could seem detrimental in the feel-good context of 1990s America where the value of a sense of shame is severely underrated. However, Gurnemanz here gives Parzival and the initiate-speaker an important hint about how they might relate to their imperfections in a new way. The sense of shame, says Gurnemanz, pricks sharply whenever one has said or done something that is dishonorable, something that is beneath one. The initiate-speaker may barely feel a twinge at first. Over time, however, one will begin to recognize quite painfully each time one's deeds or speech have been unworthy.

Gurnemanz certainly is not suggesting that Parzival and the initiate-speaker dissolve in a puddle of self-condemnation when they feel shame. Instead, he encourages Parzival to learn to value the sense of shame as a teacher, which prods his conscience when he has violated the code of honor by some word or deed. This code is only partially culturally given; each person also develops an inner sense of what words and actions befit his or her self-respect. Shame then becomes a reminder, helping Parzival and the initiate-speaker to be more "true" — in the sense of an arrow that flies true — in both doing and speaking.

This first rule is complemented in Gurnemanz's concluding

comments. He tells Parzival that "husband and wife are one," and seems to know that this wisdom cannot be taught directly or comprehended immediately. He urges Parzival to "strive to understand"[20] what marriage means. Marriage, whether to a person, to creative work, or to a quest, results from profound choice. Usually only partially aware of the source of this choice or where it will lead, one nonetheless joins with one's destiny whenever such a commitment is made. Thus, not to understand the inherent oneness of the two who are joined — husband and wife, creator and work, seeker and quest — is to risk disloyalty to and separation from one's own destiny. Gurnemanz aims to awaken Parzival to the significance of the choice to marry and the necessity of remaining loyal to that choice once it is made. Chaos and confusion in the communal realm and great hurt and pain in the personal realm are the results of failure to do otherwise.

Gurnemanz's teachings also apply to the initiate-speaker. Initiation is a marriage. The seeker and the quest are one; like content and form, neither has shape without the other. Furthermore, through this alchemical conjunction, the initiate is united with a new self-knowledge, a new understanding of the world, a new sense of responsibility. Once one is set upon the path of initiation, the transformation begins and there is no going back to the way things were before. Any attempt at reversal portends severe consequences for the initiate and perhaps for others as well. One of the reasons such care surrounds the preparation and enactment of ancestral initiatory rites is that those who conduct such rituals recognize the degree of risk present for the initiate and the community.

The initiatory significance of Gurnemanz's teachings consists of their addressing Parzival as a moral being and exhorting him to make a code of ethics the foundation of his life. Few would disagree, and yet even this advice is not perfect but black-and-white mixed. Something Gurnemanz says — "Do not ask too many questions" — will eventually cause torment, because knowing the "good" in each situation is not given and cannot be taught. Living life vigorously loyal to a moral code constitutes only a preparation, a strengthening, for those moments when each person must decide, alone, what is truly good for a specific situation.

Parzival, still quite literal-minded, swallows Gurnemanz's advice whole, unquestioned, as he did his mother's. As a result, he will dutifully resist asking any questions during his first visit to the Grail castle and will fail to deliver the Grail king from his suffering. By remaining attached to habits or codes from the past which need to be released or at least re-examined, the initiate-speaker will likewise make mistakes. But this is not to be mourned, because the bitter harvest of mistakes activates the whole journey — *if* one has cultivated a healthy sense of shame.

Maybe that is why Parzival chooses to take leave of Gurnemanz and declines his offer of love and security with Liaze. Parzival has received teachings, but he knows he has not earned his own way yet, has not striven enough with and against the world to develop his own seasoned wisdom. That will only mature after many, many battles, and it is to the first of these he now rides.

Toward Speech of the Grail

Bird images hover throughout Wolfram's story, appearing at crucial moments in Parzival's journey. Mythologies the world over associate birds and their soaring flight with the concept of spirit. Thus we can deduce that, for young Parzival, the birds he shoots represent his first exposure to his spiritual calling. The person who can represent the Grail, become a speaker of the healing word, has a nascent sense of belonging with spirit. At first, however, the attraction may be experienced more as an absence, an emptiness, than as a nourishing presence. Then some profoundly moving image or experience seems to promise connection, though the seeker may as yet not be conscious of what she or he is reaching for. As Herzeloyde notices, Parzival is struck by an aural image — the birds' voices.

That Parzival seeks to bring down the very birds that so attract him reflects the human tendency to misunderstand our relationship to spirit, to that in us which calls us to speak. The temptation is to try to conquer, control or bend those urges into something for personal security, pleasure or gain. Succumbing to such desire only assures the helpless descent and seeming demise of the power in us through which we can experience true freedom, the human equivalent of birds' flight.

Still, this spiritual force is not easily obliterated. Parzival does not understand the spirit in the image of the birds, but his potential to learn and change are indicated by his grief at the death of the birds and by the two questions he asks Herzeloyde: "What do they have against the birds?" and then, "O, what is God, mother?" These are the only words of any profundity that Parzival will say for quite a while. All through these early adventures, his speech is naive and foolish at best and downright stupid and insensitive at worst. The implication could be that, while speaking is one of the first things we do, it will be among the last things we do well. And there is no guarantee even of that.

However, Parzival's first words in the story are noteworthy because they are framed as questions, and questioning is the engine of contemporary initiation. Questions form the connective tissue by which we join the world with ourselves. A question is uniquely personal; something matters, and the questioner wishes to know about something or someone. At the same time, a question is interpersonal. It is addressed to someone or something, thereby relating the questioner to whomever or whatever is addressed. Finally, since questions concern some aspect of the cosmos we inhabit, we can follow them to realms far beyond, but inclusive of, both the personal and interpersonal.

As curious children, we ask questions. If as adults we have kept the soil of wonder well watered, we will continue to ask questions. Such questions, always leading to more questions, are the pre-eminent teachers of thought. Spiritual teachers in all traditions ply their students with riddles, koans, and perplexing parables. Through questions, Parzival and the initiate-speaker must simultaneously reach deep inside themselves and stretch out beyond themselves.

Questions free our minds to fly. The birds killed at Herzeloyde's command have been reborn in Parzival — as questions. Flying (and sometimes waddling!) in pursuit, Parzival and the initiate-speaker will learn to treasure their questions and, through them, grow closer to the spirit first glimpsed in the birds.

But, once Parzival is off into the world, if he resembles any bird, it is certainly that magpie of which Wolfram spoke at the beginning. He is a mixed-up youth, bearing "Love's color," yet dark with ignorance, misunderstanding and insensitivity. Specifically, his speaking is barely more developed than a parrot. He speaks as he has been taught to speak and rarely knows what he really means, let alone the consequences of what he says.

A counterpart for this phase of the initiation appears in the

Bible (which can also be interpreted as an initiation in speaking, becoming one with the Word[21]). The Tower of Babel, described early in Genesis (11:1–9), was built to satisfy powerful human ambitions. The people at that time, who, we are told, were "of one language, and of one speech," decided to build a tower "whose top may reach unto heaven," and whose construction would "make us a name, lest we be scattered abroad upon the face of the whole earth." In other words, their ambition to build the tower originated from a need for a center of orientation, a need to name and thereby recognize and remember who they were.

For reasons not clearly explained in the text, this ambition affronted the Deity who observed that "they have all one language and this they begin to do: and now nothing will be restrained from them, which they have imagined to do." Then the Lord "did there confound the language of all the earth," so that the people could not understand one another's speech, and scattered them across the earth.

The healing for this schism happens only much later, in the New Testament, when, at Pentecost, the Spirit descends in living flames on the Apostles (Acts 2:1–13) and they are thus empowered to speak in a language that all present can understand: "The multitude came together, and were confounded, because that every man heard them speak in his own language." Far ahead in Parzival's own journey, Pentecost will also be a turning point. We can be sure Wolfram was aware of the resonance with the Biblical narrative.

Meanwhile, in Book III, Parzival and the initiate-speaker are definitely in the Babel phase. Parzival babbles merrily on, following his ambition to connect with the radiant heights. No longer the birds, now knighthood has become the alluring image he hunts. The amusement, confusion and pain his naive babbling cause are shown, respectively, in the scenes with the three knights he thinks are gods, with Jeschute and then with the red knight, Ither. No real communication occurs in these episodes; Parzival utters words, but does not listen to or understand clearly what others say back to him. The others, meanwhile, are dumbfounded, "confounded," as it were, by this brash boy who is simultaneously so beautiful and so idiotic.

Parzival is empty-headed, "thoughtless" in the sense of both being insensitive and lacking thought. When this is added to an unconscious grasping for spirit in the glittering guise of material things, power, influence and glamour, the combination — to Ither's sorrow — is lethal. Parzival and the initiate-speaker will wreak destruction unless they develop conscience and conscientiousness. The shame at Cunneware's beating and then Gurnemanz's teachings are first steps in that direction.

The ethical advice Gurnemanz gives Parzival has ramifications for his speech as well as his general character. In antiquity, when the power of the word (to accomplish good *or* evil) was more generally acknowledged, it was assumed that a "good" speaker was a good person — that he or she aspired to the good, the true and the beautiful in thought and action as well as words. The goodness of the speech, its healing or therapeutic effect, had its source in the goodness of the speaker, as Pedro Lain Entralgo has discussed in *The Therapy of the Word in Classical Antiquity*. No less a commentator than Aristotle delineated the foundation of the orator's art: "the character of the speaker, the inclination of the hearer, and what is said in the speech."[22] Of these, the character of the speaker was deemed most critical — meaning not only the "natural qualities" of the speaker, but also the moral habits acquired in the course of life.

Rudolf Steiner adopted from antiquity and developed further many ideas about speech. He formulated the concept of "ethical speaking," the ability to know and to do what is good in each rhetorical situation and context. Werner Glas, in his dissertation on Steiner's rhetorical thought, quotes Steiner cautioning a potential speaker:

> You will only arrive at what you are aiming to achieve through the cultivation of two fundamental attitudes of soul. You must nurture a true love for what you represent, and also an insightful love of humanity. Be quite clear that if these two conditions are not met, or these attitudes are replaced by others, let us say by ambition or vanity, you may be able to present material ever so logically, you may be able to demonstrate exceptional cleverness, and you will still not achieve anything.[23]

Steiner proposes that, without love (the modern word for what, in antiquity, was called "the good"), the initiate-speaker will not be inspired by sufficient "inner powers of invention."[24] Somehow the capacity to improvise spontaneously in articulation grows out of our goodness, our moral character. We might ask why? The simplest answer is that only in our ethics are we free. Anyone can look around and see that ethical conduct receives small reward in this world. Lying, cheating, manipulating, stealing, aggression and violence usually accrue greater earthly wealth and power in the short run. But unethical action is never free; it always serves the underlying taskmasters of fear or greed. To choose honesty, generosity, forgiveness or unconditional love as the basis of one's actions cannot be "reasonable" in such a world. There is little earthly reward and therefore no reason to do so. Hence, such choice must really be free. To be free means one has the power to "begin," to create anew, which is why Christ — most moral and most free of beings — can say, "Behold, I make all things new." The conclusion can only be that our ability to heal and transform others with our speaking depends entirely on the degree to which we have become truly free.

Moral character, in individuals and in humanity as a whole, evolves over time. Cultural codes of morality foster its early development in both. But, as we will soon see in Parzival's journey, situations arise where a code will not suffice. Only strong integrity joined with inventive spontaneity can create a right course of action. Parzival and the initiate-speaker have far to travel before they possess that capability.

BOOK IV

Taking his leave from Gurnemanz, Parzival rides for a day, disturbed by thoughts of sweet Liaze. These fantasies distract him to such a degree that he does not direct his horse and allows it to trot or gallop as it will through wild and unknown country. After a while, they come to a rushing stream, which Parzival remembers to ford at a shallow place, and then to a castle whose drawbridge spans this same stream. When he arrives, the doors are locked against him. As it turns out, the castle is under siege, and those inside think Parzival is the attacker. The embattled inhabitants brandish their weapons, shouting, "Go back," and the bridge sways so wildly that Parzival must dismount and lead his horse across. Despite all this, he is finally admitted to the castle through the help of a young maiden.

Inside he discovers a weakened, wounded army of men who,

along with the townspeople, are ashen with hunger. After the rust of his armor is washed off, his beauty reassures the townspeople that he is a knight worthy of their service, and they conduct him to their queen, Condwiramurs, of whom Wolfram writes:

> In *her* God had not omitted any wish, she was the mistress of the land, and like the rose washed with the sweet dew that from its bud sends forth its new and noble glow, red and white together.[25]

Parzival is moved by her incomparable beauty, but, guided as ever by what he has been told, adheres to Gurnemanz's advice not to ask questions. Thus Condwiramurs finally decides she must speak first, even though she thinks Parzival must be put off by her thinness from so little food.

> Sir, a hostess must speak. My kiss earned me your greeting, and besides, you did offer your service when you arrived — so one of my maidens told me. Guests have not accustomed us to that, but my heart has longed for it. Sir, I inquire whence your journey has brought you?[26]

Parzival responds that he has just come from the castle of the venerable Gurnemanz. Since Condwiramurs knows Liaze very well, this identifies him as someone safe to welcome as a friend, though she is amazed that he has traveled in one day the distance requiring two days for her swiftest messengers.

As Parzival and Condwiramurs become acquainted, food coincidentally becomes available for the starving people in the castle. Two old men volunteer provisions from their remote forest home, and Condwiramurs, following Parzival's instructions, distributes the food. "Thus for the two of them [Condwiramurs and Parzival] hardly a morsel remained, but they shared it without an argument."[27] Not long after, it is time to sleep.

In the middle of the night, "not for such love as gains the name of changing maids to women, but for help and a friend's advice,"[28] Condwiramurs, with tears streaming from her eyes, steals up to Parzival's bed and wakes him. Urging her not to kneel at his bedside — an honor due only God — he asks her to sit up beside him on the bed or to let him get out of bed so she can lie where he was and he can lie somewhere else. She tells him that if he will not "wrestle" with her, she will lie beside him and tell him her woe. He readily agrees, and she tells him her story.

Left an orphan by her father, Condwiramurs has been pursued by Clamide, the knight who killed one of Gurnemanz's sons. Because she has refused to give herself to him, Clamide and his seneschal Kingrun have besieged the castle, killing half her army. She tells Parzival that she will die rather than surrender herself. When he asks her what can help her, she answers that, if Kingrun could be defeated on the morrow, she would be saved from throwing herself into the moat. Parzival swears to defend her.

In the morning, he rides forth to battle. This is his first sword fight, yet he defeats the seasoned knight Kingrun after a fierce joust. He first wants to send Kingrun to Gurnemanz with his oath of service, but Kingrun says that, since Clamide killed Gurnemanz's son, he will be killed there. Then Parzival wants him to take his oath of service to Condwiramurs, but Kingrun claims he will be hacked to pieces by her troops as well. So, finally, Parzival sends the defeated seneschal to Arthur's court, instructing him to offer his oath of surrender to the "maid who laughed" and to tell her that Parzival is in her service. Furthermore, Kingrun is to tell Arthur and Ginover that Parzival is in their service and will return to the court only when he has avenged Cunneware of the unfair beating she received, when "I have purged myself of a shame which I bear in common with her who offered me her laughter."[29]

A ship of provisions arrives soon after Condwiramurs has helped Parzival remove his armor. Parzival arranges to pay the merchants double the cost of their wares and then portions out the food to the hungry people of the castle. He is careful not to give them too much at first in case they should "overtax" their stomachs, and then he gives them more later. They have declared him their king, and Condwiramurs has offered him her love.

That night, Parzival and Condwiramurs share the same bed but they do not consummate their marriage. Nevertheless, the next day Condwiramurs ties on the headdress of a matron to designate Parzival's love for her. Two more chaste nights pass as they simply enjoy one another's affection. Parzival often thinks of embracing her, but only on the fourth night do their bodies entwine, and he finds the closeness sweet.

Meanwhile Clamide arrives with reinforcements and receives news of Kingrun's defeat. He tries unsuccessfully to storm the gates and then, upon learning that the castle is now well provisioned, offers a truce if Parzival will meet him one-on-one in battle. Parzival agrees, and they meet in ferocious combat, from which Parzival emerges the victor. He threatens to kill Clamide, but the latter asks that his life be spared. Parzival then wants to send him to Gurnemanz, but Clamide, like Kingrun, begs not to be sent there, so Parzival sends him, too, to Arthur's court to give his oath of surrender to the lady who laughed. (Back at Arthur's court, the arrival of the first of a virtual tide of defeated knights who swear their oath to Cunneware causes the seneschal Keie growing discomfort and increasing disapproval from the court. Everyone now agrees that he acted improperly in beating the lady, though he continues to defend his actions.)

Parzival and Condwiramurs live happily together for a year or so as the kingdom is rebuilt.[30] The young king is beloved for both his bravery in battle and his generosity. Then something stirs in Parzival's memory. One morning he asks Condwiramurs' leave to go "see how things are faring with my mother, for I know nothing at all as to whether she is well or ill."[31] For this purpose, and "for adventure," further to serve his lady, Parzival leaves his home and kingdom. It will be a long time before he sees his wife again.

A Brief Excursus

We should pause to consider all these besieged and sorrowing women whom we meet in this story. They are not the *only* type of women we meet, but they predominate. Who are they in the journey of the initiate-speaker? Those of us influenced by feminist thinking may feel impatient with, even offended by, the portrayal of all these mournful ladies, trapped passively in their castles, waiting helplessly for rescue. But if we can calm our sociopolitical sensitivities for a while, we may begin to hear deeper resonances of this image.

First let us recall the queen or lady in her castle. She is besieged (for one reason or another, but usually having to do with love) by an army who repeatedly attacks her stronghold. Her own forces grow weak, and she awaits one who can strengthen her forces and return peace to her castle and her country. She will usually marry the one who accomplishes this task.

A possible clue to her identity might be found in the rhythmic quality of a siege. Periods of attack alternate with retreat, and s times these rhythms are coordinated with the rhythms of the c (fighting in the daytime but not at night) or the season of the year, if the siege lasts so long. This rhythmic movement of war is a kind of "breathing" that transpires in and around the castle. The image of breathing suggests a body, specifically the human body, with its rhythmic breathing bearing witness to the equally reliable rhythm of the heart surrounded by expanding and contracting lungs. The question then becomes, what, besides the physical body, is enlivened by rhythm?

One answer might be the soul. One school of thinkers says that the soul only enters the infant with its first breath, so for them, at least, the soul is animated by the rhythm of the breath. There are other opinions, but it is not necessary here to outline the many tomes of philosophical and theological inquiry on the nature of the soul. More to the point is the general agreement that the soul is quite distinct from the spirit.

Spirit, invariably imagined in birds and their flight, is related to the wind, the breath of God. The sovereignty of the spirit is assured and immutable. It is universal, not individual (which is why its descent upon the Apostles allows their words to be understood by everyone). The spirit is always present, unchanging, but to become known, to be experienced, by humans it must be attained — by ascent or even, though less often, descent. Images of the spirit, says archetypal psychologist James Hillman,

> . . . blaze with light; there is fire, wind, sperm. Spirit is fast, and it quickens what it touches. Its direction is vertical and ascending; it is arrow-straight, knife-sharp, powder-dry, and phallic. It is masculine, the active principle, making forms, order, and clear distinctions. . . .[32]

Soul receives a quite opposite depiction. Feminine in quality, associated with moistness and depth, soul manifests in an individual way in each person, as near to one as the breath in one's body. Actually, for the ancients, the word "soul" (known as nephesh or "breath" in the Old Testament and psyche in the New Testament) refers to the unity of body and inner, experiencing self before any distinction was made between the two.[33] In James Hillman's imagining,

. . . soul sticks to the realm of experience and to reflections within experience. It moves indirectly in circular reasonings where retreats are as important as advances, preferring labyrinths and corners, giving a metaphorical sense to life through such words as "close," "near," "slow," and "deep.". . . It is the "patient" part of us. Soul is vulnerable and suffers; it is passive and remembers. It is water to spirit's fire, like a mermaid who beckons the heroic spirit into the depths of passions to extinguish its certainty. *soul is imagination*, a cavernous treasury . . . a confusion and richness, both.[34]

The sovereignty of the soul, unlike that of the spirit, is not a "given." Like a queen and the land she represents, the soul must be acknowledged, honored and protected. Rather than attained, the soul must be developed — or at least a relationship with the soul must be developed. How is such a relationship developed? It would seem that we come to know our soul, not through vertical ascent or descent, but through wavelike rhythm.

In this respect then, we can view the lady queen in her castle as the soul of the initiate-speaker. The initiate-speaker, whose name is Parzival in this story, is made aware of her presence inside by the rhythmic waves of worldly assault upon her stronghold. If the knight yearning to fly to the heights represents the spirit in the quest, the embattled lady waiting to be known in love represents the soul of the quest. It is her heart the initiate must win and marry before the quest can begin in earnest. When soul and spirit marry in the initiate-speaker, the door to the Grail castle, though still hidden, opens.

Initiatory Themes

Parzival has matured greatly since leaving the sheltering forest of his childhood. He has changed from a bumbling, uncouth, truly callow youth to a responsible and increasingly sensitive young man. Now he does not just impetuously demand and take what appeals to him in the world, but is generous, even nurturing, toward others. These qualities suggest his readiness to meet Condwiramurs whom, associated with the colors white and red, purity and passion, he will recognize as his true wife.

The first speech we hear from Condwiramurs occurs within herself. She tries to understand why Parzival does not speak to her, then overcomes her trepidation that he may be repulsed by her wasted appearance and urges herself to act appropriately as his hostess and be the first to speak. She has waited and suffered a long while until her rescuer should appear, and she will wait long again after he departs. Her capacity for inner speech obviously strengthens her for the heroic waiting that will, repeatedly in turn, strengthen Parzival for his own difficult tasks. Within the initiate-speaker, Condwiramurs represents the ability to companion oneself, to coach oneself. This inner resource sustains one who, having left childhood and the fostering care of mentors, ventures on the lonely road toward an individuated destiny.

Condwiramurs' name means "to conduct, to serve, to guide love."[35] The love to which she, the soul, guides Parzival and the initiate-speaker is not simply love for another person. Condwiramurs is the guide to all the forms of love. Her nature, as inner reflection, creates the twofoldness that allows for the very possibility of love. Without marriage to Condwiramurs, Parzival and the initiate-speaker will remain imprisoned in solipsism — with no center, no source, no destination. Conversely, without Parzival, spirit, Condwiramurs will starve, even die, for lack of the quickening light that pierces right "through the middle" of the obscuring darkness of worldly suitors claiming her attention. Only his arrival reveals her as queen-wife of the king-husband she knows as hers.

The courtship of Parzival and Condwiramurs, as spirit and soul, respectively, deserves notice. A quality of patience characterizes this coming together, a warmth rather than burning desire. Soul tells her story, describes her plight, and expresses her wish to die rather than give herself to one not worthy. Spirit responds with protectiveness and willingness to help. The gentle communion between these two, accomplished through speaking and listening, cements their bond.

The moment that soul and spirit meet, nourishment becomes available for the starving people in the castle-body. After they communicate, a ship arrives carrying an abundance of provisions. Parzival realizes this is very rich food and must be allotted carefully so the inhabitants can properly digest it. His care in the distribution shows his increasing maturity and is evidence also of the grounding that the soul provides for the restless spirit. Parzival, spirit, now in communication with Condwiramurs, soul, is much more aware of earthly needs and rhythms than he was in the previous book.

At the conclusion of Book IV, Parzival unexplainably remembers his mother. Innocuous as it may seem, this memory and his willingness to follow it are what will lead him to the Grail castle the first time. Wolfram seems to be indicating that memory and remembering are necessary and crucial for the initiatory process. So we need to ask just what memory is and why it arises at this juncture in the story?

The Greeks called her Memory, or Mnemosyne, and she is very old. She emerges near the beginning of the Greek creation myth, one of the twelve Titans, offspring of Earth (Gaia) and Heaven (Uranus). She lay with her nephew Zeus for nine days and brought forth thereby her nine daughters, the Muses — without whose inspiration neither poets, musicians nor dancers can practice their arts. We are to be reminded, however, that this is Memory as she is honored in an oral culture. There she has the character much more of a "voice" than of a "record," "filing cabinet," or "data bank." In an oral culture, Ginette Paris reminds us, the poet listened to Mnemosyne and her daughters while singing, without straining to remember, because

> . . . the individual Greek who knew Homer by heart didn't have to "search his memory" to remember a certain passage; the words came effortlessly to his lips at the right moment as if a voice had whispered them to him, thanks to Mnemosyne.[36]

With Memory, as she is known in oral cultures, there is no separation between recollecting and doing. In such cultures, the speech (or song) born from this union of the reflective and the active impulses is felt to possess great power. In ancient Hebrew culture, for example, the word for "word," *dabar,* also meant "event."[37]

Memory cannot be "searched" or "erased" in an oral culture. Rather, she "speaks out."[38] And she does not reside in the brain, contrary to what several hundred years of Western science have attempted to prove. The Greeks thought (probably remembered!) that her home is in the heart.[39] It can be no accident, then, that she whispers to Parzival just after he has found his own heart's home.

Condwiramurs awakens Parzival's heart, and out of that awakening the first hint of self-reflection emerges in Parzival. An image appears in the form of a memory: a remembrance of his mother. The sequence confirms Hillman's contention, quoted above, that "Soul is imagination." Now it is not an external sight that moves him and makes him move — not flying birds or flashing knights. Now an image whispered by memory within his own heart calls to him.[40]

With the voice of memory speaking to him, our magpie is about to become a different kind of bird. The decision to go see his mother is the first Parzival makes without an obvious reason. An inner voice prompts recollection, and he responds. No one has told him to do this. There is no obvious reward to be gained, no punishment or pain to be averted. Nonetheless, this decision will take him, in a very short while, to his momentous first visit to the Grail castle. In the choice to visit his mother, Parzival goes backward so he can move forward — and not for the last time. Now Parzival wings toward his own unique destiny, no longer simply reflecting that of his parents.

Toward Speech of the Grail

The speech of the Grail can be spoken only by a truly free human being, and therefore the first part of the journey has less to do with actual speaking than with becoming free (a process that is never complete and must, to some degree, be recapitulated — however briefly — many times). To be truly free, one must not only be able to question and to choose ethical conduct in all action. True freedom also requires imagination. If Condwiramurs represents imagination, then Parzival and the initiate-speaker travel amazingly fast in that direction once they decide to leave the comfort zone of Gurnemanz's castle. That does not mean, however, that they know where they are going. Imagination is never reached by knowing where one is going; one knows one is in the right place only after one has arrived.

Until then, imagination waits, ignored, or sometimes beset by hostile forces that would conquer her and put her to their uses. In our own time, the greatest threat comes from the destructive armies of prefabricated, electronically transmitted images commanding the soul's attention from all sides, yet leading to her starvation. Only her true bridegroom, by protecting and fostering her forces, can release her from the siege and encourage her to tell her own story and take her place as his queen. In marrying Condwiramurs, Parzival activates imagination into imagining.

For the initiate-speaker, this entails developing a relationship with inner images; dreams, fantasies, visions (and, archetypal psychologists would add, the pathological symptoms of mind and body). Strengthening of imagining can best be conceived as inner "listening." After his marriage, Parzival grows reflective for the first time, thinking back to his mother. Inner listening means noticing, honoring, even acting upon the images as they appear. For this purpose, the initiate-speaker may keep a journal or a dream diary; practice an art like painting or sculpture, dancing or movement, poetry or song writing; or work with a psychotherapist using active imagination, a term C.G. Jung coined, referring to a process of conscious visualizing in the presence of a therapist. The muscle of imagining needs to grow strong, not only because imagination is not highly valued in our present culture but also because what is presented by imagination is not always pretty or pleasant. For example, what Parzival first glimpses in the castle of imagination are starving people. Those who would know and serve imagination must learn to value and bear with the pathologized contents that inevitably appear.[41]

Jung and archetypal psychologists assert that merely becoming aware of inner images is not enough. In his autobiography, written late in his life, Jung explains:

> I took great care to try to understand every single image, every item of my psychic inventory, and to classify them scientifically — so far as this was possible — and above all, to realize them in actual life. That is what we usually neglect to do. We allow the images to rise up, and maybe we wonder about them, but that is all. We do not take the trouble to understand them, let alone draw ethical conclusions from them. This stopping-short conjures up the negative effects of the unconscious. . . . The images of the unconscious place a great responsibility upon a man. Failure to understand them, or a shirking of ethical responsibility, deprives him of his wholeness and imposes a painful fragmentariness on his life.[42]

This implies that healthy imagining does not remain a strictly inner affair. All the modes of inner listening mentioned above move the initiate-speaker toward expression. Through these modes, the initiate-speaker "tells" someone or something the image echoing within. Telling, or expressing, is what allows the image not only to remind us of the past but to take us toward the future. When Parzival tells Condwiramurs about his recollection of his mother, he asks, almost simultaneously, to go see her. If the initiate-speaker can listen to images with "innocent ears," as Russell Lockhart proposes, then honestly and personally "tell" them, the next step will be to find a way to "enact" the images so they may carry us into the future.

"Enactment" connotes formation of conscious, artistic relationship to the images. This is in sharp contrast to "acting out" which results from unconscious reaction to or unreflective possession by the image. Still, enactment stays close to image and to imagination, avoiding the deadening distance of an overly intellectual, interpretative approach. Supporting this idea, Wolfram shows Parzival and Condwiramurs snuggling close while she speaks to him. The appropriate response to the symbolic is symbolic. To quote Lockhart, the image found in a dream, fantasy or vision

> . . . calls out not as much for interpretation as for *relationship,* and that will be found not only in its telling but in what one *does* in response. . . . Meaning would then be experienced not only as something formulated in words, but as something enacted. Meaning would be achieved not through reflection only, but through enactment of the psyche's urge toward manifestation.[43]

Now that Parzival and the initiate-speaker are more closely in touch with imagination, the next movement should be toward manifestation. In the story, Parzival has an urge to act upon the memory-image of his mother by returning to his place of origin and becoming reacquainted with her. Analogously, the initiate-speaker will remember and be drawn toward the origins of speech. The roots of speaking stretch far back into rich loam of the oral tradition. For the initiate-speaker, storytelling becomes a means to become reacquainted with this tradition through practicing it.

The oral tradition as we can become reacquainted with it is not the oral tradition as it lived before alphabets and print.[44] Nevertheless, the initiate-speaker can experience an echo of what it might have been like to speak "out of" oneself (though the sense of a "self" — created, in large part, by literacy — is radically different from the "I" experienced in totally oral cultures only at the moment of speaking).[45] To speak "out of" oneself means to experience "word" and "event" as the same substance, and that experience is more likely if one does not memorize the words.

Story

Working without memorization,the storyteller speaks the words that arise from the images and themes appearing to his or her awareness in the moment of the telling and simultaneously shapes them through voice modulation, facial expressions and bodily gestures. In that sense, the speech is coming "out of" the self. In addition, however, the storyteller surrenders to the story, to the specific tradition from which it grew — even when, as is so for modern tellers, the tradition is not their own — and to the particular situation in which it is being told. In this sense, the speech is "out of" the self in the sense that it does not "belong" to the self; the self is the expressive medium through which the story moves and breathes amidst certain people at a unique moment in time. Storyteller John Harrell declares

> . . . we can only tell stories, truly, from the inside out. The outside of a story is simply its words. . . . The hard thing is to understand a story from the inside, and once we have that insight and sense of the story's reality, then moving from inside out we will find that the traditional way of telling is just right and cannot be any other way. And then when we are ready to tell the story, we do not tell it to the Muse. The Muse already knows the story. She it was who made it come alive for us in our contemplation of it. Rather, we tell the story to those around us to whom the Muse wants to speak through us. If this strikes you as too mystical then you have not had your first experience of being a real storyteller.[46]

Learning to live inside a story and then speaking out of that experience in one's "own" words constitutes the practice of the initiate-speaker in storytelling. Riding in the chariot of language, the storyteller must bring five headstrong horses into even, harmonious movement. Those horses, the means of language's movement, are: the storyteller's imagination, voice, body (including the face), sense of connection with a spiritual tradition or source,[47] and relationship established with the listeners. If the telling is to be truly alive, the speaker-storyteller must convince the five to work together for an overall coherence.

The quality of aliveness meant here refers less to the entertainment value in the telling — how much it "grabs" listeners or gives them pleasure — and more to the power of a telling to arouse listeners from the passivity of being merely audience and invite them to create the story within themselves — that is to make it their own. This can happen, of course, only if the storyteller has done so — by means of the craft outlined briefly above. The deeper portent of Parzival's marriage for the initiate-speaker is that it represents a first step toward becoming a "witness," a word that philosopher Georg Kühlewind warns

> . . . should not be taken lightly. It bears weight. *Martyria* is not merely an ability to report something, but to report and describe in such a way that one's testimony convinces men directly, and allows them to believe. . . . The word *martyria* (verb, *martyrein*) is related to "remembering." It suggests older stages of consciousness, when a human being could be reminded of what he really knows. This idea still echoes in Plato's theory of *anamnesis* or "unforgetting."[48]

In the practice of storytelling, the initiate-speaker confronts challenges similar to that of any artistic discipline and, in the process, begins, more and more, to "unforget." Wrestling with the aesthetic problems posed by the discipline exposes one to oneself, and thus the initiate-speaker grows in self-knowledge as well as in skill. The unveiling of Parzival and the initiate-speaker has begun with their marriage to imaginative soul.

NOTES

[1] Wolfram, Book II, 118.

[2] Wolfram, Book II, 118–19.

[3] Wolfram, Book III, 119.

[4] Wolfram, Book III, 119.

[5] Wolfram, Book III, 119.

[6] Wolfram, Book III, 126.

[7] Wolfram tells us that Schianatulander was killed by Orilus.

[8] Wolfram, Book III, 140.

[9] Wolfram, Book III, 149.

[10] Wolfram, Book III, 154.

[11] Wolfram, Book III, 156.

[12] Wolfram, Book III, 158.

[13] Wolfram, Book III, 161.

[14] Wolfram, Book III, 170.

[15] Wolfram, Book III, 171.

[16] Wolfram, Book III, 173.

[17] Wolfram, Book III, 177.

[18] Northrup Frye, *The Great Code,* 168.

[19] Wolfram, Book III, 171–73.

[20] Wolfram, Book III, 171–73.

[21] The Tower of Babel, and its resolution at the first Pentecost, is one of the themes Northrup Frye discusses to show the Bible as a unitary work in *The Great Code* and *Words with Power.*

[22] Pedro Lain Entralgo, *The Therapy of the Word in Classical Antiquity,* 177–78.

[23] Werner Glas, *An Analytical Study of the Rhetorical Thought of Rudolf Steiner with Some Implications for the Teaching of Speech,* 156.

[24] Glas, 161.

[25] Wolfram, Book IV, 188.

[26] Wolfram, Book IV, 189.

[27] Wolfram, Book IV, 190–91.

[28] Wolfram, Book, IV, 192.

[29] Wolfram, Book IV, 199.

[30] Some scholars who have plotted the time line in Parzival estimate he stayed about fifteen months in Pelrapeire. See note from translators regarding time sequence in Wolfram, 120.

[31] Wolfram, Book IV, 223.

[32] James Hillman, *Re-Visioning Psychology,* 68–69.

[33] *A Handbook of Christian Theology,* 355.

[34] Hillman, 69.

[35] Campbell, *The Masks of God,* 459.

[36] Ginette Paris, *Pagan Grace: Dionysos,* 130.

[37] For in-depth elaboration, see Walter Ong, *Orality and Literacy,* 31–77.

[38] Paris, 121.

[39] Paris, 122.

[40] For an excellent study of the connection between imagination and memory, see Edward Casey, *Spirit and Soul: Essays in Philosophical Psychology.*

[41] For James Hillman's complete argument, see *Re-Visioning Psychology,* particularly the chapter "Pathologizing or Falling Apart," 55–112.

[42] C.G. Jung, *Memories, Dreams, Reflections,* 192–93.

[43] Russell Lockhart, *Psyche Speaks: A Jungian Approach to Self and World,* 16.

[44] Three books concerning language and speech in preliterate culture and the changes wrought by print are: Walter Ong, *Orality and Literacy: The Technologizing of the Word;* Eric A. Havelock, *The Muse Learns to Write: Reflections on Orality and Literacy from Antiquity to the Present;* Ivan Illich and Barry Sanders, *ABC: The Alphabetization of the Popular Mind.*

[45] For fuller exposition, see Illich and Sanders, 71–83.

[46] John Harrell, *Origins and Early Traditions of Storytelling,* 64.

[47] The spiritual basis of the great epics from the traditions is evident. In my opinion, almost all traditional stories, including fairy tales, are similarly spiritual. In the distant time of oral culture, spiritual significance permeated all aspects of life and must have extended to the stories as well. My contention then is that the only way a storyteller can authentically embody traditional stories is through relationship with a spiritual source or tradition.

[48] Georg Kühlewind, *Becoming Aware of the Logos,* 44.

"May Your Mouth Become Empty of the Tongue within It"

The Grail King Speaks

Oh, Speaker your guiding vision will appear
And vanish because you do not apprehend it.
And then, awareness of past misdeeds,
Will be the stony road to awakening,
With only silence to assuage your shame.
Scourged, castigated, worse than foolish
Will you appear, until you feel
Even God has abandoned you.

BOOK V

Parzival starts back to his mother's forest home to find out what has happened since he left, but he is so distracted by thoughts of Condwiramurs that he allows the reins to dangle, letting the horse find its own way. At dusk, he comes to the edge of a lake where he finds a richly attired fisherman, with a hat trimmed in peacock feathers, sitting in a small boat. Parzival inquires whether the fisherman knows where he might find lodging for the night, and the wealthy fisherman invites him to be his guest. Then he advises Parzival to go on ahead up the steep and curving road to the castle but to be careful as "it is easy to ride astray."[1]

Parzival finds his way to the castle with no difficulty and is welcomed when he informs the gatekeeper that the fisherman has sent him. The inhabitants of the castle do not let Parzival see their sadness, instead welcoming him most hospitably. His armor is removed, and he is loaned the silk cloak of the queen to wear until clothes have been made for him. Then he is ushered to the great hall, where three huge fireplaces spout flames from aromatic woods, and couches to accommodate four hundred knights are arranged for the dinner soon to be served.

The fisherman, who is lord of the castle, is brought in and placed on a cot facing the central fireplace. Warmly dressed because "his life was but a dying"[2] from a long-term illness, the king nonetheless courteously invites Parzival to sit next to him. Then a wondrous spectacle occurs. A squire dashes in bearing a lance, whose point is gushing blood. Weeping and wailing, his sleeves dripping blood, the squire runs along all four walls and then out of the room.

Next, a procession of twenty-four maidens brings, in succession, two ivory stools, a tabletop carved from a precious, transparent stone, knives for cutting meat, and clear glass vessels in which sweet balsam is burning. The first group of maidens wears gowns of soft brown wool, the second wears flowing green dresses, and the third group wears silk interwoven with gold. The tabletop is set up on the ivory stools in front of the king, and the maidens arrange themselves in two groups of twelve. Finally, the queen, Repanse de Schoye, dressed in silk and so radiant that a soft light seems to emanate from her, enters the hall bearing "a thing called the Grail"[3] on a dark green cloth. She sets the Grail before the host, and then moves to join the two groups of maidens so that she is exactly in the middle between them. Parzival is now aware that the cloak he was given to wear when he arrived is hers.

Parzival and the fisher king share the same bowl for washing, and the knights also wash their hands, just before golden eating vessels are put on the tables. Squires then serve the knights by approaching the Grail and receiving from it whatever food or drink is desired. "Its delights were very like what we are told of the kingdom of heaven."[4]

Watching all this fills Parzival with wonder. Many questions stir in him, but, remembering Gurnemanz's advice not to ask questions, he remains silent, thinking all will be revealed to him in good time. Even when the King gives him a beautifully carved sword with hilt made of ruby — which, Wolfram tells us, signals the moment to speak — Parzival remains silent.

The feast ends. The maidens, in reverse order, remove the implements. As they disappear behind the great doors at the end of the hall, Parzival glimpses beyond them "the most beautiful old man he had ever beheld," but this sight also does not loosen his tongue. After his host commends him to his rest, Parzival is led to a luxurious bedroom, accompanied by four maidens who serve him. Soon, he falls into a fitful sleep, beset with violent nightmares of jousts — visions of future suffering not unlike the dream his mother had just before hearing of his father's death.

In the morning he wakes to find no pages there to help him, so he falls asleep again and does not wake until midmorning. Since there still are no pages, he dresses himself in his armor, including the two swords, and goes outside to find his horse waiting, saddled and with spear and shield nearby. Otherwise, the castle seems deserted, as no one is roused by Parzival's calls.

Angry now at what he sees as inhospitable neglect, Parzival follows the horse tracks he sees in the courtyard and rides out across the drawbridge. An unseen squire pulls up the bridge behind him so sharply that it almost strikes Parzival's horse and knocks him down. When Parzival looks back, he hears the stinging words:

> Ride on . . . and bear the hatred of the sun. You are a goose. If you had only moved your jaws and asked your host the question! But you weren't interested in winning great honor.[5]

When Parzival shouts back for an explanation, he is met only with silence.

He follows the tracks, hoping to fight in this company of knights and thus earn the sword he has been given, but the trail soon grows faint, and then the tracks go off in different directions. Just as the trail comes to an end, Parzival hears the voice of a woman lamenting and, looking around, finds a nearly bald, ashen-faced lady sitting in a linden tree, an embalmed knight in her arms.

Though he does not recognize this lady as his cousin Sigune, he quickly greets her and says he is in her service if she needs him. She does not recognize Parzival either and merely asks how he comes to be in this dangerous region, warns him to "turn back" and then asks where he spent the night. When he describes the rich castle nearby, she at first refuses to believe he has been there because

> rich it is in all earthly perfection. He who diligently seeks it will not find it, alas. Yet many do search for it. He who shall see the castle must chance upon it unaware.[6]

She tells him about the rulers of the castle and its name, Munsal-vaesche, saying that if indeed he has come from there, then its king, Anfortas, will have been freed of his suffering.

When Parzival reiterates that he has been there, Sigune at last recognizes his voice. She eagerly asks him if Anfortas has been released from his suffering and if Parzival saw the Grail. Parzival's only response is to ask how she knows him, at which she reintroduces herself. Amazed that she has grown so grey, Parzival urges her to let him bury the dead knight in her lap. She replies that the only joy she could have now would be the knowledge that Anfortas has been healed.

Then Sigune notices the sword Parzival received from the fisher king. She tells him it was wrought by noble artisans and wonders if he learned the magic spell which ensures the sword's owner success in battle. She explains that the sword will withstand any first blow but will always break on the second and can only "become whole again by the flow of water"[7] at a spring named Lac near Karnant. Before daybreak, the sword must be dipped in the water at its source beneath a rock. The sword will emerge repaired, even stronger than before, with the engravings on its blade shining clearly. That Parzival possesses this sword suggests to Sigune that he must have asked the right question, and so she predicts that all happiness will be his, that he will have whatever he wishes on earth.

Parzival replies simply, "I did not ask." Aghast, Sigune severely castigates him and bemoans his even being in her presence. "Oh, alas, that my eyes behold you . . . since you were too faint of heart to ask a question."[8] He pleads with her for kindness and says he will make atonement, but she angrily tells him to spare himself his atonement. She declares he has already lost all honor, and then refuses to speak with him further. Parzival rides away smitten with remorse.

The day is so hot that he removes his helmet and carries it, but Parzival must cope with more heat than just the sun's. His next travail is not far off, as he comes upon the fresh track of two horses, one shod and the other not. Following these tracks, he soon overtakes the latter, a poor unshod beast whose rider, a lady, is not much better covered than the horse's hooves. Recognizing Parzival immediately as the one who caused all her sorrows, the ragged lady begins lamenting all the woe he has caused her. Thus is Parzival reintroduced to Jeschute, whom he so rudely mistreated just after leaving his mother.

Parzival at first denies Jeschute's charges, saying he has never brought shame to anyone since becoming a knight, and he offers her his gambeson to cover herself. She warns him away, worried that he will meet his death from her husband, who is riding just ahead. Parzival says he would rather die than flee, and just then Duke Orilus, dragons on helmet and shield, wheels his horse around and challenges him to joust.

The two men fight with swords while still mounted on their horses, and the battle is long and fierce. When Parzival proves the victor, he says he will allow Orilus to live if he returns Jeschute to his favor. Saying he cannot do that, Orilus instead offers Parzival his oath and great wealth as well. Parzival declines this offer and commends Orilus to Cunneware at Arthur's court, again insisting that Orilus reconcile with Jeschute or be killed.

Orilus wishes to live, so he agrees to the terms. He receives Jeschute's grateful kiss, and the three ride to a nearby hermit's cave wherein is an altar with holy relics and a brightly painted spear leaning against it. Of "his own free will,"[9] Parzival swears an oath upon the holy relics that Jeschute did nothing amiss when he bumbled into her tent. He confesses to being "a fool then, not a man, and not yet grown to wisdom,"[10] who had stolen her ring and her brooch. He returns the ring to Jeschute, admitting that the brooch is lost because he gave it away.

Then, Parzival takes the spear beside the altar and, declining Orilus's invitation to join them for a meal, rides away. Orilus and Jeschute celebrate their reconciliation, riding afterward to Arthur's court where Cunneware — Orilus's sister — reluctantly receives an oath of service from her own brother.

Initiatory Themes

Every initiation has, at its core, a vision. From the moment of its appearance — often during a mystical experience — the alluring ideal defines and animates the novice. The intention of a vision quest is to become open to receiving such a vision, and even quests undertaken less consciously — like Parzival's at first — eventually cohere around a central, activating image. Once the vision has emerged, the work is to build and maintain a relationship with it. The vision will be at once a prod and guide, a helpful familiar and a fearsome mystery. One day it will seem as close and real as one's own hand and the next day only a distant illusion.

The content of Parzival's vision — all the components of the ceremony at the Grail castle — will not receive detailed attention in this study. Emma Jung's investigation of the symbolism of the motifs in the ceremony is substantial,[11] and a summary could not do it justice. Just those contents relevant to the speech of the Grail will be considered. Primary among these is the Grail stone, which, as Wolfram describes it, exemplifies the fundamental qualities of any genuine initiatory vision.

Like the Grail stone, the energy of the vision always flows in two directions at once; it nourishes and sustains the individual and, through that individual, nourishes and sustains the wider community. An initiatory vision is never strictly personal or for oneself. A true vision always leads the individual into service of the community, not only the human community but also the earth and her creatures. Initiation is the process through which the initiate absorbs and becomes the vision.

Other interpreters provide evidence that the Grail castle is, in fact, the world and that therefore the Grail and all who serve it sustain the whole community of earthly forms. Robert Sardello notes that, in another of Wolfram's poems, the Grail castle is described as having seventy-two towers, that being the medieval conception of the number of earthly nations. In addition, Sardello thinks that the colors of the Grail maidens' gowns suggest the plant world which supports all life. The brown would be the soil, the green would be the stem and leaf, and the silk interwoven with gold would be the flower and fruit.[12] Going even further, Hermetic scholars Henry and Renee Kahane conclude that the procession portrays the entire cosmos:

The first four maidens, dressed in brown wool, represent the four elements of earth, water, air and fire. The eight maidens, dressed in green samite, represent the seven planetary spheres and the sphere of the fixed stars. The twelve maidens dressed in silk interwoven with gold, and pfellel-silk from Ninevah, represent the twelve zodiacal signs, while Repanse de Schoye, glowing like the sun in Arabian silk, represents and bears the Grail, the divine Monad. The procession, therefore, relates to the soul's ascent through the cosmic spheres . . . a central doctrine of the Hermetic writings.[13]

We now can understand that an initiatory vision imposes an awesome responsibility on its recipient. In tribal cultures, the whole community supported the novice until she or he could assimilate the vision's import. When there is no tribe or when an individual initiatory vision is not culturally sanctioned, a person may deny it, run from it, forget it, or not even recognize it as a vision. The latter seems to be the case with Parzival. He has quite an unusual adventure, but it does not seem to have any impact on him. If he did not subsequently meet others who tell him the significance of what he experienced, he would probably go right on in life, dismissing the whole event as an unexplainable, unattainable dream of his youth.

Yet something ineradicable has happened which results, for quite a while thereafter, in Parzival's life seeming to flow backwards. He encounters Sigune, then Jeschute, in reverse order of the first meetings, but nonetheless in close succession. In the next episode, he will once again be welcomed at Arthur's court and then, also as before, be publicly shamed. All of these encounters can be seen as a continuation of what he experienced at the Grail castle. Each shocks him with self-confrontation, wresting him from his dull self-satisfaction, his attachment to attitudes and behaviors that, though he has been taught them, are not his own. Parzival's trip down memory lane, begun with the desire to return to his mother, will not be comfortable, as anyone who has experienced deep psychotherapy knows. Parzival must learn, writes Walter Johannes Stein,

> . . . that Anfortas suffers because he, Parzival, has not recognized himself to be the cause of his suffering. Who seeks the imagination of the Grail and thinks that he sees anything other than the slaying of what is noblest through his own imperfection, cannot redeem the suffering Grail King. The QUESTION is what brings redemption.[14]

To be empowered by a vision, the individual who receives the vision may have to be disempowered first, divested, that is, of the sense of power generated by his or her accomplishments in the world and maybe even of the inflation of receiving the vision itself. No matter how grand the vision, the initial consequence often feels like suffering, a kind of dismemberment of the sense of self that has been so carefully constructed. We, the readers, can see that Parzival's suffering is exactly what will awaken him to the meaning of what he experienced at the Grail castle. But the person caught in the whirlwind of deconstruction, feels like a victim, and the first question is "why me?" This sense of victimization can escalate to a feeling of complete abandonment by God.

Following his painful meeting with Sigune, when Parzival removes his helmet in the heat, we can remember that Gahmuret was killed after a similar gesture and can guess that, subsequently, Parzival will endure a kind of death. It cannot be coincidental that this foreshadowing comes right after his meeting with Sigune. Twice more will he find this lady who seems to do nothing but sit grieving in the forest, and after each of the four visits, he will go away with a stronger sense of who he is and of his mission. We might wonder, why?

The first two encounters, at least, reveal Sigune as the one in Parzival and the initiate-speaker who relates them to death, awareness of which strangely accompanies and assists the whole initiatory journey. In all authentic initiations, the novices must come to terms with death and the existential loneliness that attends consciousness of the transience of all things. Any attempt to avoid the confrontation immediately enslaves one to fear and greed, both of which are predicated by the effort to turn away from death's leering countenance. To be free, to possess oneself and therefore be self-possessed, Parzival and the initiate-speaker rely on Sigune for an evolving relationship with death. Urges to wail helplessly, fight it in externalized, vengeful battles, or abuse oneself — reactions seen in Sigune or Parzival in these first two meetings — will be transformed during the journey so that Parzival and the initiate-speaker can see past death's awful appearance.

Meanwhile, however, all that Parzival knows at present is that he has stumbled onto a vision he never asked for that imposes expectations he has no idea how to satisfy. Wolfram tells us later that the names of those called to the Grail appear inscribed on it and fade once the person arrives. Parzival has not been presented with an all-powerful animal totem or the fiery wheels within wheels Ezekiel beheld. Parzival has been granted a vision that needs him — a vision that has a vision. The fate of the vision depends on Parzival just as much as the fate of Parzival resides in the vision.

Meanwhile our flashy magpie has become just a common, stupid "goose," as the squire shouts when he leaves the Grail castle. That heavy domestic bird, for all its honking protests, can fly neither far nor high. Its tasks are closer to home. By the time Parzival, "of his own free will," swears his oath to Orilus and Jeschute, he can humbly admit his former foolishness, demonstrating not only new maturity but strengthened self-perception. This goose is not cooked yet. Without knowing it, he has made progress and is about ready for the roasting that feels like death.

Toward Speech of the Grail

A person who has the yearning and determination to learn to speak in a way that heals and transforms must have been, at one time or another, the recipient of such an act of speech, or, at the very least, had a fantasy of the possibility. Someone — maybe a parent, a friend, a teacher, a minister — said something that allowed the initiate-speaker to understand a situation in a new way, to see an opening for taking the next step, to be released from a constraining thought, feeling or habit. Maybe the initiate-speaker listened to a story and never could forget it, saw a play, or heard a poem and then comprehended something differently than before. These aural experiences introduce the initiate-speaker to the "vision" of the speech of the Grail.

For one driven or guided by such a vision, there is, in addition, an increasingly insistent feeling that something from the domain of language is calling — a sense that one's vocation is expressed in inspirational, educational or healing speech. There will be one or many moments when the properly prepared initiate-speaker will have the most helpful words or just the right story. One grows to realize that, if the words calling to be articulated are not expressed through oneself, they will go unsaid. Attunement to this responsibility comprises the initiate-speaker's calling to the speech of the Grail. Parzival is also

coming to understand this: he is the one through whom the words —
the question — are waiting to be asked.

The Grail saga itself can inspire the vision of this calling — as
indeed it has for the author of this study. Walter Johannes Stein
reports Rudolf Steiner's visit to a high school class where Steiner
referred to the knights of the Round Table as "Knights of the Sword,"
and to the Grail knights as "Knights of the Word." Steiner pointed
out that the Grail sword breaks when it has grown old from use and
that its fragments must be "renewed at a living spiritual source."[15]
Stein suggests that the Grail story, likewise, comes to us in fragments
and that anyone wishing to take up the calling of being a "Knight of
the Word"

> . . . must come provided with the fragments of the sword and must
> appear by night beside the rock that is unillumined by the sunlight
> of waking consciousness. Here at the Source of Inspiration . . . the
> Spiritual Sword will again be made whole out of the fragments of
> lingering tradition.[16]

Inheritance of those fragments, though, can feel less like a gift
than a burden, more a process of subtraction than addition. Parzival
has a confusing experience at the Grail castle. For him, it certainly
does not feel like anything ranking as a vision. Then he meets Signe
again and learns from her some of the significance of what he has
experienced, as well as what he has failed to do. After Signe refuses
to speak with him further, he rides on to encounter Jeschute and is
forced to recognize the hurtful consequences of his former, foolish
choices. It is a beleaguered Parzival who, taking his leave of Orilus
and Jeschute, rides away from the hermit's cave. He is probably too
numb to notice that he is carrying a new sword — a magical one! —
as well as the spear he found, which Wolfram identifies as coming
from the Round Table.

The sword and the spear are aspects of his visionary experience
that Parzival carries away with him. Each has distinct properties. The
spear from the Round Table, found by the altar in the cave when
Parzival admits his error to Orilus, belongs to this world — the world
of Arthur and all the codes and conduct required for participation
in it. A spear is hurled and strikes at a distance, and thus its essential function is aimed penetration from afar.[17] Once sent forth, like

words from the mouth, the spear flies free of its user's control. If not employed with skill and care, spears and words will fail to reach the target and may unintentionally pierce and wound something else. Training for use of such tools must be sober and include full knowledge of the consequences of their misuse. With these earthly instruments, Parzival and the initiate-speaker are able to aim consciously at something at a distance. They may not yet know what to aim at, or even that they can do so, but what they have acquired as a result of taking responsibility for foolish mistakes gives them this greater power of penetration.

Hurtling across space, a spear takes some time to reach its mark. We will not hear of this spear again until Parzival returns to the hermit's cave, at the turning point of the quest. At that time, Parzival will finally understand his destiny and choose it. The spear, aimed here, will then have found its mark. All the while, Parzival and the initiate-speaker will have been aiming at themselves from afar, wanting to penetrate to the meaning of their destiny — to embody the speech of the Grail.

Parzival's new sword, on the other hand, is a weapon not completely of this world; it is "magical," activated by magical words and capable of being mended by certain waters when it has broken. And it *will* break, Sigune tells Parzival, at the second blow. It has to be constantly returned to the water's source to be made whole again. The sword is held closely and therefore represents its owner. It does not penetrate from a distance, but cuts and separates. It is not pointed and piercing, but sharp and two-edged. This particular sword is directly connected to words; a spoken spell allows its owner to fight without fear, so assured is victory.

During Parzival's visit at the Grail castle, Wolfram never mentions the charm so we can assume Parzival did not learn it from Anfortas (probably because he did not ask the question), but he still received the sword. He and the initiate-speaker, from their vision at the Grail castle, now have something that allows for cutting-through. This could be a distinction-making ability that is connected to words but that must be constantly renewed at a water source. The water flows under a rock where the sword must be placed before the light of day strikes it. In the darkness of the mother earth from which it comes, the hard metal is healed in her fluids. If it is to be strong, this sword of words, magically empowered to fight on the surface, requires very close contact with the underground source of the waters. Wielding such a sword, speaking in such a way, Parzival and the initiate-speaker will have the cutting edge necessary to separate from the foolish, dull self of the past and grow toward the awakened self who can fulfill the vocation apprehended in the vision.

The trail is arduous, though, and at times a kind of numb dumbness would be a relief. Too often the right words do not come or the wrong ones do; riding on a mood or rash whim, they intrude abrasively, and regret cannot retract them. The effort to become awakened in speech can feel like a ride on an unruly bronco; one almost gets into a rhythm with the ride and then, suddenly, there is a leaning and lurching, and speech and speaker have separated like rider and horse. Many times, the initiate-speaker will have to apologize or wish for atonement for words unwisely said.

BOOK VI

Something is always coming from the future toward Parzival and toward the initiate-speaker, even as they might be wishing some relief or escape from their distress. As it turns out, Arthur and his court have been eight days in search of Parzival. Arthur, having now received at court a number of knights Parzival has defeated and sent there, wishes to invite Parzival to become a member of the Round Table. Meanwhile, he has decreed that all his knights must give their word not to joust without first asking his permission.

While hawking in the early evening, Arthur's falconers lost their best falcon, and all night it has perched near Parzival in the forest. The falcon follows Parzival in the early morning as he meanders through a meadow where a thousand geese are at rest. With a swift plunge, the fierce hunting bird dives among the geese and strikes at one so violently that it barely manages to escape. On the unseasonal May snow, three drops of blood fall from the bird's wounds.

The bright red on the dazzling white catches Parzival's attention. He is hypnotized by these colors that remind him of the beautiful body of his bride, Condwiramurs. Thoughts of her fill his mind, and he inwardly praises God for this image in the snow, flooding him with such deep feeling. Meanwhile, he appears as one does while sleepwalking. He sits on his horse in a trance, staring at the drops of blood on the snow, oblivious to everything else around him.

Having been spied by a squire from Arthur's retinue who assumes he is an alien knight, Parzival is soon challenged by one of the eager young knights from the court. He does not respond, however, but continues to stare at the ground while his well-trained horse turns and gallops toward the oncoming challenger. This momentarily releases Parzival from his trance, and he lowers his spear and handily knocks the brash young knight out of his saddle. Without a word, Parzival rides back to stare down again at the blood on the snow.

Keie, Arthur's cranky seneschal, then asks permission to take up the battle. Parzival is equally unresponsive when Keie accosts him with insults but, thanks again to his horse, is even more effective against the challenge. He receives a blow on the head from Keie, but Keie is sent flying off his horse with such force that his right arm and left leg are broken and his horse is killed when it falls over the tree where the injured goose took refuge. Once more, Parzival turns to stare at the crimson streaks on the snow:

> His thoughts about the Grail and the Queen's likeness here — each was a painful burden, but heavier lay on him the leaden weight of love. Sorrow and Love can break the strongest spirit. Can these be called adventure? They both could better be called pain.[18]

Keie is carried to Arthur's tent where Gawan, Arthur's nephew and foster son, tries to comfort him to no avail. The injury has not crippled Keie's sharp tongue, and he angrily rejects Gawan's consolations, accusing him of womanly softness if he does not ride out to meet the strange and irksome knight who has wounded him. So Gawan does ride out, but without spur or sword. "He wanted to come in peace and discover who it was who had done this fighting."[19]

Parzival is oblivious to Gawan's greeting, even though it includes an offer of "mercy and pardon" for bringing such shame on the two other knights. Yet the observant Gawan, noticing Parzival's entranced stare at the snow, suspects that "love holds this man enslaved."[20] He throws a scarf over the drops of blood in the snow, and Parzival immediately returns to his senses. He mourns aloud for the loss of Condwiramurs and then notices his spear is gone and wonders aloud how he lost it.

Gawan explains that it was lost in jousting and, at Parzival's further questioning, reports the events that have preceded their meeting. Parzival asks Gawan who he is, and Gawan introduces himself as the nephew of King Arthur, pledged to the king's service.

"Are you Gawan?" says Parzival, adding, "I have always heard it said of you that you treat everyone with kindness."[21] He thanks Gawan and expresses regret that he cannot go with him to the encampment because he was dishonored when Arthur's seneschal struck the lady who laughed.

Gawan assures him that wrong has now been avenged and tells him of Keie's injuries, showing Parzival's broken spear in the snow as proof. So they ride together into the camp where they are welcomed gratefully by Cunneware, whose tent is pitched next to Gawan's. She kisses Parzival and sees that his armor is removed, the rust is washed off his skin and fine clothes are put on him.

Word reaches Arthur, while he is at Mass, that Parzival has arrived in camp. He comes to meet Parzival with the fool Antanor, who had also been soundly thrashed by Keie, capering ahead. Arthur welcomes Parzival, who "looked, save that he had no wings, like an angel come into flower upon this earth,"[22] and honors him with an invitation to join the Round Table. Then all the knights voice their wish that he join the company. Parzival accepts, and, since the Round Table was left at Nantes, a flowering field is chosen for the ceremony and covered with a great circular cloth.

Dressed in their finest and joyous with the occasion, the members of the court have just been seated around the cloth when an incredibly loathsome-looking woman rides up on an equally miserable-looking mule. She is the remarkable Cundrie, *la sorcière*. Her dress and saddle trappings are regal, and she is so learned that she knows "all languages" ("Latin, French and heathen")[23] as well as dialectic, geometry, and astronomy. But hear how she appears:

> Over her hat swung a braid of her hair, so long that it touched the mule. It was black and hard, not pretty, and soft as the bristles of a pig. She had a nose like a dog's, and two boar's teeth stuck out from her mouth, each a span in length. Both eyebrows were braided and the braids drawn up to the ribbon that held her hair. . . . Cundrie had ears like a bear's, and no lover could desire a face like hers, hairy and rough. . . . the hands of this charming dear looked like a monkey's skin. Her fingernails were none too fine, and, . . . they stuck out like a lion's claws.[24]

However crippled Cundrie's appearance, her tongue is "far from lame," Wolfram tells us, and she wastes no time in getting to the purpose of her visit. She shames Arthur for accepting a knight into the ranks of the Round Table who is a knight in "outward signs" only.

"You think me an unnatural monster, yet I am more natural and pleasing than you, Sir Parzival."[25] She continues:

> May your mouth become empty, I mean of the tongue within it, as your heart is empty of real feeling! You are destined for hell, in heaven before the hand of the Highest, and also upon this earth if noble men come to their senses. You bar to all salvation, you curse of bliss, you scorn of perfect merit! You are so shy of manly honor and so sick in knightly virtue that no physician can cure you. I will swear by your head, if someone will administer the oath to me, that never was greater falsity found in any man so fair. You baited lure! You adder's fang! Your host gave you a sword, of which you were never worthy. Your silence earned you there the sin supreme. You are the sport of the shepherds of hell. Dishonored are you, Sir Parzival. Yet you saw the Grail borne before you and the silver knives and the bloody spear. You death of joy and bestowal of grief![26]

Cundrie does not stop with this condemnation. She goes on to describe the riches that might have been Parzival's if he had asked the question, riches that far surpass those of the richest kingdom on this earth won by his half-brother Feirefiz, that remarkable son of the Queen of Zazamanc who is "both black and white." Then she bemoans Parzival's actions in light of both his noble parents, whom she describes in detail.

As she succumbs to weeping and wailing, Cundrie turns to leave the company. But first she issues a challenge, asking if any knight there craves a great adventure. At the Castle of Wonders, she says, four queens and four hundred maidens are held captive, and no other adventure could equal the freeing of these ladies. Then she turns and rides away.

The court is in shock, with Cunneware being the first to weep that Parzival has been so abused. With no time for recovery, another uninvited visitor appears. A knight clad in costly armor rides up and demands to speak to Arthur and Gawan. When he is conducted to their presence, this knight, named Kingrimursel, denounces Gawan as the man who killed his lord just as he greeted Gawan. To avenge this misdeed, Kingrimursel challenges Gawan to face him in single combat forty days hence in a distant kingdom. He declares that if Gawan does not agree to this challenge, he does not deserve to sit at the Round Table.

Angered by this unfounded slander, Gawan's brother, Beacurs, begs Gawan to let him go in his place. But Gawan gently replies that he must answer this challenge himself, though "Indeed, I do not know why I am to fight, and fighting for its own sake gives me no pleasure."[27] Kingrimursel approves this response and, before riding away, guarantees Gawan safe conduct through all the land until they meet in combat.

Aggrieved by these events, Gawan and Parzival stand together amid the court, receiving comfort from all sides. Clamide, Condwiramurs' spurned suitor, takes this opportunity to pursue his own agenda with Parzival, asking him to intercede in his behalf with Cunneware, whose love he wishes to win. Distraught as he is with missing his own wife, Parzival agrees to help him. Meanwhile, another courtier, a woman from heathen lands, approaches to tell Parzival more about his brother.

> Nothing can compare with his wealth . . . save that of the Baruch . . . He is worshipped like a god. His skin has a wonderful sheen, but in color it is different from that of other men, for it is both white and black. . . . He is a noble king. . . . In a joust with him, no man has ever kept his seat. He is known for lavishness, and a more generous man never sucked at a mother's breast. His conduct is without falsity. Feirefiz, the Angevin — he has endured suffering in women's service.[28]

Parzival thanks her for the kind words of encouragement she gives him after her description of Feirefiz. We are not told what, if any, response he has to the news about having a brother. Instead, Parzival tells the woman that he feels scorned and greatly misunderstood, that his suffering is so great he can "find no words" for it. What is more,

> I will allow myself no joy until I have seen the Grail, be the time short or long. My thoughts drive me toward that goal, and never will I swerve from it as long as I shall live. If I am to hear the scorn of the world because I obeyed the law of courtesy, then his counsel may not have been wholly wise. It was the noble Gurnemanz who advised me to refrain from impertinent questions and resist all unseemly behavior.[29]

Both Parzival and Gawan then prepare to leave the court. Gawan approaches Parzival, kisses him, and asks God's blessing on him in all his battles. Parzival responds with almost the last words[30] we shall hear from him until Book IX, a time span of nearly five years.

> Alas, what is God? If He were mighty, if God could rule with power, He would never have imposed such disgrace on us both. I was in His service, since I hoped to receive His grace. But now I shall renounce His service, and if He hates me, that hate I will bear. Friend, when it comes your time to fight, may a woman be your shield in battle and may she guide your hand — a woman in whom you have found both virtue and womanly kindness. May her love keep guard over you! I do not know when I shall see you again. May my wish for you be fulfilled![31]

He and Gawan, having been outfitted for their journeys, depart separately. Then, all the knights of the court disperse, lured forth by Cundrie's description of the riches and honor awaiting them if they should find and free the Castle of Wonders.

Initiatory Themes

Parzival's disturbing dreams during his night in the Grail castle, like his mother's before Gahmuret's death, foreshadow the future. It just takes some time for the nightmare to manifest in his waking life. The failure at the Grail castle apparently behind him, he is warmly welcomed into Arthur's court, accorded the status due the finest knights in the realm. In terms of worldly success and in the eyes of others, he has reached an apex of achievement. So who should complain?

The objection comes from a source that appears monstrous. Who is this learned, loathly lady? She is not only well educated in the scholarly sense but seems to know what is in people's hearts. She lives in this landscape of people and events so intimately that it seems part of her body. She seems to know everything that is going on in and between the worlds. Wolfram informs us later that Cundrie, and her grotesque companion, Malcreatiure, came from the East, sent as a gift from Queen Secundille to the Grail king Anfortas before he was wounded. Cundrie is a messenger and traveler between the worlds. She does not seem really to reside anywhere, but moves with equal ease among the Grail host, Arthur's court, and the court of the Castle of Wonders. We will eventually learn that she also manages to keep Sigune nourished in her forest hermitage, bringing her food from the Grail.

Popular as she is in medieval tales, this loathly lady has qualities that hark back to even earlier times. Is she in disguise? In another medieval story, "The Marriage of Gawain and Dame Ragnall, the Loathly Damsel," her appearance *is* a disguise of sorts, caused by a spell. It does not seem too big a jump to recognize in her many of the qualities of the goddess the Greeks honored as Hecate, who, some scholars think, came from Asia Minor — and who herself bore characteristics of even earlier goddesses.

Hecate is the goddess of the Triple Way; her statues at the meeting of three roads often showed three forms, back to back, one each with the head of a dog, a mare, and a lion (or snake). According to Patricia Monaghan, "This threefold goddess was best honored where one could look three ways at once."[32] Her threefold aspect reveals her as connected with the moon and its distinctive three phases. Like Cundrie, she wanders among the worlds: overseeing from the sky as moon; giving companionship to Persephone in Hades; assisting forest-roving Artemis in her various duties; accompanying grieving Demeter across the earth in search of her daughter. Some sources say she carried a torch and a scourge, and some associate her with Erinnyes or Furies, those three bony crones who pursue people who have a bad conscience. Hecate can move in the daytime, but she is more truly Queen of the Night. Her fire may singe, but ultimately her light is reflective and eerily penetrating, like the moon's. Not even Zeus could take away her ancient power to confer upon mortals their dearest wish.

But it will be a while before Cundrie offers such a boon to Parzival. She offers him, instead, what he least would want — a public shaming and curse right at the moment of his highest glory to date. She curses him to silence, and thus he will remain for quite some time. We are about to lose sight of the person we have been identifying as Parzival; his disappearance directly follows Cundrie's visit.

What has happened to our magpie-turned-goose? A fierce falcon has followed him and struck at his very breast, piercing it, deflating any puffed-upness. We can be reminded of the sacred history of the goose: the bone called "Merry Thought" (our wishbone) was close to the breast of the fowl and, at the end of the traditional feast of

Michaelmas, was examined for portents of future events or weather conditions.[33] The speech from the bone could only appear after the death of the goose. Cundrie's words have penetrated Parzival to his core. Her curse is that his "mouth become empty" because his "heart is empty of real feeling." This wounding must have a healing intention — to open Parzival's breast, his heart. And yet, for now, he appears only to have become more closed, denouncing even his faith in God.

Nevertheless, even as the fire of her words has incinerated Parzival's sense of accomplishment, Cundrie has left a glowing ember of warmth in his hardened heart. She has told him of his radiant half brother, that fiery one in the East who already may be heading toward Parzival from the future. Cundrie's words will later help Parzival to identify Feirefiz, and Parzival's return to the Grail castle can only happen after that meeting.

Parzival, as we have known him, has disappeared. He is no longer the callow youth, nor a buoyant young warrior. His parting words to Gawan resound with the world-weariness of a broken old man. He has pledged to return to the Grail Castle, and now, we must realize, it is for his own healing as well as the Grail King's. That healing act will happen when Parzival has developed his own way of "feeling" in the world — when his heart, home of his soul, has grown stronger and opened again.

Toward Speech of the Grail

The confrontation with Cundrie marks the moments when the initiate-speaker descends into silence. Through that fertile descent, like a root seeking its primary nourishment, the initiate-speaker will come to know the gifts silence proffers, and, acquainted with its full presence, learn to speak out of silence instead of *against* it.

In his richly illuminating book, *The World of Silence*, Swiss philosopher Max Picard not only discusses but actually evokes this silence, which bequeaths such value to our lives and to our speech.

> Silence is a basic phenomenon. That is to say, it is a primary, objective reality, which cannot be traced back to anything else. . . . Silence is original and self-evident like the other basic phenomena; like love and loyalty and death and life itself. But it existed before all these

and is in all of them. Silence is the firstborn of the basic phenomena. It envelops the other basic phenomena — love, loyalty and death; and there is more silence than speech in them, more of the invisible than the visible. There is also more silence in one person than can be used in a single human life. That is why every human utterance is surrounded by a mystery.[34]

Silence is "useless," points out Picard, while "all the other great phenomena have been appropriated by the world of profit and utility."[35] Earth, air, water and fire all have been bent and distorted to serve human purposes. Silence cannot be exploited and therefore, perhaps, poses a threat to our sense of control. Evidence abounds for our uneasiness. Besides greed, one explanation for the wholesale destruction of wilderness could be that it is a refuge for this useless and fearsome silence. Death, another sanctuary of silence, is made ever more noisy with desperate "life-support" measures. Even the silence of learning is besieged, as ear-splitting bells punctuate the school day everywhere.

But, "there is more help and healing in silence than in all the 'useful things'," says Picard, because "it makes things whole again, by taking them back from the world of dissipation into the world of wholeness."[36] In its unity of existence and activity, silence is generous with its autonomy. It "gives to things inside it something of the power of its own autonomous being"[37] and thereby strengthens their autonomy.

In *The Grail Legend*, Emma Jung muses about the emergence of the Self. This occurs not long after she distinguishes the aspects of ego-consciousness represented by the spear and sword. But she does not make the connection between Parzival's possession of these tools and the development of the Self, but her idea supports the necessity of Parzival's confrontation with Cundrie and all his imperfections as soon as he obtains them:

As the threads of fabric are woven into a pattern, so the Self as the living garment of divinity is woven out of the many decisions and crises . . . by which we are affected in the course of our lives. Such occasions present themselves at every level of life and intelligence and in every milieu. Whether or not they lead to a manifestation of the Self depends solely on our own response. Many of us have observed that children, even small children, when faced with some difficulty, possess an attitude which many adults could only envy. That "something," the lack of which we experience as soullessness, is a "someone" who takes a position, who is accountable and who feels committed. Where this higher, responsible ego is lacking there can be no Self. Ethos and Self are therefore mutually interdependent. For this reason, too, an attitude of "beyond good and evil," such as has been commended in many quarters in modern times and especially since Nietzsche, is the best way to prevent the emergence of the Self.[38]

Both Parzival and the initiate-speaker are becoming an autonomous "someone" who is committed and accountable — in their actions and in their speech. Aware now that automatically heeding Gurnemanz's advice led to failure, Parzival pledges loyalty to the vision formed out of his own life; he vows to see the Grail again, no matter how long it takes. But first he must submit to the embrace of silence, which can feel like the kiss of death.

Shattered, as his sword will be again and again, Parzival and the initiate-speaker must repeatedly return to silence, the source of speech. With Picard, they will recognize that "there is something silent in every word, as an abiding token of the origin of speech" and that in every silence as well, "there is something of the spoken word, as an abiding token of the power of silence to create speech."[39]

When language is no longer related to silence it loses its source of refreshment and renewal and therefore something of its substance. Language today seems to talk automatically, out of its own strength and, emptying and scattering itself, it seems to be hastening to an end. There is something hard and obstinate in language today, as though it were making a great effort to remain alive in spite of its emptiness. There is also something desperate in it, as though it were expecting its emptiness to lead it to a relentless end, and it is this alternation of obstinacy and despair which makes it so restless. By taking it away from silence, we have made language an orphan. The tongue we speak today is no longer a mother-tongue but rather an orphaned tongue. . . .[40]

For both speaker and speech, repair and renewal flow from silence, which the initiate-speaker increasingly feels not just as an absence of noise and babble, but as an active, gentle presence in which to rest and re-orient. But, meanwhile, Parzival's old life is dead, and, as we have known him, he will soon disappear from the text. Our initiate-speaker is succumbing to silence. How can the story continue?

Wolfram offers his solution in the opening sentences of the next book:

> Now for a while, he whose conduct was never dishonorable shall claim this adventure for his own, a man known to all as noble — Gawan. In this story, many a man appears beside or even above the one who is its hero — Parzival.[41]

Using a not uncommon device in medieval literature — character substitution — Wolfram contends this is the only way for his story not to be a "false and lying tale" that would "better lie homeless out in the snow so that the lips ache that spread it as the truth."[42]

Like Parzival, Gawan is accused of a dishonorable deed and also embarks on a journey to clear his name and regain his honor. With the exception of the pivotal Book IX, Gawan's adventures will occupy the next seven books. Some commentators have declined to consider these chapters an integral part of the epic, and yet even a cursory examination reveals their intimate connection to the main thread of Parzival's journey.

We will become acquainted with Gawan much better in upcoming adventures, but we have some clue to his character already. We first meet him when he offers words of consolation to an unreceptive Keie, who has just been defeated by the entranced Parzival. When Keie lambastes and taunts him, Gawan, unlike the other knights, does not climb into his armor and gallop forth to confront Parzival. He rides out thoughtfully to see what is going on and, ever observant of details, notices why the strange knight stares so raptly at the snow. Upon learning Gawan's identity, Parzival thanks him for his kindness and remarks on Gawan's reputation for being kind to everyone. As to his lineage, Gawan is nephew to King Arthur and, having been fostered by Arthur, is like his son. Gawan is also a distant cousin of Parzival's, because Arthur and Gandin (Parzival's grandfather) were offspring of two brothers.

Gawan and Parzival are related, as are subject and mirror image. The mirror reflects back the picture, but in reverse! In the ensuing chapters, Gawan's words will mean little. What matters in Gawan's adventure is what he *does,* not what he *says.* His actions are always connected with genuine feeling, as distinguished from mere emotion. A subtitle for the Gawan chapters could be the old adage, "Actions speak louder than words."

What do we express as the silent mirror of speech? Gesture. Not the same as body language, which often betrays one's unauthentic words, by revealing one's actual emotional attitude, gesture aligns with and accentuates spoken communication. The descent to silence opens the possibility for gesture. The initiate-speaker will learn from Gawan's adventure to speak from the whole body, not just from the mouth.

NOTES

[1] Wolfram, Book V, 226.

[2] Wolfram, Book V, 230.

[3] Wolfram, Book V, 235.

[4] Wolfram, Book V, 238.

[5] Wolfram, Book V, 247.

[6] Wolfram, Book V, 250.

[7] Wolfram, Book V, 254.

[8] Wolfram, Book V, 255.

[9] Wolfram, Book V, 269.

[10] Wolfram, Book V, 269.

[11] Emma Jung and Marie-Louise von Franz, *The Grail Legend,* 113–212.

[12] Comments made during a 1989 seminar concerning the Grail at the Dallas Institute of Humanities and Culture, Dallas, Texas

[13] Summarized by David Fideler in his article "The Path Toward the Grail," from Henry and Renee Kahane, *The Krater and the Grail.*

[14] Walter Johannes Stein, *The Ninth Century and the Holy Grail,* 107.

[15] Stein, 2.

[16] Stein, 4.

[17] See Emma Jung and Marie-Louise von Franz (79–97) for a whole chapter contrasting spear and sword as symbols.

[18] Wolfram, Book VI, 296.

[19] Wolfram, Book VI, 300.

[20] Wolfram, Book VI, 301.

[21] Wolfram, Book VI, 304.

[22] Wolfram, Book VI, 308.

[23] Wolfram, Book VI, 312.

[24] Wolfram, Book VI, 313.

[25] Wolfram, Book VI, 315.

[26] Wolfram, Book VI, 316.

[27] Wolfram, Book VI, 323.

[28] Wolfram, Book VI, 328.

[29] Wolfram, Book VI, 329–30.

[30] He does speak briefly after a battle in the next book when he sends some defeated knights to give their oath of service to Condwiramurs.

[31] Wolfram, Book VI, 332.

[32] Patricia Monaghan, *The Book of Goddesses and Heroines*, 131–32.

[33] Beryl Rowland, *Birds with Human Souls*, 67.

[34] Max Picard, *The World of Silence*, 21.

[35] Picard, 18.

[36] Picard, 19.

[37] Picard, 19.

[38] Jung and von Franz, 134.

[39] Picard, 24.

[40] Picard, 41.

[41] Wolfram, Book VII, 338.

[42] Wolfram, Book VII, 338.

"In Reality You Are Me, Even If Our Names Are Different"

The Grail King Speaks

In the mirror land, one is expected
To know answers, not questions,
And answers must be enacted
Rather than spoken.
Oh, Speaker, permit gesture,
Mirror of speech,
To penetrate every action.
And take heart from the child within,
The only one who will
Recognize who you are.
Discipline your impulses
And, by stopping, stay straightforward
In the world of complexity
Where entanglements can obscure
The path to the Grail.

BOOK VII

Gawan has ridden forth with his company to keep his appointment to fight Kingrimursel and reinstate his good name. Well into the journey, Gawan sees a large army approaching, their banners waving and spears bristling. He quickly quells any urge to flee and, instead, orders his aides to saddle for him the white horse with red ears that Orilus had captured from a Grail knight and given him. Mounted on proud Gringuljete, Gawan trots forward to meet the army, thinking to himself, "Anyone who is such a coward that he flees before he is pursued is too hasty for his own honor."[1]

Gawan encounters one of the squires from the army who is amazed at Gawan's questions about this host. The squire thinks Gawan should know everything already but finally explains that there are actually two armies here, though both are fighting for the same cause. The armies, one led by a young knight, Meljanz, and the other by his uncle, are besieging the castle at Bearosche where Obie, daughter of Meljanz's vassal Lippaut, has refused to accept Meljanz's offer of love and insulted him in the process. In a war of words between the lovers, Meljanz took offense at Obie's suggestion that he was too unseasoned a knight to deserve her love. He had reminded her caustically that her father is his vassal, to which Obie had retorted:

> Then let him to whom you give a fief serve you for it. . . . I do not want a fief from anyone. My sovereign freedom is great enough for any crown which earthly head has ever borne.[2]

Obie's haughtiness has ignited Meljanz's prideful hostility, and many good knights will die in the resulting battle.

The squire rushes off to help his newly knighted lord to win honor by being first into the fray. Gawan is left alone, feeling very ambivalent. One part of him advises leaving this battle to the instigators, and another part urges joining in, lest "all my earthly fame will be destroyed."[3] After brief and distressed deliberation, he rides toward Bearosche, asking God's blessing in his endeavor.

Even so, he has committed himself only to see what is happening, not necessarily to participate. "Doubt cut his heart like a plane with sharp anxiety."[4] He particularly does not want to be viewed as one of the profiteers who were often bystanders at battles, and reassures himself, "I am looking for no profit — I just want to keep what is mine."[5] which means his knightly honor. He rides on through the army camp and up to the well-fortified castle, which bustles with preparations for battle. Just outside the castle wall, his squires set up a temporary camp so Gawan can observe the scene. Above him the old queen, her daughters and all the women surge to the windows to watch the battle.

Gawan will find no welcome here, except from one small girl, Obilot — sister of the haughty Obie. Within earshot of Gawan, these two sisters disagree vehemently as to who or what he is. Obie labels him as a merchant, but Obilot says, "You're accusing him of something that never happened, sister. . . . No one ever called HIM a merchant. He is so handsome, I want to have him for my knight."[6] Obie's acidic remarks about Gawan intensify, as Obilot defends her choice of a knight and condemns her older sister's manners, both in regard to her chosen one and to Meljanz. Gawan hears every word of this exchange.

Meanwhile Prince Lippaut, the girls' father, is distraught about having to fight his own lord, whom he actually had fostered after Meljanz's father died. A court of inquiry has declared Prince Lippaut innocent of any wrongdoing, yet still this battle threatens. Now his counselors advise him to send his ablest knights to joust with Meljanz's armies, so that perhaps a wholesale battle can be averted. Lippaut concurs, and a fine tournament results, with young Meljanz shining in knightly vigor and courage.

Meljanz's prowess seems to affect Obie's attitude toward her spurned suitor, and she begins to contrast Gawan, her little sister's chosen, quite unfavorably with Meljanz. She does more than just talk, however. First she sends a squire to Gawan, supposedly to buy some cloth or a horse. Gawan's eyes flash with anger, and he sends the squire away. Then Obie sends word to the burgrave of the town that Gawan is a peddler who is trying to cheat them. When the burgrave goes to accost the unscrupulous merchant, he finds only a fine knight whom he is proud to welcome. Finally Obie sends word to her father that Gawan is a counterfeiter whose goods should be confiscated. When Lippaut goes to see for himself, the burgrave defends Gawan, declaring him to be a knight. With his eyes and his heart, Lippaut sees this is true and asks Gawan for help in the battle. Gawan cordially replies that he must decline "until my own battle has been fought."[7] Lippaut implores him to reconsider until Gawan reluctantly responds with a promise to think about it overnight and give his final answer in the morning.

That evening, little Lady Obilot finds her way to Gawan to ask him to serve her. He greets her respectfully and thanks her generously for defending him when he was being maligned by her sister. A tender dialogue blooms as the child speaks "without any shyness":

> Sir, as God is my witness, you are the very first man with whom I have talked in private. If I do keep my good breeding and my woman's modesty, this talk will make me happy, for my teacher told me that speech is the housing of the mind.[8]

She goes on to say that she sees him as one with herself, and thus her plea to him is a plea to herself. "In reality you are me, even if our names are different. You shall now bear my name and be both maid and man."[9] Her great distress, she says, motivates her to seek refuge in his kindness and to ask him to serve her. She knows she is "worthy of being served,"[10] and in return vows she will love him with all her heart.

At first, Gawan gently resists, pointing out quite reasonably that it will be at least five years before Obilot is old enough to give any man her love. But then he remembers Parzival telling him to trust women rather than God, "and this counsel was a messenger of the maiden to Gawan's heart."[11] Clasping her small hands in his own, he gives Obilot his pledge of service, meeting and matching her own words when he says:

> Into your hands I give my sword. If anyone challenges me to a joust, it is you who must ride to meet him and do the fighting for me. Others may think they see ME in the battle, but I shall know it was you who did it.[12]

She responds in kind, promising him that she will be "your protection and your shield, your solace and your heart."[13] Then Obilot excuses herself to go prepare her token for him, the sleeve from a special new dress that her parents agree to have made for her when she tells them that Gawan will fight in her service.

Under moonlight, the castle inhabitants prepare for the day's fighting ahead. When the sun rises, the fighting begins, and Gawan fights against the armies of both Meljanz and his uncle. After one brief joust with a young knight who winds up prostrate on the flowering field, Gawan notices his squire is the one who so courteously informed him when he first saw these armies. Gawan returns to the squire the horse he has just won from his lord. Later Gawan learns that, the fiercest combatant fighting for Meljanz was "The Nameless Knight," dressed all in red armor. Gawan feels grateful that they did not meet one another in battle, since he knows this knight must have been Parzival. Gawan and Parzival, both nameless to their comrades in this battle, have excelled over all the other warriors.

Finally, Meljanz challenges Gawan to joust. Gawan wounds and defeats him, and takes him prisoner. When the Red Knight hears this, he goes to his own prisoners and makes them swear an oath that they will either free Meljanz or win the Grail for him. When they reply that they do not know how to find the Grail, only that a king named Anfortas has it in his keeping, the Red Knight sends them instead to Condwiramurs to tell her that he "yearns for the Grail and yet also for her love. Both are always in my thoughts."[14] Then the Red Knight chooses a horse named Ingliart, which had escaped from Gawan when he took Meljanz prisoner. and rides away, leaving others to divide the wealth obtained in the battle.

Prince Lippaut is relieved that Meljanz has been captured and the war is over. Meljanz is treated with hospitality and respect in the castle where he grew up and contritely confesses that Obie's mockery of him drove him to this war. Meanwhile, Obilot parades before the enraged Obie with her token, the sleeve, which Gawan has returned to her. Gawan conveys his prisoners' pledges to the burgrave, but delivers Meljanz into the care of Obilot. In turn, Obilot directs Meljanz to give his pledge to Obie. After some resistance from Meljanz, love springs anew between the two estranged lovers, and they soon wed.

Before long, Gawan takes leave of the court to continue his own journey, but not before a tearful Obilot has begged to go with him. He hugs her, but says she must stay. He is given provisions and a huntsman for a guide and leaves the court with heavy heart.

Initiatory Themes

In Books I and II, we learned that the marriage of yearning and determination creates the conditions for the spiritual quest. Born from this inner marriage is a spiritually aimed mannequin — someone not quite fully human, as he stumbles along, living out of his yearning and determination, but not very aware of or concerned about what is going on around him. He acts out of what he is told or what he thinks is expected of him, gradually awakening as a result of all the difficulties and confusions that ensue.

Nonetheless, this mannequin takes a curiously uncomplicated path; he yearns, he leaves his mother, goes to Arthur's court with little interference, gets the red knight's armor, finds a mentor, wins his wife, arrives at the Grail castle, fails, is punished for his failure. He is only minimally involved with intricate intrigues and subplots. Like a rocket launched toward the infinite universe, Parzival represents the vertical path.

Gawan's path, on the other hand, traverses the horizontal plane. Like a patient weaver, he will have to untangle, then knit together again, several complicated situations. If Parzival is the arrow set loose in flight toward a target, Gawan is its feathers. The arrow flies direct, as circumstances permit, perhaps breaking in the process but bending very little. The feathers further the arrow in flight and help to "true" its aim by moving, bending, adjusting to all the nuances of the circumstances during the flight. We disdain a "feather in the wind," knowing that to be blown about by every passing breeze gives a person little power or direction in life. What our contemptuous glance may miss is the positive qualities of such a feather: It is very responsive to what comes toward it, and such responsiveness assists an arrow in flight to hold its established direction.

Another way of understanding Gawan's strength can be gained from Jung's ideas about the "feeling function," which he characterizes as "rational" and, therefore, to be distinguished from strictly emotional reactions. One gets carried away by emotion, as evidenced by the measurable physiological changes that occur.[15] Feeling, on the other hand, is not evidenced by physiological effects:

> Feeling informs you through its feeling-tones of the values of things. Feeling tells you for instance whether a thing is acceptable or agreeable or not. It tells you what a thing is WORTH to you. . . . It is, like thinking, a rational function. . . .[16]

The world that feeling perceives differs from the single-focused world of spiritually-aimed yearning and determination. For feathery feeling, responsive to the slightest shifts in currents, the world brims with many-sided complexity. Gawan's skill in sorting through the numerous and sometimes frustrating details of life on this horizontal plane receives more focus than his prowess on the battlefield. Informed by discernment and discrimination, Gawan's feeling responsiveness guides him in evaluating situations and thereby discovering what he can or must do. He never has to let go the reins of his horse just to be able to move on. His feeling moves him. We will see that, through the part of himself called Gawan, Parzival gains "real feeling," the sensitivity and confidence of a "feeling heart," which Cundrie so harshly accused him of not having.

Meanwhile, as a preliminary, Wolfram provides a picture of Gawan before his pivotal adventures begin. He does not describe Gawan's background, as he did with Parzival. Rather, Gawan arrives in the story fully grown and becomes known by how he acts in certain situations. Intricately related to Parzival, Gawan is revealed in Book VII and especially in Book VIII, to be, at first, no more complete a character.

Wolfram introduced us first to Parzival as a young boy listening to the birds, moved by inchoate desire somehow to grasp the heights in which they so joyfully sing. In the opening pages of Gawan's first adventure, Wolfram describes him camped in trees beneath a castle wall listening to "an army of women" surging "like a flood" on the battlements above him. What he hears is not so pleasant as what entered Parzival's ears. Obie's insulting remarks testify to her anger that her "sovereign freedom" has not been respected by the man who sought to claim her on his terms and not hers. In this word "sovereign" lies the clue to Gawan's calling, just as surely as the bird songs are hints of Parzival's calling.

In *sovereignty*, we meet an ancient conception, important particularly to the Celtic world but no longer much in fashion as a term except in political circles.[17] Celtic tradition held that Sovereignty was a goddess immanent in the land. The embodiment of this divine earth was the queen, who served also as high priestess and whose king pledged his service to her. The spiritual values of these connections faded over time, leaving the word "sovereignty" impoverished. It came to mean only an exercise of power over a certain territory, and thus is often interpreted, psychologically, to mean the right to do whatever one wants without interference. Through Gawan's adventures, Parzival and the initiate-speaker learn the difference between sovereignty and self-indulgence. Self-mastery, which, psychologically speaking, is the same as sovereignty, relies primarily on the ability to discern the subtle distinctions that only the heart, not the mind, can initially perceive.

Right off, Gawan is confronted with the choice of whether or not to get involved with the tangled war at Bearosche. Such ambivalence is not all that uncommon for Gawan. Yet, the ability to bear ambivalence typifies the life of feeling.[18] Things are not always immediately clear in the life of feeling. Because of all the complications, subplots and subtle consequences perceived by feeling, it often takes some time to become aware of the "true" path. Being directed is not enough. If it were, Gawan would not be tempted to get involved in the skirmish between Meljanz and Prince Lippaut.

True to his style, Gawan first goes to see what is going on, to listen to what is being said. In other words, to reach the heart of feeling, the feeling in the heart, one must become alive and awake in one's senses. Gawan clearly demonstrates his sense-ability (sensibility) during his time at Bearosche. Whereas Parzival follows imaginative envisioning, his experiences mediated by images and memories, Gawan experiences first with the senses. He sees, and carefully observes — as when he detected that Parzival was entranced by the drops of blood on the snow and when he goes to see what is happening in Bearosche. He also listens carefully, not merely to parrot back what is told to him but to discern the meaning of what is being said. He does not think literally. Compare his dialogue with Obilot to the comedy of misunderstanding in Parzival's first encounter with Jeschute. Gawan remembers Parzival's advice about trusting women more than God but allows this suggestion to have meaning in the context of a little girl asking for his service. He listens so carefully to the speech of Obilot that he is able to respond with a perfectly matched speech of his own.

Who is this woman-child whom he honors so graciously, who is able to see Gawan despite the slandering of her sister and the doubts of the burgrave and her father? Obilot, a child, sees with her heart, just as Parzival the child sees with his imagination. A kind of marriage takes place between Gawan and Obilot through the words they say to one another. They each say that Gawan is Obilot and Obilot is Gawan, reflecting, despite their difference in years, old

Gurnemanz's last teaching to Parzival that "husband and wife are one, as are the sun that shone today and the thing called day itself."

In agreeing to serve Obilot and to accept her linguistic context for their relationship ("In reality you are me, even if our names are different"), Gawan has taken Parzival a long way toward the ability to see with his heart. As she shows so plainly when she reunites her irritable sister with Meljanz, this child is wise beyond her years in her feeling for the truth. The dialogue with Obilot also reveals Gawan as a willing "double," a patient servant of the more singly directed, restless arrow that is Parzival. Gawan, for Parzival, follows Christ's injunction to "become as a little child" and to let the child lead.

Parzival's parting advice, gleaned from his own life experience, opens a new possibility for Gawan. Gawan's usual way of thinking is not literal-minded but reasonable, very rational. He always cogitates about situations, and, though Obie intends slander when depicting him as a merchant, her remark has some validity. Gawan is not unfamiliar with the balance sheet, with assessing the profits and losses of his options in each situation. Memory of Parzival's words spurs him to take a leap — only the first of several he will make. In this leap, he relinquishes his habit of reasonableness — which starts to convince Obilot that she is too young to ask a knight's service. Instead, against all reason, he steps into her service and therefore into the silly battle which is just a lovers' quarrel blown out of all proportion.

As later episodes will prove, Gawan's leaping is counterpart to Parzival's wandering — and, in fact, directly expedites Parzival's journey. After the battle at Bearosche, Parzival returns to his wandering, mounted on a new horse — Gawan's. Because Gawan did not act out of habit but let his heart be guided to respond to Obilot, Parzival's means of momentum is no longer the horse he shamelessly pilfered but now is something he has earned — albeit on the dubious side in this battle.

It must be noted, however, that the discriminating feeling and sense-ability characteristic of Gawan are not always met kindly by the world. Gawan receives more actual disrespect than Parzival. He does not cause pain, as Parzival did, and then endure shame for it. Rather, he is continually accused unfairly and mocked. He is on his way to a joust because of an untrue accusation and then decides to interrupt his journey to help out at Bearosche, despite being rudely insulted by Obie. Hers will seem a relatively mild disrespect compared to what he receives later.

The restraint and patience he demonstrates here will be characteristic of Gawan throughout the epic. That he chooses to exercise such restraint and patience — and that they do not merely reflect weak passivity — is evidenced by his flashing eyes when he dismisses the squire sent by Obie to purchase goods from him. Gawan represents not only discerning and discriminating feeling, but also disciplined emotion.

Cundrie's accusation of Parzival has produced a split in the consciousness of the seeker of the Grail. One of the pair leaves the scene silent and determined; the other, connected to the senses and to feeling, comes into the foreground, attending to the complexity of life on the horizontal plane. Only when Gawan has re-established order in this confused realm can Parzival proceed on his vertical path.

There is a division but as yet no overt conflict. Gawan and Parzival are fighting in the same war on different sides, but they do not meet face to face. They each remain nameless to the people they are fighting with, though they would be known to each other. Only Gawan realizes how close they have come to battling each other. Parzival, as usual, is too preoccupied with his worries and goals to recognize the leader of the other army as Gawan. Though he is suffering, Parzival has not yet developed his feeling heart. However, it is significant that he begins sending knights he defeats back to Condwiramurs rather than to Arthur's court. No longer spurred only by swollen ambition, Parzival now acknowledges the connection between his spiritual destiny and his soul's love; the Grail and Condwiramurs wait, calling him silently. He has promised is to keep them "always in my thoughts."

Toward Speech of the Grail

After Parzival's condemnation by Cundrie, the initiate-speaker starts to become acquainted with silence. This is not an enforced, monastic silence or the wordlessness of the hermit. One will continue to talk, but now awareness of the limitations of language and shame of one's seeming inability to speak in a truly healing and transforming way, will lead to an increasing silence under the surface talk. At first there will be no conflict between this invisible, inner silence and the busy concerns of outer talkativeness.

The spaciousness of silence nurtures new sensitivities, new sense-abilities. During this phase of the speaker's initiation, the emphasis will not be directly on speaking but on perceiving: on *seeing* instead of just looking, on *listening* instead of just hearing. Eyes and ears are not sufficient. The ancients in Greece, Palestine and Persia knew that the heart is the organ for seeing "into" and listening "into" people, things, and events.[19]

To speak from the heart, Parzival and the initiate-speaker must listen to the speech of the heart, which grows articulate in being "moved." James Hillman proposes that what moves the heart is beauty. Such beauty is not an evaluated quality ascribed to people, things or events but something that breathes forth from every part of creation when it is perceived through the eyes of a child's heart. To see beauty in the world is to see the divine revealing itself. This beauty is "neither transcendent to the manifest or hiddenly immanent within" but, rather, refers to appearances as they are given. Beauty is thus "the very sensibility of the cosmos, that it has textures, tones, tastes, that it is attractive."[20]

The speech of the heart is animated by the speech of the world. The eyes of the heart do not find nouns in the world, but verbs. The heart is moved because it perceives the world as moving and gesturing. The verbalizing heart orients itself not by labeling and declaring the independent, isolated existence of objects but, as Russell Lockhart suggests, by joining the dance of interrelationship that verbs presuppose.

> Nouns and adjectives work for distance, keeping the ego in a superior position of naming and hence having power over, standing over, the objects of our experience. . . . Verbs relativize the ego, immersing it in something else: "he shadows you," "she animates you," "it projects you." Verb language takes the *is* out of the superior position, emphasizing not the existence of things, but the relationship between things.[21]

The sense-abilities of the heart, exemplified so well by children, release Gawan and the initiate-speaker for aesthetic relationship with the world. This aesthetic relationship is mediated by imagination, but notice that this mode of imagining has a different direction than Parzival's. The images that move Parzival are from the "other" world or the "inner" world. He does not really see the birds; just his own unconscious spiritual yearning. He does not see Ither behind his gorgeous armor, just an image of himself wearing it into glory. His vision at the Grail castle, which is definitely not in the "real" world, will so possess him from now on that he will hardly know where he is or what day it is.

This is not to say that Parzival's mode of imagining is inferior to Gawan's. In fact, this mode — which so values dreams, fantasies and visions — essentially sustains the foolish oddball on the path of a spiritual calling. Imaginal images companion such a person on the lonely road through a world of people who find him or her incomprehensible. Images encourage the seeker's perseverance in pursuit of the calling. But, to develop the speech of the Grail, Parzival's mode of imagination must be complemented by Gawan's mode of imagination — which values (i.e., compassionately sees and listens to) the people, things and events of the everyday world.

With Parzival's silence, Gawan's mode of imagining can be enlivened in the initiate-speaker. The experience of wonder-filled breathing in of the world may not, at first, have much to do with speaking, however. Seeing or listening "into" someone or something is always a journey into something that is too great to be put into words but that grows increasingly palpable to ever stronger sense-abilities. The thirteenth-century Sufi poet Rumi poignantly expresses this experience:

> A whole afternoon field inside me from one stem of
> reed,
> The messenger comes running toward me, irritated:
> *"Why be so hard to find?"*
>
> Last night I asked the moon about the Moon, my
> one question
> for the visible world, Where is God?

The moon says, *"I am dust stirred up when he passed by."*
The sun, *"My face is pale yellow*
from just now seeing him." Water: *"I slide on*
    my head and face
like a snake, from a spell" he said. Fire: *"His*
    lightning,
I want to be that restless." Wind, why so light?
"I would burn if I had a choice." Earth, quiet
    and thoughtful? *"Inside me I have a garden*
and an underground spring."

This world hurts my head with its answers,
wine filling my hand, not my glass.
If I could wake completely, I would say without
    speaking
why I'm ashamed of using words.[22]

The seeing and listening of the heart enable the initiate-speaker to appreciate the world and all its phenomena as animate. Such awareness inevitably awakens wonder and respect for the silent mystery of one's own body. Movement and rest; pulses and undulations; building up, tearing down — similar structural forms and mineral elements belong both to body and world and are confirmation that body and world belong to one another.

Increasingly, one gains the strength of perception to recognize that the world and one's body are not vacuous and dumb but abound with speaking gestures that can be "read" as wise, living texts.[23] Everything is moving and changing in this world, from ever-active subatomic energies to blossoms opening to tigers bounding after prey to slow shifts in stone formations carved by the wind. Thus everything can be experienced as gesture. The initiate-speaker must simply become quiet enough, heartfully sense-able enough, to perceive and inwardly honor this silent speech of the world. Then one's responses can be as expertly attuned as Gawan's words to Obilot. However, this dialogue is never given, never guaranteed. The initiate-speaker must actively re-create the conditions for it in each moment, and even Gawan has much to learn in this regard.

BOOK VIII

Gawan has traveled over high mountains and desolate moors and finally arrives at Schanpfanzun, where he agreed to joust with Kingrimursel. The splendid fortress rises above a plain, which spreads out for a mile in front of it, and there Gawan encounters its king, Vergulaht, his knights and his falconers, who are out for a day of hunting. A wounded heron has escaped to a swamplike pond, dragging a falcon with it.

King Vergulaht, though drenched by the effort, has just saved the unlucky falcon from drowning, but since the falconers have exercised their right to claim his garments and horse, the king must be furnished with different garments and another mount. At this moment, Gawan arrives.

Asking Gawan's permission to continue his hunting for a while, Vergulaht commends Gawan to the castle where, he says, his sister will be pleased to entertain him. Gawan enters the castle and is welcomed most warmly by beautiful Antikonie. The warmth is returned and rapidly becomes heat, as they exchange a "nongreeting-like kiss"[24] and sit down for a precipitously frank discussion of whether or not they will repair to the bedroom. Antikonie expresses mild reluctance, reminding Gawan that she is his hostess and thus wishes to treat him well, but that, after all, "I don't know who you are, and yet in such a short space of time you want to have my love."[25]

Gawan is so aroused that his thinking has become uncharacteristically literal. He responds to her comment by assuring the young woman his noble ancestry is certainly on a par with her own. Then, since her ladies and courtiers seem to be tactfully occupying themselves elsewhere, and since, as Gawan reflects, "a weak eaglet will often catch the large ostrich,"[26] he proceeds to slip his hand under her mantle. Wolfram "thinks" he may even have touched her thigh. This secret touch inflames Antikonie's desire as well, but their passion is not to be consummated.

In rushes an old knight who recognizes Gawan and shouts his name as a call-to-arms, yelling, "Alas! and hey — hey! for my master whom you murdered, and, as if that weren't enough, here you are about to rape his daughter."[27] Immediately the knights rise to attack. Gawan is without his sword and can see he is in trouble. He asks Antikonie for her advice because "neither of us has much in the way of weapons of defense."[28]

She suggests they move to a more defensible location, and they run up into the tower. Antikonie keeps shouting at the knights to desist, but no one can hear her in the clamor. In the tower, Gawan and Antikonie look for something they might use to stave off the attack. She finds a heavy inlaid chessboard with an iron ring for hanging and gives it to Gawan; by grasping the iron ring he flails the oncoming knights with the board. Antikonie tearfully hurls the large and heavy chess pieces at the attacking knights. Whoever gets hit falls, so accurate and strong is her aim. Meanwhile, Gawan's fighting intensifies with every glance he steals of her beautiful face and figure.

At this juncture Vergulaht rides up and orders the tower be torn down to expose the combatants. The landgrave Kingrimursel, who had promised Gawan safe passage until such time as they would joust, also arrives. Greatly dismayed at the attack, Kingrimursel asks Gawan and Antikonie for a truce so that he can join them. This causes the attacking knights to pause, allowing both Gawan and Kingrimursel to get to more open ground, and enraging Vergulaht. He urges the knights to attack again, but they hesitate. A spokesman explains that many of the knights do not want to fight the landgrave because they respect and honor him. He also advises Vergulaht that he risks his own honor if he murders a guest who had been promised safety. In addition, the Lady Antikonie is in peril, and if she is killed or injured it will be Vergulaht's fault. The spokesman then begs him to call off the battle.

Vergulaht declares an armistice until he has more time to consider how his father's death might be avenged on Gawan. (Wolfram tells us now that Gawan did not kill the man.) In the meantime, Antikonie kisses Kingrimursel and Gawan and proceeds to upbraid her brother for his shameful attack. Kingrimursel, also offended by the attack on Gawan, to whom he had given his oath, threatens to withdraw his service from his cousin Vergulaht. Another vassal goads Vergulaht to kill Gawan. Then everyone argues with everyone else.

Vergulaht finally interrupts the dispute, saying that this wrangling is disrespectful to him. He bids Antikonie and Kingrimursel to dine with Gawan while he withdraws to his chambers with his allies to determine the best course of action. In his chambers with a council of wise men, Vergulaht confides that he was defeated in the forest by a knight who forced him to swear to "get the Grail for him,"[29] or, if he was not able to do that, to go to Pelrapeire and give his oath of service to the queen there, Condwiramurs. Vergulaht asks the council's advice.

The vassal who was so eager that Gawan be killed speaks forcefully:

> For the thing into which you were forced by that lone man, let Sir Gawan here be the hostage — he's flapping his wings in your trap. Ask him to take an oath here before us all that he will get the Grail for you.[30]

The other counselors concur, and Vergulaht determines to tell Gawan in the morning.

The next morning Antikonie intercedes for Gawan, calling upon her brother to be a model of manly honor. Vergulaht acknowledges that he wants her love and forgiveness, and asks Gawan to help him by swearing to seek the Grail in his place. Gawan so pledges. At the same time, the landgrave Kingrimursel is reconciled with Vergulaht. Gawan's squires are then reunited with him, having been imprisoned all this time. He commends them to Kingrimursel, who is to guide them back to Bearosche where they can be led back to Arthur and Ginover. After a sad farewell to Antikonie, who assures him she will keep him in her thoughts no matter what happens, Gawan mounts sturdy Gringuljete,[31] who formerly belonged to a Grail knight, and rides forth in search of the Grail.

Initiatory Themes

Gawan's exploits in Book VIII show that feeling one's way on the horizontal plane is no easier or more sure of success than Parzival's vertical path toward spiritual vision. The opening paragraphs give us the image of a high-flying falcon brought low by its prey into a swampy pool, and then having to be rescued just before it drowns. The image foretells the rest of the episode, as Gawan — whose name means "Hawk of May"[32] — winds up flapping helplessly in a trap of his own making.

It is quite a different Gawan we meet here. Finally he has arrived at his destination, the castle where he is to meet Kingrimursel and clear his name. But, instead of remaining poised to meet this test, Gawan tries to seduce Antikonie the moment he enters the castle. Though not exactly crude, he suddenly seems bereft of the subtle sensitivity he demonstrated with little Obilot, and displays an atypical literal-mindedness for one who responded so beautifully and

appropriately to Obilot's speech. Did he misunderstand his relinquishment of reasonableness and assume it meant going to the other
extreme of acting out of sheer appetite?

Sensitivity and sense-ability seem overrun by sensuality, over-
shadowing Gawan's more gallant virtues. As a consequence, he must
wield the chessboard in a futile battle against his assailants. Indeed,
with the exception of the escape to the tower, Gawan becomes
unusually inactive, even passive, in this episode. He is subject to
various discussions regarding his fate, but he is not privy to, let alone
a participant in, these talks. He is informed of the decisions, after
both Kingrimursel and Antikonie have spoken up in his behalf.

No falcon's eye view prevails here; little in this episode could be
described as uplifting. The summary may not capture the tedium of
the long, convoluted arguments before the final decision is reached.
The characters here are heavily mired in the misunderstandings, the
petty jealousies and quarrels, the dullness of this world. This is definitely the horizontal plane, with little access to, or even hints of, the
depths and the heights of the vertical plane which can give one perspective. When the horizontal so predominates, the world appears
quite flat and terribly turbulent.

Despite Gawan's manly beauty, sensitivity, articulateness, gal-
lantry and courage, this episode exposes him as no more perfect than
Parzival. He must also struggle for a middle path of balance. Just as
Parzival saw the Red Knight and desired his possessions, so Gawan
meets Antikonie and desires her. In each case, the young man's finer
attributes are obscured in his efforts to grab what he desires.

Greedily grasping and grabbing are devoid of the expressiveness
that enlivens gesture. Grasping and grabbing belong to the realm of
reflex, of mechanical reaction to desire or fear, and therefore are driven rather than consciously chosen movements. If Gawan is to
develop for Parzival the "real feeling" of the heart through which
mechanical bodily movements become freely chosen gestures full of
expression and meaning, this incident at Vergulaht's castle shows
the challenge that lies ahead.

The temptation here is specifically sexual; Gawan's reflexive grabbing is stimulated by sexual desire. The chessgame of life — that
royal game of the eternal dance of opposites — certainly has, at its
base, the attraction between the sexes. The sexual act, quite literally,

draws us into this world, the world of phenomena and material things which can seem so real as to preclude awareness of any spiritual realm. In a solely material world, no reason exists to exercise any consciousness, discipline, or restraint in one's sexuality. A person can just "do what comes naturally" and "be happy" like the other creatures.

Yet what is natural for a human being seems more complex. All traditions have taught that human beings belong naturally to a cultural and spiritual sphere as well. In puberty initiations everywhere, tribal traditions impress upon the young person that something of the sexual has to be sacrificed (which originally meant "made sacred") so that she or he belongs not only to *this* world but also to the *other* worlds, the cultural and spiritual worlds.[33] The culture and the community mediate this passage with ritual enactments, sometimes entailing operations on the sexual organs, which signify that one's sexuality belongs to the community as much as to oneself. The procreative power of the young person links the communities of past and present to the community of the future. Thus it is a sacred power, godlike in its assurance of continuity. The sacrifices involved in the puberty rite are performed to make known and sacred this spiritual responsibility.[34] Only after the puberty rite is the young person considered mature enough to marry, marriage being the place where sexuality and community are joined.

Disciplines, codes, and moral axioms regarding sexuality belong to human cultures, not the animal and plant worlds. Thus any choice to limit one's sexual behavior constitutes an important first step away from that more creaturely existence toward something else. Like initiates of ancient mystery cults, persons who consciously commit their lives to spiritual endeavor know their path to be *contra naturam*, against nature. The disciplining of sexual impulses always attends initiation to spiritual life — which is, almost always, life given in service to the wider community as well as to the gods.

Those not prepared to choose such discipline appear and often feel more foolish than the true fool — who may be naive and idealistic, but is not merely stupidly driven. Instead of really "playing" the game of chess — being outside it and above it in a certain sense — such people are flailing the chessboard, tossing the pieces, and utterly sunk in the game until all the pieces are thrown away and the board is broken.

What rescues Gawan and the initiate-speaker from living turbulently on the surface of things, driven by desires and fears, is Parzival — the spiritual seeker within. Because of Parzival's advice, Gawan released his habitual reasonableness to accommodate Obilot, and now, again because of Parzival, Gawan is moved in a new direction. Parzival defeated Vergulaht, a man very much of this world who does not look very deeply into things but responds to their appearances. He is too easily convinced, for example, that Gawan has killed his father and so seeks revenge. He almost kills his sister in the blind rage he directs at Gawan in the tower. He listens to the unending arguments of his vassals and then finally makes a decision based on their advice. In order to appease his own need for revenge, to keep the respect and love of his sister, *and* to avoid a dangerous mission himself, Vergulaht transfers to Gawan the oath he gave to Parzival to seek the Grail. Parzival may feel a long way from the Grail, but because he now knows where he is going, his actions no longer place someone in jeopardy — as they did with Jeschute and Cunneware — but actually remove Gawan from jeopardy.

From another perspective, what rescues Gawan from the tyranny of automatic impulses is stopping, having to wait, becoming "passive." According to Patricia Berry, stopping can be a "mode of animation."[35] Her idea may require some amplification in a society where busyness means one is well occupied, where constant activity is a sign of one's worth and waiting is experienced as degrading dependence. Berry recalls Medusa, the sight of whose face stopped everyone in their tracks, turning them to stone. Undaunted, the hero Perseus did not look her in the face but, instead, touched her body, became acquainted through his fingertips, before cutting off the gruesome head and strapping it to his back:

> Through touch Perseus gets the Medusa's head, her very essence, and straps it to his back, backs himself with her immobility, her eternal deathlike vision. . . . He's protected because he is backed by a vision which sees the immobility, the stasis, the rock in all things. If one can experience the stasis, can back oneself with that vision, then movement is possible, because movement is her nature too, is part of her very image — her eternally writhing hair.[36]

Paradoxically, "within stasis we find movement," within stony immobility hides airy flight. Pegasus, the winged stallion, prances

forth from Medusa's headless body. "In that awe-full image of stopping there is a rush of wings, an animal power in the insubstantial
air."[37]

W.H. Vanstone, a Canon Residentiary in the Church of England,
establishes the spiritual value of waiting by showing its place in the
life of Jesus Christ. He re-evaluates the "passion" of Jesus, noting that
the image conveyed by Paul and the gospel accounts of events preceding the crucifixion is not "betrayal" or "treachery" but "being
handed over." In all the Gospels, after the "handing over," Jesus —
whose activity, heretofore, in speech and deed, has been entirely
potent — becomes inactive, passive, and largely ineffectual. Vanstone
thinks it incorrect to associate the passion of Christ solely with the
crucifixion; the Greek words suggest to him that the passion was the
entire series of events that occurred after being "handed over."[38]
From then on, Jesus becomes less subject than object, waiting upon
decisions made by others. In this way, God is revealed as

> . . . One Who hands Himself over to be affected by the world, to
> receive the impact and the meaning of the world, to wait upon the
> world. It is of this God that we bear the image — an image that
> includes passion no less than action, waiting no less than working.[39]

In all waiting, there is learning. All conditions of being "subject
to" teach us about our needs, our vulnerability, our interdependence.
Self-imposed waiting, like that of the lover or the artist, presents even
greater gifts. One's awareness of the need that constrains one to wait
engenders a "heightened sensitivity, a more intense receptivity,"[40] to
the meaning of that for which one waits.

By stopping and waiting, Gawan restrains impulsiveness and
expands his capacity to recognize and receive the meaning of what he
is willing to wait for. It is true that Gawan did not stop himself; he
was stopped. He will soon have opportunity to demonstrate how
much he has learned in that process. Meanwhile, mounted again on
his "animal power," renewed by waiting, Gawan departs atop red-
eared Gringuljete in quest of the Grail.

We know, of course, that finding the Grail castle is not Gawan's
task. The Grail calls to its own; it cannot be assigned from one person to another. Gawan, like Parzival before, thinks he is headed one
place when, in fact, he is going to quite another. Like Parzival at the

Grail castle, he will be tested to see if he has mastered the lessons from these recent events. Much depends on whether or not he succeeds.

Toward Speech of the Grail

Becoming generative through the body, as ritualized with ordeals and scarification in puberty rites the world over, is a kind of death — or, to put it another way, a second birth. Becoming generative in speech imposes no less a trial upon the initiate-speaker. This too can feel more like a death than a second birth.

The question as to how sexuality is connected with language and speech plunges any investigator into the furthest depths of what it means to be human. The domain remains mostly uncharted[41] and cannot be adequately plumbed in a few pages. Nonetheless, Wolfram's Book VIII compels us to confront the issue.

Even casual consideration of human beings immediately discloses the fundamental nature of the question. Along with relatively little skin covering, two characteristics distinguish humans from other creatures — our sexuality and our language and speech. Our sexual rhythms and cerebral sounds differ from those in the animal world. And our spine, connecting pelvis and head, must somehow be involved since it supports that other unusual trait, our upright, two-legged stance.

The depth of the question is revealed also by Genesis, the founding creation myth of Western civilization, in which speech and sexuality are both prominent themes. In the beginning, after God has created the earth and all its creatures, he welcomes Adam to the fruitful garden and invites him to eat of everything except the tree of knowledge of good and evil. He warns Adam he will die if he eats of this tree. Then,

> out of the ground the Lord God formed every beast of the field, and every fowl of the air; and brought them unto Adam to see what he would call them: and whatsoever Adam called every living creature, that was the name thereof. (Genesis 2:19)

So, before the Fall onto the horizontal, black-and-white chessboard of good and evil, it was the human being whom God consulted for names. We can assume that these were more than just labels. Because Adam was absolutely one with God's creation, feeling neither separate nor filled with value judgments about the greater worth of some beings over others, he was able to ascribe names out of a depth of perception unavailable to us now. Adam lives in the image of his creator in giving these names; in fact, he seems to create things a second time.

It is not explained why God felt names were necessary, only that He brings things to Adam to be named. Naming seems to complete things and therefore must be central to Adam's role in God's creation. Names divide things from one another; they differentiate and distinguish. In this granting of distinction, Adam resembles God who, out of the formless void, separated the elements of light and darkness, air and water, water and earth.

But to make distinctions is not to cut asunder. God looked upon the creation as "good" because it was whole and harmonious, nothing disconnected or discordant. Then, Adam's and Woman's (so named by Adam) eyes "were opened" by eating the forbidden fruit. Such was the death about which God had warned them. Noticing their nakedness and the differences between them, they sewed fig leaves into aprons. Awareness of and shame about sexual distinction changed Adam's role in the scheme of things — because his perception of the scheme of things changed.

From then on Adam's way of "knowing," in the Biblical sense, is sexual. Instead of namer, he becomes progenitor. Instead of caretaking an ever-flowering garden, he labors amid the interplay of good and evil, life and death, on the chessboard of existence. Instead of effortlessly naming things in the clear light of Eden, Adam must grope his way across the strobe-lighted earth, where darkness and light alternate and clarity is so momentary that finding a permanent name for anything seems impossible.

Is it not understandable that Adam and his descendants dream of return to the kind of perception they had before the Fall onto the chessboard? Does it not make sense that we seek a way to assuage the pain of separation — from God and from creation — that the awareness of good and evil and of sexual difference engendered? How can we reestablish that sense of belonging, that sense of self-worth and trust, that sense of being in a blessed world well tended by its Creator?

Certainly a clear echo of that sense of connection, relaxation, and fullness is experienced in the love act. Which is why, from medieval mystical poetry to contemporary popular music, the love act is idealized. Sexual union with a beloved mirrors the experience of oneness Adam knew in the garden. The problem is that a mirrored experience is still only a pale reflection of the real thing. The union of bodies alone, no matter how pleasurable, will not recreate in the initiate-speaker a unifying perception in accord with the Creator's[42] That can happen only when one is able to *be in* the mirror and *look into* the mirror simultaneously.

If one stays lost in the mirror, captive to unexamined habits and impulsivity, one will not be able to develop the inner witness who can look into the mirror. To gain that perspective, one must become silent and stop — which is to say, meditate. The particular form of the practice matters less than the regular *activity* of doing it, which gives the initiate-speaker increasing command of his or her own powers of attention.

Meditation not only assists the initiate-speaker in restraining impulsiveness and avoiding unconscious susceptibility to empty distractions that clamor to hold attention hostage. To have command of one's attention, to experience oneself as perceiver, moves one closer to an experience of the unconditioned "I." Experiencing oneself as an I-being then enables one, much like Adam, to "read creation together again,"[43] says Georg Kühlewind, who adds:

> As we become aware of our attention as a creative reality, it lights up for us as the most intimate and individual activity of the I. When our I-experience occurs in perceptive attention, it reaches a level where the I becomes able to take in the language of natural phenomena. Then we discover that these phenomena have always been *speaking* to us, but we lacked the ability to understand this powerful language.[44]

Now the initiate-speaker starts working backward in Genesis, as Parzival does in his story. Beginning with the shaming awareness of difference after eating the forbidden fruit, one gradually works back to naming one's own sexuality and, in the naming, will recognize and choose who or what that sexuality belongs to and serves beyond oneself. The process can include submitting to a code of sexual behavior

— celibacy or monogamy, for example — but little will change if one adopts a code out of desire (for a "higher" life, for example) or out of fear (of being shamed for one's sexual inclinations). The essence is the decision itself — the choice to act consciously — rather than adherence to a strict code. This is true "sexual freedom," with sexuality no longer shamefully split off from consciousness, hidden behind fig leaves.

One might experience a sense of loss when one freely decides not to yield thoughtlessly to physical and emotional urges. Something of the purely personal must be sacrificed, even if it is just impulsive self-indulgence or comfortable habit. Enduring that death, however, permits a birth. By stopping and choosing to practice a meditative discipline and a code of restraint, one steps toward a new life — a life of being subject to one's choices. Birthed within the initiate-speaker is the one-who-chooses, and the one-who-chooses is the first inhabitant of that brave new world, sovereign self-mastery.

Any choice to stop or wait is based at least in caring and at most in love. Something matters, and so we stop and wait for it.[45] The meaning of what we have chosen to wait for grows as one continues to "stop," out of love for the choosing, out of love for the one-who-chooses within oneself. Growing into the strength of this one-who-chooses is, in common parlance, called "maturity," sexual and otherwise. Alignment with the one-who-stops-and-chooses out of love indicates the initiate-speaker is well into the second birth at the core of initiation and has gone back a long way toward the unifying perception that connected Adam with God.[46]

Through meditation and discipline of impulsivity, the initiate-speaker actually fosters the increase of meaning in his or her life. Such caretaking in the garden of meaning re-establishes connection with God, because, when we are given in service to meaning, we are like Him. As Vanstone reminds us, God also stops and waits, subject to all his creation as it slowly grows into Him:

> By the exercise of [H]is freedom, [H]e surrenders [H]is freedom and takes upon [H]imself a constraint. . . . One might say that the ultimate glory of God's creativity is the creation of His own exposure to that which He has created. . . . He has handed Himself over to the world, that He has given to the world not only the power of being but also that power to affect Himself which is best described as power of meaning.[47]

The speech of the Grail requires a sense of worth based not in pride of worldly accomplishment or acquisition but in a security of knowing and honoring oneself as one-who-chooses. At this point, however, neither Gawan, who was stopped during his sojourn at Schanpfanzun, nor Parzival who was stopped by Cundrie, is much in touch with the one-who-chooses in himself. That is about to change for both of them, but in quite different ways. Sometimes being stopped — becoming ill, experiencing failure, feeling ashamed — can lead to choosing to stop. Such chosen stopping, taking the time to name and claim all aspects of one's identity, can be guided by another person — a confessor, a psychotherapist, a teacher — who has passed through a similar ordeal. Having been stopped, Parzival and Gawan and the initiate-speaker must now choose to stop — must choose to receive forgiveness and choose to forgive.

NOTES

[1] Wolfram, Book VII, 340.

[2] Wolfram, Book VII, 347.

[3] Wolfram, Book VII, 350.

[4] Wolfram, Book VII, 350.

[5] Wolfram, Book VII, 351.

[6] Wolfram, Book VII, 352.

[7] Wolfram, Book VII, 366.

[8] Wolfram, Book VII, 369.

[9] Wolfram, Book VII, 369.

[10] Wolfram, Book VII, 370.

[11] Wolfram, Book VII, 370.

[12] Wolfram, Book VII, 370.

[13] Wolfram, Book VII, 371.

[14] Wolfram, Book VII, 389.

[15] C.G. Jung, *Analytical Psychology,* 26.

[16] Jung, 12.

[17] A thorough discussion of sovereignty in Celtic tradition can be found in Caitlin Matthews' *Arthur and the Sovereignty of Britain*, 13–30.

[18] Jung, in *Analytical Psychology*, states, "An English philosopher has said, 'A superior mind is never quite clear.' That is true, and also superior feeling is never quite clear. You will only enjoy a feeling that is above-board when it is slightly doubtful, and a thought that does not have a slight contradiction in it is not convincing" (52).

[19] For amplification of the seeing, imagining heart, see James Hillman, "The Thought of the Heart."

[20] Hillman, 28.

[21] Russell A Lockhart, *Psyche Speaks: A Jungian Approach to Self and World*, 32–33.

[22] John Moyne and Coleman Barks, *Open Secret: Versions of Rumi*, 41.

[23] Georg Kühlewind, in *The Logos-Structure of the World*, incisively discusses the silent speaking of the world. His intention is "to show that the world, including human beings and their consciousness, is not originally a world of things but a world of words; that, fundamentally, it is structured like a text and can therefore be read like a text" (13).

[24] Wolfram, Book VIII, 405.

[25] Wolfram, Book VIII, 406.

[26] Wolfram, Book VIII, 407.

[27] Wolfram, Book VIII, 407.

[28] Wolfram, Book VIII, 407.

[29] Wolfram, Book VIII, 424.

[30] Wolfram, Book VIII, 425.

[31] Gringuljete, like the heroic horses of Celtic legend, is probably white with red ears. Wolfram, Book III, 340, tells us his ears are red, and his name probably has a Welsh root which means "white-hardy." (See note in Mustard and Passage translation, page 183.)

[32] John Matthews, *Gawain: Knight of the Goddess*, 19.

[33] This is a very general interpretation of puberty initiations and what they mean. I am not suggesting this description is complete or that tribal peoples would describe their rituals this way.

[34] Modern youngsters, reaching puberty in the AIDS era, suffer from lack of corresponding rites. The relationship of sexuality to spirituality has

received no definitive thought in our times. Meanwhile, the churches weakly promulgate irrelevant-sounding axioms, and from other quarters comes loud insistence that sexuality is strictly personal, for one's own pleasure. Georg Kühlewind comments that "sexuality, in the widest sense, is the most endangered activity of modern man" (*From Normal to Healthy*, 139).

[35] Patricia Berry, "Stopping: A Mode of Animation," *Echo's Subtle Body*, 147–61.

[36] Berry, 160.

[37] Berry, 161.

[38] W.H. Vanstone, *The Stature of Waiting*, 102.

[39] Vanstone, 102.

[40] Vanstone, 107.

[41] Two scholars who have approached the subject are Norman O. Brown in *Love's Body*, especially in the chapter entitled "Head" (126–40), and William Irwin Thompson in *The Time Falling Bodies Take to Light: Mythology, Sexuality and the Origins of Culture*, especially in the Prologue (3–40).

[42] A unifying perception must be distinguished, of course, from a unitary perceiving, which would be seeing things in only one way or from one perspective, another word for which is fundamentalism.

[43] Kühlewind, *The Logos-Structure of the World*, 17.

[44] Kühlewind, 138.

[45] Vanstone, 102.

[46] In the attempt to illuminate some of the connection between sexuality and speech, I have placed more emphasis on discipline of the former. It is possible that restraint of impulsivity in speech might lead to more conscious choice in regard to sexuality as well. (Georg Kühlewind offers such speech exercises in *From Normal to Healthy*, 97–107, though not with the intention of curbing sexual impulsivity.) However, what I see in Wolfram's Book VIII is that the tendency for unconsciousness in sexuality is so strong that, like initiates in tribal cultures, mystery cults and spiritual vocations, the initiate-speaker must confront it directly.

[47] Vanstone, 93–95.

CHAPTER FIVE

"Open Up! . . . I Want to Come into Your Heart"

The Grail King Speaks

Shall I say it again? In order to arrive there,
To arrive where you are, to get from where you are not,
You must go by a way wherein there is no ecstasy.
In order to arrive at what you do not know
You must go by a way which is the way of ignorance.
In order to possess what you do not possess
You must go by the way of dispossession.
In order to arrive at what you are not
You must go through the way in which you are not.
And what you do not know is the only thing you know
And what you own is what you do not own
And where you are is where you are not.

> — T.S. Eliot
> "East Coker" from "Four Quartets"[1]

BOOK IX

"Open up!"
To whom? Who are you?
"I want to come into your heart to you."
Then it is a small space you wish.
"What does that matter? Though I scarcely find room, you will
have no need to complain of crowding. I will tell you now of won-
drous things."
Oh, is it you Lady Adventure? How fares that lovable knight? I
mean the noble Parzival whom Cundrie with harsh words drove
forth to seek the Grail. . . .[2]

A brief, but pithy dialogue with Lady Adventure calls Wolfram's
attention back to Parzival, who has wandered over many lands and
seas, never having been beaten in any of the numberless jousts he
has fought. The sword Anfortas gave him has broken and been made
whole again by the power of the spring. After entering a forest, Parzival discovers a newly constructed hermit's hut situated over a fast-
flowing stream. Within, Sigune is kneeling in prayer beside her
knight's coffin.

Parzival rides up to the window of the hermitage to ask directions through the forest and feels embarrassed he has not dismounted
when a feminine voice answers his call. After he dismounts, tethers
his horse and goes into the cell, he again does not recognize his sorrowing cousin. They sit together on a bench by the window and he
inquires how she is able to live in this place. She tells him that her
food comes "directly from the Grail";[3] Cundrie *la sorcière* brings her
a week's food every Saturday night.

Thinking she might be lying to mislead him, he asks her about
the ring she wears, a strange ornament, he thinks, for a hermit. When
she tells him about her knight and his death, he finally realizes she is
Sigune. At that, he takes off his coif of mail, allowing her to recognize
him, whereupon she asks: "How fares it with your search for the
Grail? Have you at last discovered its true nature? How has your
journey been?"[4]

Parzival laments that he sorely misses his wife Condwiramurs but
that he mourns even more for the "high goal, to behold Munsalvaesche and the Grail."[5] He expresses his dismay that she bears him
such ill will when he is so full of woe. She withdraws all her former
censure, saying she understands how he has suffered by "being so

slow and not asking the precious question."[6] Then she encourages him in his search, relating that Cundrie has just now ridden away and that he may be able to follow her track and overtake her.

Parzival rides after Cundrie forthwith but soon loses the track in the pathless forest. Instead he encounters a knight, fully armed, who rebukes Parzival for riding on his lord's land and summons him to joust. The templar's challenge identifies him as a Grail knight because he declares that "Munsalvaesche is not accustomed to let anyone come so near unless he were ready to face perilous strife or make the atonement which outside this forest is known as Death."[7]

Though Parzival wonders why he must fight when he has only been riding over ferns and not a man's wheat field, he nonetheless complies and promptly defeats the knight, knocking him off his horse into a ravine from which he escapes on foot on the other side. Meanwhile, Parzival's horse has rushed over the cliff and died, leaving Parzival clinging to the branch of a cedar tree. He is able to clamber back onto the cliff and finds the templar's horse standing there obediently. Parzival mounts this horse from the Grail castle and sadly rides off, feeling as far as ever from his goal.

After riding for weeks more, he finds himself in another forest where an unexpected light snow has fallen. There he meets an elderly knight with his wife and daughters. They are on a pilgrimage and, though they appear to be nobility, all of them are clothed in rough, grey sackcloth. Parzival, clad as ever in richly adorned armor, pulls his horse off the path to let them pass and asks the meaning of their pilgrimage and their dress.

The old knight cordially responds that this is Good Friday, "when the whole world can rejoice, yet at the same time sigh in grief."[8] He expresses regret that this holy day has not moved Parzival to remove his armor, cease riding and go barefoot, as is customary. Parzival replies that he has no idea when the year began, how many weeks have passed, or what day of the week it is. Besides, the God whom he had served with faith has granted him only disgrace and offered no help when he asked for it.

The old knight reproaches Parzival for this attitude and reminds him of the sacrifice God made in sending his son to die and thereby redeem humankind. He advises Parzival to follow their tracks back to the cell of a holy man they met nearby, where he might receive counsel and forgiveness. When his daughters intercede for Parzival — reminding their father how cold Parzival must be in that armor, pleading for understanding, forgiveness and hospitality — he concedes and invites Parzival to join them in their Good Friday meal which they eat each year here in this wild forest. Though he feels drawn to the warmth of the daughters, Parzival admits to himself that he would feel uncomfortable in this company of believers since he "hates Him Whom they love with all their hearts."[9] Declining the invitation, he rides away.

But he is not at peace with his decision. "Now for the first time he [thinks] on his Creator," of His great power in creating the universe, and wonders if there is some chance that "God will give help to overcome my sadness."[10] He decides to let God help "if help He can," and turns back to find the family, who are still lamenting his departure. There, he declares:

> If God's power is so great that it can guide both horse and beast, and men as well, then I will praise His power. If God's art possesses such help, then let it show this Castilian of mine the road that is best for me. Thus His kindness shall show its help — Now go, whichever way God chooses![11]

He drops the reins over the horse's neck and urges him on with his spurs. Without delay, the horse conveys him to the cell of the hermit Trevrizent who, Parzival will discover, is his own maternal uncle as well as brother of Anfortas, the Grail King. Finally, it is time for Parzival to learn about the mysteries of the Grail.

But first, Wolfram says he can now tell his readers a mystery of his own, the source for this story. He claims that Kyot, the Provencal poet from Toledo had sworn him to reveal the source only when "she herself, Adventure, should invite the telling, and then one must speak of it, of course."[12] Kyot himself had first read this story in "heathen writing," by Flegetanis, a "scholar of nature" who was descended from Solomon and, on his father's side, from calf-worshipping heathens. Flegetanis was apparently an astronomer/ astrologer because he "saw with his own eyes in the constellations things he was shy to talk about, hidden mysteries," and among these was a "thing called the Grail whose name he had read clearly in the constellations."[13] He discovered that angels had brought the Grail to earth and given it to the guardianship of Christian men of great nobility and discipline. Kyot further investigated this story, tracing the tale through Latin books. Reading in chronicles from Britain,

France, Ireland, and in "Anjou," Kyot uncovered the lineage of those who were bequeathed the Grail.

After disclosing his source, Wolfram returns to Parzival, who, having arrived at Trevrizent's cell, soon recognizes it to be the place where he swore to Orilus that he had not violated Jeschute. The hermit, Trevrizent, welcomes Parzival, reminding him he should not be wearing his armor on this day. "If your longing is for true love, then love with the love that belongs to this day," he advises.[14] Parzival dismounts, tells the hermit he has been sent there by the old knight, and asks Trevrizent to give him counsel because "I am a man who has sinned." When Parzival inquires why Trevrizent was not afraid when he rode up, the hermit explains that he too was a knight once and that nothing human frightens him.

After they have seen to Parzival's horse, they go to Trevrizent's warm cave where Parzival takes off his frigid armor and accepts a cloak from Trevrizent. Parzival asks how much time has passed since he took the spear of bright colors from the adjoining cave, where the altar is, and Trevrizent tells him it has been four and one-half years and three days. Parzival admits that it also has been that long since he has spoken any praise of God, that he has thought of nothing but fighting in that period. Then he tells Trevrizent of his bottomless grief and of his anger at God for being no help to him in his distress.

Trevrizent responds with a lengthy teaching on the love and power of God and the fall of humankind into the world of bliss and sorrow. He urges Parzival to recognize, through the example of Lucifer, that nothing can be wrenched from God through anger. He gives Parzival these teachings, and others, with the invitation to "Hear now age-old tales as if they were new that they may teach you to speak true"[15] and encourages Parzival to turn his heart toward God.

But Parzival says that he has spent his youth in care and, for his faithfulness, received only sorrow. When Trevrizent invites him to talk about his sorrow so that he can give him counsel, Parzival explains "My greatest grief is for the Grail, after that, for my own wife."[16] Trevrizent approves his suffering for his wife because remaining faithful in marriage will in due time be rewarded with God's blessing and help. However, he points out that "no man can ever win the Grail unless he is known in heaven and he be called by name to the Grail."[17]

Since he seems to know so much about the Grail castle, Parzival asks if Trevrizent has been there, though he does not reveal that he himself was there. Trevrizent says he has been to the castle and tells Parzival about it. Knights live there who are sustained "from a stone of the purest kind. . . . By the power of that stone the phoenix burns to ashes but the ashes give him life again."[18] The Grail rejuvenates all who look upon it and nourishes everyone through its own renewal by the dove who descends from heaven each Good Friday and places a small white wafer on it.

Around the edge of the stone appears the name and lineage of each person — maiden or youth — who is called "to take this blessed journey."[19] Rich and poor alike, from many lands they come. Once they read their names, the inscription fades away. When a person is summoned by the Grail, everyone rejoices because being in its service assures a person greater protection from "sinful shame" and "good reward in heaven."

Parzival declares that he has accomplished much in his striving for knighthood and therefore should be fit to be summoned to the Grail. Trevrizent warns him, tearfully, against the pride of youth that all too easily violates the virtue of moderation. He urges Parzival to take heed from the folly of Anfortas, whose "youth and power brought grief to all around him and his desire for love beyond all restraint and bounds."[20] Trevrizent emphasizes that all the Grail company humbly guard against excess. Only one person came unbidden, a "foolish man who took sin away with him, since he said not a word to the king about the distress he could see in him."[21]

Remembering the turtledove of the Grail knights on the saddle of Parzival's horse, Trevrizent asks who he is. Parzival identifies himself as the son of Gahmuret and confesses also that he killed Ither, the Red Knight, and despoiled his corpse by taking his armor. Trevrizent now sadly realizes that this is his nephew and tells Parzival, "You have slain your own flesh and blood" — not only because he killed Ither, who was a kinsman, but because Herzeloyde, his mother, "died because of you."[22]

Shocked, Parzival demands to know if this is really true. Trevrizent fully describes Herzeloyde, even telling of the dream she had before learning of Gahmuret's death, and thus proves what he says is true. He continues with even more detailed information about the rest of Parzival's family, which includes his aunt Repanse de Schoye, the Grail carrier, and Anfortas, his uncle.

He describes Anfortas's exploits when "Amour was his battle cry,"[23] even after he inherited the kingship of the Grail castle. In violation of his duty to love only whom the Grail named, he served a noble lady of his own choosing. In her service, he was pierced through the testicles by the poisoned spear of a heathen who sought the Grail for its power. Despite an extensive search for a curative herb and Trevrizent's renunciation of knightly life for a hermit's calling, Anfortas's wound never healed, nor could any relief be found for his pain. When, in despair, the Grail company kneeled before the Grail and prayed, they had seen written on it that a knight would come who must ask a certain question but that no one could prompt him. If the question was not asked the first night, its power would vanish. If it was asked, then the wound would heal and that knight would become the new Grail king. They waited until a knight did come, but he did not ask the question, "Sir, why is it you suffer so?"[24] and so the suffering goes on.

Both men are heavy with sadness as they go out to feed Parzival's horse and dig some roots for dinner. Despite the meager meal, Parzival has such affection for his pious host that he feels more substantially nourished here than at Gurnemanz's or even at the Grail castle. Later that evening, telling Trevrizent that "My trust seeks refuge in you,"[25] Parzival confesses that it was he who came to the Grail castle and failed to ask the question.

Trevrizent grieves anew at this admission but does not reject Parzival:

> God gave you five senses, but they denied you their aid. How did they help you then, at the wound of Anfortas, to preserve your loyalty? Yet I will do my best to give you counsel And you must not grieve too much. You should in right measure grieve and abstain from grief.[26]

Now, in response to Parzival's questions, he clarifies certain aspects of what Parzival experienced at the Grail castle, starting with his meeting Anfortas supposedly fishing on the lake. Trevrizent describes the cyclical nature of the pain in Anfortas's wound and also the nature of service in the Grail company. He himself violated the vow of celibacy that all but the Grail king must swear when he entered the service of a woman and went on missions for Anfortas.

During this conversation, Trevrizent also extracts from Parzival the story of how he happens to be riding a Grail horse. He reminds Parzival that, for the sins of killing his clansman and causing the death of his mother, he must do penance and make atonement. In the days afterward, again responding to Parzival's questions, Trevrizent explains that Repanse de Schoye is his aunt and that the beautiful white-haired man Parzival briefly glimpsed within the Grail castle is beloved Titurel, whose rosy, young complexion contrasts with his white hair. Though bedridden, he sees the Grail so often that he cannot die, and he is often sought for his counsel by the Grail company.

Parzival stays fifteen days with his uncle, eating roots and herbs, enduring "privation willingly for the sake of gladdening words — for his host absolved him of sin and yet counseled him to live as a knight."[27] Among these teachings are commandments never to mistreat a woman and to show good will toward priests. If Parzival will follow these teachings, they guarantee a "life of true worth" and a "good end."

On the day of their parting, Trevrizent tells Parzival to hand over his sins to him. In the sight of God, Trevrizent will now be the guarantor of Parzival's atonement. Thus forgiven, Parzival rides off and "disappears" again for several episodes.

Initiatory Themes

A brief dialogue with Lady Adventure begins Wolfram's telling of the pivotal Book IX, yet what happens here takes place mostly in words, rather than in adventuresome feats. This is a very interior episode. Sigune, the mourning widow, is now lodged in a hut; for the first time we get inside Parzival's head to hear him think (after he meets the old knight); Trevrizent's teachings are given mostly in a cave, and, while hearing them, we also enter the other "cave" of Parzival's ear. Trevrizent's teachings themselves are interior; they do not, until the very end, concern actions or attitudes in this world, unlike the instructions given by Herzeloyde and Gurnemanz. Rather, these teachings concern the inner story of the Grail and its company, and also provide Parzival information about his inner heritage, his bloodline. If these are the "wondrous things" which Lady Adventure has to tell, surely it implies that the greatest adventure is the one taken by a seeker within his or her own being.

The Lady Adventure to whom Wolfram speaks seems to determine, or at least be profoundly connected with, the timing of matters and events. Only now does she allow Wolfram to reveal the source of his story. Only now has she led Parzival to the person who can guide him on his inner journey. The chapter itself is rhythmical, almost musical as, fuguelike, the dialogue between Parzival and Trevrizent transpires. Trevrizent, with the artfulness of an experienced confessor or a skilled psychotherapist, shows an excellent sense of timing in drawing forth Parzival's story, and much of what he himself says concerns time: how long Parzival has been traveling since he was last at the cell; the history surrounding the Grail; the cyclical pain of Anfortas's wound which is influenced by planetary and lunar rhythms.

Enough time has passed and enough battles have been fought that Parzival is ready to receive deeper knowledge about himself and the Grail path. His turning point, like a conversion, comes at that moment when he *chooses* to stop and listen to the advice of the old knight in sackcloth. He decides to let God help him by choosing to drop the reins of his horse. Previously, he left the reins loose only because he was preoccupied. The horse always took him to the next step in his journey, but, while the horse (his greater will) was with him, he was not really *with* his horse. Now, in giving himself to God, he also joins with his own will, even spurring it on. He chooses to accept the help of something bigger than himself and allow it to take him where he needs to go.

His own yearning, determination, and effort have finally mounted him on the Grail horse. But to make any progress from this point, he must cultivate a different image of himself than that of angry warrior, unfairly victimized by God. Parzival's wound is to his faith, his spiritual force, and, like Anfortas's wound, the pain can be relieved only by what he thinks wounded him — which is God. Now that the time is right for him to choose this course, we know a healing has begun.

As in any thorough therapy, however, the pain will get a lot worse before it starts getting better. One reason for this is that, to stop seeing oneself as a victim, one must be willing honestly and accurately to name one's own culpability. In medieval terms, this means to acknowledge one's own "sins and sinfulness." Thus Parzival, strong enough at last to hear the truth, learns that he killed his own kin in killing Ither and that, as well, he caused his mother's death. Now he knows that his negligence at the Grail castle is only part of why his life has seemed so hard.

Owning up to one's errors and shadowy side constitutes a preliminary phase in developing a broader sense of responsibility. The
next phase occurs when one accepts one's role in healing the world.
Initiation is never just for oneself, even though "Know thyself" is
the first injunction to all initiates. The less repeated but thoroughly
companion summons is "Love the world." "Love" here is fully a verb,
not an emotion. Each initiate has the task to love and heal the world
actively, out of the knowledge of who she or he is. The "voice of conscience" and the voice of one's calling are never far apart.[28]

Many persons, like Parzival, have no more certainty of their
responsibility to heal the world than of their responsibility to know
themselves, and particularly the unpleasant aspects. There may be a
dim intuition of "calling," as Gahmuret felt in his yearning for the
heights, but all too often, one's ideas about one's role are not only
misguided but arrogant. Trevrizent's very first teaching, not coincidentally, concerns Lucifer, prototype of overweening pride, who
apparently thought he knew what role he deserved in creation and
invited humankind to join him in that kind of dangerously prema-
ture knowledge when he urged them to eat of the apple. Trevrizent
warns Parzival against such conceit when Parzival comments that his
success as a knight should qualify him to be called by God to the
Grail.

Before the meeting with Trevrizent, Parzival does not experience
the events in his life as having any interconnection. Things have just
seemed to "happen" to him, and he has had no sense that they might
be leading him somewhere. After the interlude with Trevrizent, Parzival outwardly shows little change, as he continues wandering, fighting his battles. But internally he departs quite transformed. We saw
how this was accomplished: through sharing stories. Parzival has
told his story, and Trevrizent has told him stories, all the while connecting them to Parzival's.

Little by little, Parzival dares to relate his experiences and mistakes to Trevrizent, saving for last the worst shame of all, his negligence at the Grail castle. Piece by piece, as he is given them,
Trevrizent skillfully fashions these formless lumps into a containing
whole, an overarching story that includes the mythical container of
their times (the Christian narrative), the lineage into which Parzival
was born, and the history of the Grail company and its service to the
world. Parzival's personal struggle, which was not even a "story" for

him earlier, is now intricately woven into a much larger story. As James Wiggins suggests:

> What one needs precisely is to come to the conviction that out of the myriad possibilities of human life there is embodied in one's own story sufficient particularity to mark one as an authentic individual human being who does not simply replicate some inevitable round of existence. At the same time one longs to discover the universal dimensions embodied in one's story to a degree that marks one's life as an authentic individual human being. Without both distinctiveness and commonality the story will ultimately be unsatisfying and one will continue to retell it agonizingly until both dimensions are uncovered in some fulfilling fashion. . . .[29]

Perhaps this defines an essential difference between psychotherapy and spiritual initiation. In therapy, a person finds ways to live more harmoniously in personal time. One is put together with oneself. In spiritual initiation something else happens as well. One aligns with personal time but also transcends time — locating oneself in the context of a timeless story in which, nonetheless, one plays a role in time. This places one's sins and imperfections in a different light, literally arranges them in a wider space, a cosmic story that can feel more forgiving even as it calls one to do better. Having been transported out of himself into a greater time, Parzival now inhabits time differently.

One must empty oneself in order to re-enter, and re-create, the world in love and forgiveness. Only very large stories provide an adequate crucible to contain the process, stories that bear within themselves a cosmology and, therefore, are "sacred." Every spiritual tradition proffers examples. The Christian story, which Trevrizent frames for Parzival, begins with a Fall — first Lucifer's and then Adam and Eve's — whose effects humans still experience. Each human being can mitigate these consequences by freely choosing to follow God's example and "emptying" — the word that best translates Paul's phrase for the Incarnation of Christ.[30]

Parzival leaves Trevrizent's cave with deeper understanding of all that he has come from — his lineage as well as his life's events — and a more defined knowledge of where he is going. For the first time, he knows what question to ask if he does reach the Grail castle, although nothing Trevrizent has said encourages him to persist in the quest. Trevrizent has done his best to convince Parzival that no one can reach the Grail by fighting for it out of personal ambition. Parzival has been fed only herbs and roots in the hermit's cave but has been nourished on stories. He leaves full of them instead of full of himself. Commended to the knightly life, he apparently plans to follow it humbly as the role appropriate for him.

Trevrizent notices that a new bird is associated with Parzival now — the turtledove. This symbol of the Grail knights is carved on his saddle. The dove has rich and seemingly ambiguous associations. In many mythologies the dove is associated with the Great Goddess, particularly in her role of seductress, goddess of love and fertility. In Christian iconography, the dove represents the purest spiritual reality, flying above and untainted by the crass world. The turtledove, particularly, is renowned for its loyalty to its mate, retaining that loyalty, as Sigune does, even after the mate has died. Moreover, painters often depicted the dove hovering above the head of the Virgin, murmuring the announcement of her calling to be the mother of God. Some medieval writers even imagined that Mary conceived through her ear.[31]

Certainly Parzival has conceived through his ears. He has conceived a new way of looking at himself and his life. Now begins an incubation so that this spiritual pregnancy can unfold.

Toward Speech of the Grail

Parzival lives very simply and eats sparse food during his stay at Trevrizent's, yet "endured the privation willingly for the sake of the gladdening words." It is difficult to imagine that anyone aspiring to the speech of the Grail would undertake this arduous journey unless she or he had experienced receiving such words. This implies, of course, that the initiate-speaker has been wounded painfully enough that she or he has sought help, support or forgiveness in a therapeutic, dialogic encounter with another person. The encounter can last for only a moment or many years. Parzival and the initiate-speaker have taken off their cold, heavy armor at last.

Less burdened now by heavy defenses, the initiate-speaker can become more sensitive to time and timing. Exquisite attunement to time — knowing when to speak, just how much to speak, and when not to speak at all — takes time to learn. The question, one may ask, is where can timing be learned? Training programs for psychotherapists and pastoral counselors — and sometimes those for educators — have as a subtext the timing of comments and commentary, but this is not necessarily part of the intended curriculum. In becoming a client or student or patient, one can grow more aware of timing in one's speech, as one tells one's own life story, gradually noticing the effect of remaining silent too long or speaking too much or not at the right time. Such lessons can also be learned by the initiate-speaker in any intimate relationship: with parent(s), children, spouse, partners and friends.

The oral tradition of storytelling has long served not only to transmit stories but also to train the timing of speech. Storytellers in traditional cultures often have to be called forth by their community to tell a story. They have to be convinced it is the right time — that people are ready to listen. Then the storyteller chooses a story from the repertoire that is most appropriate for those people at that moment. The choosing actually is a "listening," a waiting by the storyteller, tuning to the moment and trusting that the story most meaningful for that time will be recollected, thereby indicating it is the one to be told. There are times and seasons when some stories are fitting and times and seasons when they are not. (Native Americans knew that the darkness of the winter was the most fertile time for telling certain stories.)

Careful attention to timing offers the best chance for teller and listeners to step into the timeless, into a different perspective on personal time which every really good story allows. Traditional storytellers know they contain and celebrate all the times of their communities — the tribal time with its history of kings, queens, lineages, and events; the personal time of individuals as they move through birth, puberty, marriage, death; *and* the transpersonal timelessness held in the "once upon a time" of myth and fairy tale, the time beyond time that is always only now in the latest timely telling of the tale. In his skillful weaving of his own story and Parzival's into the greater tapestry of the Grail castle history and Christian cosmology, Trevrizent epitomizes the storyteller-as-healer.

Trevrizent entreats Parzival to "hear now age-old tales as if they were new, that they may teach you to speak true." To hear an age-old tale "as if it were new," means to hear the story as if it is a teaching pertinent to the listener's own life and times. This imaginative leap opens the initiate-speaker's ability to hear stories metaphorically.[32]

Now the initiate-speaker begins to reconcile Parzival's mode of imagining with Gawan's, renouncing one-sided imagining where either stirring inner visions or stimulating outer perceptions predominate. Metaphorical imagining marries "inner" experiencing with "outer" perceiving, creating a "fluid interaction of reality and self which will allow a more articulate telling of that interdependent experience," claims James Wiggins.[33] Philip Wheelwright suggests further that "a genuine responsiveness is imaginative, and a genuine imaginativeness is responsive" and that a "suitably responsive-imaginative act" confers astonishing potentials of meaning upon the most ordinary objects, situations and people.[34]

This means that, when age-old tales are heard "new," the initiate-speaker achieves something beyond the relevance of the stories for his or her life. Hearing stories metaphorically separates them from the domain of "information" and directs the listener as well as the speaker toward the type of truth which can never be told, only experienced.

Metaphor is labile compared to the supposed solidity of fact or information. Imaging through metaphor, we more readily can admit that our act of understanding is an interpretation — not THE truth. Humbling but not humiliating, the realization frees the initiate-speaker from the anxious hunt for one truth and opens him or her to the playful juggling of many possibilities. When many interpretations are possible, truth is more likely to be *felt* — albeit perhaps only as a momentary insight, like the brief moment when the ball rests in the juggler's hand. Norman O. Brown reminds us that "The God of Delphi, who always spoke the truth, never gave a straight answer."[35] Learning to listen between, behind and underneath the words, actively imagining into metaphor what is said, strengthens one's tolerance for ambiguity and enhances the sense of oneself as creator — an artisan of images, of stories.

Parzival and the initiate-speaker learn this most readily with a person like Trevrizent, whose presence speaks as articulately as his words. Only a very receptive, responsive person can develop responsive-imaginative ability solely from reading texts. It is not stories by themselves that heal and free the listeners; it is the presence of the person telling the stories. Presence is the outward manifestation of attention; we recognize it by the open, listening, responsive attitude the other person demonstrates. Since attention is a free activity of the "I-being," someone's presence invites us to be more present — which is to say, to grow strong in our own I-being as well as to grow more cognizant of presence as an independent dimension of reality.[36]

James Hillman has explored the significance of oral presence in psychotherapy, suggesting that "the entire therapeutic business . . . picks up again the oral tradition of telling stories."[37] In his view, psychotherapy crafts memory and imagination into guiding metaphors, and situates them in a "fiction," capacious enough to contain one's past and also one's future possibilities:

> . . . Healing begins when we move out of the audience and onto the stage of the psyche, become characters in a fiction (even the God-like voice of Truth, a fiction), and as the drama intensifies, the catharsis occurs, we are purged from attachments to literal destinies, find freedom in playing parts, partial, dismembered, Dionysian, never being whole but participating in the whole that is a play, remembered by it as actor of it. And the task set by the play and its God is to play a part with craft, sensitively.[38]

Trevrizent's teaching presence has been forged in his own similar healing, his own previous journey toward initiation. Trevrizent tells Parzival he too has been a knight, he too made mistakes and violated his calling as a Grail templar, he too was stunned to silence in the hermit's cave, he too has made sacrifices in the name of healing his brother, Anfortas. Trevrizent never stations himself as superior to Parzival nor as unable to empathize with Parzival's pain. At moments, he seems even to suffer with Parzival. Yet, he speaks dispassionately of his errors and misjudgments. He has forgiven himself and, therefore, is truly empowered to forgive another. The more Parzival feels this forgiveness flowing toward him, the more encouraged he feels to reveal his own errors.

All the while, gently but tenaciously, Trevrizent proceeds to re-contextualize Parzival's thinking. Through his stories, he introduces Parzival to the profound drama unfolding in his life. If Parzival responds imaginatively, if he resonates to the presence radiating within Trevrizent's words, then he will no longer sing dreary dirges about his life but will play the role of dramaturge. Indeed, what Parzival and the initiate-speaker have conceived through their ears is the "artist" in themselves. "The art of healing is the healing into art,"[39] declares James Hillman.

Reinvigorated and renewed through his reconnection to a larger pattern, self-forgiving because he has been courageously honest enough to receive forgiveness, Parzival rides out of Wolfram's story for now. Gestating within him is the presence that will heal Anfortas even more dramatically than Parzival has been healed by Trevrizent. The pregnancy unfolds through Gawan, the one within Parzival and the initiate-speaker whose task remains, in Cundrie's words, to develop the heart of "real feeling" that enables the initiate-speaker to marry inner and outer in each moment of life. Gawan, and therefore Parzival and the initiate-speaker are on their way to a wedding.

BOOK X

A year has passed since the incident at Vergulaht's castle. In search of the Grail, Gawan rides into a meadow where he finds a lady with a mortally wounded knight on her lap. Being "no fool in the matter of wounds,"[40] Gawan deftly strips a tube of bark from a tree branch and directs the woman to insert it in the wound and suck on it until the blood flows out toward her instead of inward. Quickly the knight is revived and gushes gratitude.

In response to Gawan's inquiry about his wound, the knight replies that, on his way to Logrois for knightly adventure, he was unexplainably attacked by a knight named Lischois Gwelljus. Gawan says he will find Lischois to learn the reason for this attack, but the wounded knight begs him not to go, warning it will lead to disaster. Nevertheless, Gawan intends to find out what happened and, after saying a healing spell over the wound, proceeds toward the castle of Logrois.

The bloodied trail shows the way to the mountaintop citadel, which gives the appearance of a spinning top because of the winding road leading up to it. Gawan follows this spiral road upward and, at its end, "sees both his heart's joy and his heart's sorrow."[41] By a spring bubbling forth from the rock sits Orgeluse de Logrois, a maiden whose radiant beauty matches Parzival's and Condwiramurs. Smitten with love, Gawan asks permission to dismount and keep her company. "May I die if ever a woman pleased me so."[42]

Orgeluse says she knows all that but does not "like one pronouncing opinions of me." Only a *wise* man's her, and she coldly warns Gawan that his praise and win him only sorrow and dishonor.

> You desire my love? How do you come to lay claim to my love. Many cast their eyes, but they would cast them more gently with a sling if they don't refrain from looking at what cuts their hearts. Turn your hopeless desires toward some other love than mine, if your hand must serve love. If adventure has sent you out on knightly quest for love, you won't get any reward for it from me. But you could get disgrace out of it, if you want to know the truth.[43]

Gawan readily agrees that "My eyes are a peril to my heart" but that it is too late; he is her captive. To her repeated warnings, he responds that he does, of course, wish to *earn* her love, that this is only to be expected, "before and after," by anyone who is "eager for noble love."[44]

She reminds him that "to do me service, you must live warlike, yet you might achieve disgrace from it after all. My service will tolerate no cowards."[45] Then she sends him down to a meadow with instructions to retrieve her horse. She tells him to pay no attention to the merry crowd of people there, dancing and singing, but to go directly to her horse, untie him, and lead him out.

Gawan leaps from his horse to do her bidding, but can find nowhere to tie his horse. When he asks Orgeluse to hold the reins, she refuses because she doesn't want her hand to touch anything he has touched. She agrees only when he points out that he has not been holding the front part of the reins. Then she orders him to hurry; Gawan follows a path leading over a bridge, finds the meadow where the people are dancing, and goes to the horse. The people there lament his choice, knowing that this lady's service only brings sorrow, and one old knight in particular tries to dissuade him. But Gawan insists upon his course. He unties the horse and leads him out of the meadow.

When he returns to Orgeluse, she has untied the ribbons of her headdress from under her chin and put them up on her head. Any woman so dressed, Wolfram tells us, is "all set for battle." Orgeluse does not thank Gawan but merely says, "Welcome, you goose! No man ever lugged such stupidity around as you do, wanting to do service for me. O, but you would do well to give it up."[46] Gawan esponds that her "bad temper" *now* implies that her "graciousness must come afterward" and that she will have "the honor of making up for it later."[47] When he offers to help her onto her horse, she retorts, "I didn't ask you to." She nimbly mounts and orders him to ride after her, adding rudely, "May God throw you from that horse."[48]

As they ride onto a heath, Gawan sees an herb growing that is good for wounds. He dismounts to pick the herb, and Orgeluse sarcastically comments that someone who is both doctor and knight can earn a good living provided he learns how to seal ointment jars. Unperturbed by the insult, Gawan tells her about the wounded knight he helped earlier and explains that this herb can cure him. This seems to make Orgeluse pensive, because she says, "I'm glad to see this. . . . Maybe I'll learn something."[49]

Not much later, a monstrous-looking man hails them from behind, coming with a message for Orgeluse. This is Malcreatiure, brother of Cundrie *la sorcière*. Both were sent to Anfortas as a gift from Queen Secundille whose kingdom in the East has rivers of gems and mountains of gold. She sent the pair to Anfortas so "she could find out about this man to whom the Grail is subject."[50] Anfortas, in turn, had given Malcreatiure to Orgeluse as her squire.

Malcreatiure, "kinsman of the herb and the stars,"[51] is mounted on a stumbling, broken-down horse, whose legs are all lame. When he reaches them, Malcreatiure immediately launches into a tirade against Gawan, who has been waiting courteously for him. Gawan is not as patient with these insults as he was with Orgeluse's. Saying he will not tolerate such abuse, he grabs hold of Malcreatiure's boar-bristle hair, cutting his hands as he does so, and throws him off his nag. Orgeluse laughs, saying, "I love to see you both in such a fury."[52] Then the three set off to find the wounded knight.

While Gawan binds the herb to the wound, the knight warns him to leave Orgeluse, who has caused him to be lying here wounded. He tells Gawan he wants to get to a hospital where he can rest, and asks Gawan to help his lady onto his horse and him behind her. Gawan gets the knight's horse, but the knight angrily shouts that he has brought the horse too close and it may step on him. So Gawan leads the knight's horse off to a distance and helps the lady onto it. Meanwhile, the wounded knight suddenly mounts Gawan's horse and gallops off with his lady.

Orgeluse laughs when Gawan bitterly complains about this treatment.

First I took you for a knight; a few hours after that you turned sur-
geon for wounds; now you have to be a page. If anyone has to live by
his skills, you can fall back on your numerous aptitudes.[53]

When she asks if he still wants her love, he reasserts that she is

dearer to me than anything. There isn't a living soul on earth beneath
a crown, nor any that wear crowns and pursue joyous fame, who
could offer me their winnings in place of you, but that my heart's
sense would bid me reject it.[54]

The wounded knight rides back to identify himself as Urians,
gloat on the revenge he's had on Gawan, and scoff at Gawan for helping him. Then he digs his spurs into the horse's sides and rides off.
Having finally recognized the rogue, Gawan tells Orgeluse the story.
Contrary to Urians' accusation, Gawan actually had interceded with
King Arthur in Urians' behalf or he might have received a worse punishment than he was given. Urians' crime was raping a maiden, and,
instead of hanging for it, he was made to eat with the dogs for four
weeks.

Since this is her country, Orgeluse now pronounces herself the
judge of this affair and, still claiming she will never be well disposed
toward Gawan, she nonetheless guarantees Urians will be repaid for
his offenses. Gawan claims Malcreatiure's sway-backed horse for
himself while Malcreatiure confers with Orgeluse, who speaks to him
in his language, giving him orders to take back on foot to those at
her castle. When she sees Gawan about to mount the crippled horse,
she taunts him again, inquires if he still seeks her service, and warns
him that it will lead to no happiness for him. Nonetheless, he continues to declare his love and loyalty to her, and ties his shield to the rope
saddle of the sorry horse, deciding its back would cave in if he rode it.
Alluding to the pack on the horse's back, Orgeluse then asks ironi-
cally if Gawan is bringing trade goods for sale into her country. "Who
ever gave me a doctor and then a tradesman for a companion? Watch
out for tollgates along the way; some of my customs officials will take
your joy right out of you."[55]

Their journey continues with Gawan walking part of the way,
then mounting the horse. Finally they come to a large plain of
cultivated land above which rises a castle more magnificent than
any Gawan has seen before. Four hundred ladies peer out of the

windows. A mounted knight canters across the jousting meadow to the quay at the river's edge. Orgeluse tells Gawan he must joust with this knight, that she promised him disgrace and now he is about to receive it, along with embarrassment if his breeches split in front of all those ladies. Then she gets into the ferryman's boat, shouting angrily to Gawan not to try and follow her, while Gawan is left to despair that she seems in such a hurry to get away from him.

However, once the knight, Lischois Gwelljus, charges, Gawan has plenty to occupy him. Both are unhorsed at the impact, and they fight on foot, all the while reproaching one another for fighting with no apparent cause. Gawan finally wins by wrestling the man to the ground. He demands an oath of surrender, but Lischois says he's never been beaten before and he'd rather die than give his oath of surrender. Gawan, however, sees no reason to kill this man and decides to let him go. At that, they both rest among the flowers.

Gawan is so pleased that he has won Lischois' horse and no longer must ride Malcreatiure's feeble nag that he mounts the silk-draped, well-armored charger. He expresses great delight when he thinks he recognizes the gait of his own Gringuljete, the Grail horse whom Urians had recently stolen. To confirm his discovery, Gawan dismounts to check the horse's hock for the brand of the turtledove, coat of arms of the Grail company. Meanwhile, Lischois has recovered his sword and attacks Gawan again. They fight — this time without their shields which have been cut so small they are of no use. Once again, Lischois is defeated and asks for death rather than surrender. For Orgeluse's sake, Gawan once more decides to let him live.

Then the ferryman comes up to claim the horse of the defeated knight, as is his right. Instead, Gawan gives him the sway-backed horse and the knight. Pleased enough with this exchange, the ferryman accepts Gawan's help in loading Lischois on his boat and then offers Gawan hospitality in his house for the evening. Gawan is very grateful, saying he was going to request such refuge, and then tells the ferryman of his weariness.

> . . . I am in need of rest. The lady that ordered me into this discomfort, she can well turn sweet things sour and make the heart's joys dear, and make its sorrows rich. She bestows incommensurately. . . . [S]he who can hurt me so should also multiply my joy.[56]

The ferryman listens sympathetically and informs Gawan that this is the way of things in this country which is ruled by the wizard Clinschor:

Sir, that is the way here, in the open and in the forest, and everywhere Clinschor is lord, and neither cowardice nor manly subtlety
will make it otherwise: today sad, tomorrow glad.[57]

Gawan is welcomed most hospitably by the ferryman and his
daughter, Bene. Quite attracted to Gawan, Bene helps him remove
his armor, serves him a dinner of three larks caught by her brothers,
and later lingers suggestively as they all prepare to sleep. But Gawan
does not pursue her, perhaps not even noticing she is willing, and simply goes to sleep. He is going to need this rest.

Initiatory Themes

In the previous episode, Parzival has learned, through Trevrizent's
stories, that his suffering has a deeper significance than he was able
to perceive while so totally absorbed in his pain. Things are not
always, or only, what they seem to be. Gawan also will now learn this
but in an entirely different way. Through actions, not through teachings, Gawan must also pass beyond the world of appearances to
release what is held hostage behind it. And throughout the struggle,
he will have to hold faithfully firm to the feeling in his heart.

Early on, we can see a change in Gawan. He no longer impul-
sively chases skirts like he did at Vergulaht's castle. Gawan proceeds
through this episode with a kindness, courtesy and courage more
refined even than he demonstrated with Obilot. He is also amazingly
resourceful, showing his skill as a healer with the wounded knight.
His instantaneous devotion to Orgeluse is no instinctual whim.
Though he claims to be her captive, it is evident that he repeatedly
chooses his captivity, even celebrates it. His continually affirmative
responses to her questions whether he still wants her love verify his
choosing. Also, in his scuffle with Malcreatiure, Gawan shows that he
does not tolerate abuse unless he has chosen to tolerate it.

Wolfram, by the way, defends Orgeluse and admonishes his readers that "anyone wishing to follow me further should refrain from
abusive talk about her. No one should talk out of turn unless he
knows what it is he is damning and until he is informed how things
stood with her heart." Wolfram announces that he "absolves her
from all condemnation"[58] and apparently expects the readers to do so
as well — and in advance! — if they want to gain any real understanding from this story.

Gawan apparently sees or senses something in Orgeluse that is not apparent to the naked eye. Attracted by her beauty, he agrees with her warning and admits,"my eyes are a peril to my heart." Yet he chooses this peril again and again. This is a very different kind of love than Parzival's with Condwiramurs. There, the spirit and soul seem to have found safe harbor with one another. The anchorage, however, did not create in Parzival what Cundrie accused him of lacking — real feeling in the heart. For this, Gawan must accomplish an additional healing, or "making whole." He must bring Parzival and the initiate-speaker home to the world: teaching them to marry the most inner world of the human heart, with all its ideals and longings, with the outer world of life in all its unspeakable horror and indescribable beauty.

Life, as we hear in Genesis (3:14–20), is Eve's realm. Just after God punishes Adam and Woman for eating the forbidden fruit and has announced that "dust thou art and unto dust shalt thou return," Adam grants his last name. He names his wife Eve, "Because she was the mother of all living." Eve rules the domain of earthly life, so anyone who wants to find a home here must develop right relationship with her.

Gawan's trials with Orgeluse indicate how difficult this can be. With its rainbow of desires, the human heart toddles toward life, seeking fulfillment. Life lures the heart onward while at the same time testing its perseverance to the utmost. Life is bliss and sorrow, says Wolfram. If one truly seeks to serve life, to win life's love, one will be severely tested. Yet only by loving life and winning the love of life is one able to give life. That is why Gawan's adventures must precede Parzival's return to the Grail castle. Parzival will be able to release the ailing Grail king from the deadly cycle of woundedness and pain only if his own heart has learned to love life, thereby becoming itself a Grail cup brimful of life's reviving nectar.

The distillation of that brew can taste bitter, though. Only a true king has the substance for the challenge, and the distillation, as the ancients knew, is the process through which his identity as king is made manifest. In ancient Ireland and elsewhere, the king's initiation culminated in a marriage, and his bride was the land, whose name is "Sovereignty."[59] Before the marriage, she is "a hag or woman whose mind is deranged,"[60] who demands from the king-to-be his love and service. When he has proved himself strong and courageous enough to accept her on her terms, not rejecting her loathly look or bitter taste, then they are wed — and she transforms. "Sovereignty is a bride, the server of a powerful drink, and the drink itself."[61]

If we can hear the inner name of Condwiramurs to be "Soul," then the inner name of Orgeluse must be "Sovereignty." By winning Orgeluse, Gawan (and thus Parzival and the initiate-speaker) is proving himself worthy to be king of a realm, granted "sovereign" rule by the bride he has won. He surrenders to his choice to love her, no matter what, and thereby gains himself.

Like Parzival before him, Gawan has chosen this time to stop. Parzival chooses to stop and listen; he lets the horse carry him to Trevrizent and allows the hermit's gladdening words to lead him to self-forgiveness. Gawan chooses to stop and look; he sees the beauty behind Orgeluse's insolence and allows what he sees to lead him to forgiveness of she who is none other than life and the world. In forgiving her, he can serve her and, by lending her his strength, invite her to reveal herself more fully to him.

If Parzival has laid claim to himself through his meeting with Trevrizent, Gawan has laid claim to the world — or a part of it. This is the stage of initiation when one knows and claims one's "belonging" to something in the world. It represents the choosing of a place to live, a mate, a work, a spiritual path, something "outside" of oneself, and therefore "sovereign," which, given enough loyalty and service, will transmit sovereignty to him or her who has chosen and served. Time and again, to stay loyal to the choice, Gawan and the initiate-speaker will have to see beyond appearances. In Gawan's struggles, we will see just how much devotion and effort is required for mastery in this looking-glass realm.

Toward Speech of the Grail

The ability to listen and to create metaphoric understanding of stories, events and situations can help the initiate-speaker in relinquishing judgment and emotional reactivity based on judgment. Gawan can be patient with Orgeluse because he chooses to see past her loathliness — assuming her goodness, or "graciousness," lies behind it — and because he avoids being overly reactive to her mistreatment of him. With Malcreatiure and with his continual choosing to stay with Orgeluse rather than escape her "slings and arrows,"

Gawan shows that this patience and forbearance are not the result of passivity, resignation or fear. His is a very active choice not to judge her.

It is also a free choice — which is to say, the choice is made only because it is "true" for him. There is no compelling reason for Gawan's choice of Orgeluse. Gawan's popularity outshines all the other knights at Arthur's court, and any woman there would be his for the asking. But this woman is his life, and he knows it. (He repeatedly says that not to serve her would be death for him.) So he will persevere, though most people would call him a fool when she treats him so rudely. Orgeluse herself calls him a "goose," weighed down by his stupidity.

We can recall that Parzival was called the same as he rode out of the deserted Grail castle. One thing about geese — wild, free ones anyway — is their famed ability to endure very long migrations to return to what they know is their true place. Both our "geese" knights, having made clear, free choices, are mounted on Grail horses now and, without really knowing it yet, are more accurately aimed in their respective journeys. After meeting Trevrizent, Parzival knows the question he is to ask at the place he has claimed for his own — the Grail castle. Gawan has chosen the love of his life, who has led him to Clinschor's castle, which he will win.

The initiate-speaker, in equal freedom, learns to suspend judgment. This is not an easy matter, as Gawan's ordeals demonstrate. A person who wishes truly to love life and suspend judgments must be willing to endure mockery and bruising. The initiate-speaker will often appear like a goose or a fool, because to release negative judgments requires the relinquishment of all attachment to being "right" or "special." The release of such attachments can make one appear irritatingly ordinary, even stupid.

But avoiding the temptation to judge is very different from stupidity. Gawan and the initiate-speaker retain and develop increasingly penetrating powers of discernment and discrimination. They do not abandon the perception of their senses or their faculty of thinking. Gawan and the initiate-speaker must be able to see themselves and others accurately, to find appropriate actions and words and, at the same time, to restrain their tendency to be judgmental and reactive.

Sovereignty in listening results, in part, from the initiate-speaker's willingness to listen metaphorically, resisting the temptation to listen habitually or literally. Sovereignty in speaking results, in part, from the initiate-speaker's willingness to resist habitual kinds of speaking. Common habitual modes of speaking are complaint, criticism or cynicism when life or the world seems painful, unpleasing or difficult. Gossip and backbiting, as well as feigned politeness, are other habits of talking that undermine the initiate-speaker's self-mastery.

But curbing one's habits of negative speech does not go far enough. When Gawan is served larks for dinner at the end of Book X, Wolfram ingeniously employs another bird image to indicate the further development. The lark, admired for its soaring flight and flute-like song despite its unremarkable appearance, acquired its widespread reputation for singing at heaven's gates because medieval writers thought that its Latin name, *alauda,* derived from *laus,* meaning "praise." They were mistaken; *alauda* was of Celtic origin, from *al* meaning "high" or" great" and *aud,* meaning "song."[62] They may have been mistaken, but they were not wrong; a "high song" consists of praise. Gifted speakers of the ancient Greek world were called "praise singers," and those seeking the speech of the Grail must heed the wisdom of that epithet. From his meditations concerning the mythical poet-singer Orpheus, German poet Rainer Maria Rilke came to realize that

> To praise is the whole thing! A man who can praise
> comes toward us like ore out of the silences
> of rock. His heart, that dies, presses out
> for others a wine that is fresh forever.
>
> When the god's energy takes hold of him,
> his voice never collapses in the dust.
> Everything turns to vineyards, everything turns to grapes,
> made ready for harvest by his powerful south.
>
> The mold in the catacomb of the king
> does not suggest that his praising is lies, nor
> the fact that the gods cast shadows.
>
> He is one of the servants who does not go away,
> who still holds through the doors
> of the tomb trays of shining fruit.[63]

Praise that "comes toward us like ore out of the silences of rock" is neither empty flattery nor undiscriminating affirmation. To discover the praiseworthy in a world that can seem so unfair and full of suffering, to enable oneself to praise authentically anyone or anything, requires a "scientific" attitude in the most encompassing sense of that word. One's loyalty lies not with opinion but with inquiry, not with critique but with curiosity. One seeks to distinguish what makes each person, thing, or situation unique as well as to discover larger patterns of connection and causation. Appreciation evolves as ever more subtle distinctions are found and the context of inquiry unfurls in ever-greater mysteries.

The "harvest" that the praise singer Rilke describes comes after long, caring and careful work in the fields of the world. To turn everything into a vineyard filled with fruit by one's perceptive speech, the initiate-speaker, like Gawan, must dig beneath the hard surface of the thorny plain of appearances. For Parzival to become king of the Grail castle, Gawan must become lord of the Castle Merveil, the upside-down mirror land where facts are reflected but the Queens of Life are held hostage. One cannot speak from any of the wisdom of the Grail unless one has also penetrated the illusory but powerful magic of Clinschor's world.

NOTES

[1] T.S. Eliot, "East Coker" from "Four Quartets," *Collected Poems, 1900–1962*, 187.

[2] Wolfram, Book IX, 433.

[3] Wolfram, Book IX, 438.

[4] Wolfram, Book IX, 440–41.

[5] Wolfram, Book IX, 441.

[6] Wolfram, Book IX, 441.

[7] Wolfram, Book IX, 443.

[8] Wolfram, Book IX, 448.

[9] Wolfram, Book IX, 450.

[10] Wolfram, Book IX, 451.

[11] Wolfram, Book IX, 452.

[12] Wolfram, Book IX, 453.

[13] Wolfram, Book IX, 454.

[14] Wolfram, Book IX, 456.

[15] Wolfram, Book IX, 465.

[16] Wolfram, Book IX, 467.

[17] Wolfram, Book IX, 468.

[18] Wolfram, Book IX, 469.

[19] Wolfram, Book IX, 470.

[20] Wolfram, Book IX, 472.

[21] Wolfram, Book IX, 473.

[22] Wolfram, Book IX, 475–76.

[23] Wolfram, Book IX, 478.

[24] Wolfram, Book IX, 484.

[25] Wolfram, Book IX, 488.

[26] Wolfram, Book IX, 488.

[27] Wolfram, Book IX, 501.

[28] Philip Wheelwright, *Metaphor and Reality:* "The sense of being addressed — not by a hallucinatory voice, but by the silent voice which murmurs in some secret place beyond the inner ear — is felt in one way or another by every person of moral sensitivity. . . . Thus the word, the Logos, tends to become an auditory image symbolizing rightness, the What Ought, which gives meaning to moral judgment. At a primitive level the divine command finds symbolization in certain physical noises: the rushing wind serves frequently as such a symbol, and the so-called bull-roarer, which imitates the wind's tone, is used by some American Indian tribes and elsewhere, to mime the supernatural voice and magically to invite and encourage it. . . . As religions become more developed spiritually such outward noises cease to matter, but the auditory image-symbol of Logos persists, as is shown in such a phrase as the 'voice of conscience' and in such a word as 'vocation'"(124–25).

[29] James Wiggins, "Within and Without Stories," *Religion as Story,* 17.

[30] Northrup Frye, *The Great Code:* "Paul's brilliant phrase for the Incarnation is 'He emptied himself' (Philippians 2:7; the AV's rendering is not a translation but an inept gloss)" (129).

[31] Beryl Rowland, *Birds with Human Souls,* 43.

32 The only other option is to hear them literally — as worn out messages or as a programming that, if we are compliant children, we must mindlessly follow or, if we are rebellious children, we must reject, declaring such tales "untrue".

[33] Wiggins, 18.

[34] Wheelwright, 156.

[35] Norman O. Brown, *Love's Body,* 245.

[36] The Tibetan teacher Govinda, quoted by Brown at the very end of *Love's Body* says: "It is not the audible word through which people are converted and transformed in their innermost being, but through that which goes beyond words and flows directly from the presence of the saint: the inaudible mantric sound that emanates from his heart" (266).

[37] James Hillman, *Healing Fiction,* 47. Hillman states a little earlier: "I have found that the person with a sense of story built in from childhood is in better shape than one who has not had stories, who has not heard them, read them, acted them, or made them up. And here I mean oral story, those depending mainly on speech — and reading too has an oral aspect even when one reads alone in silence — rather than story watched on screen or in a picture book" (46).

[38] Hillman, 38.

[39] Hillman, 43.

[40] Wolfram, Book X, 506.

[41] Wolfram, Book X, 508.

[42] Wolfram, Book X, 509.

[43] Wolfram, Book X, 510.

[44] Wolfram, Book X, 511.

[45] Wolfram, Book X, 511.

[46] Wolfram, Book X, 515.

[47] Wolfram, Book X, 515.

[48] Wolfram, Book X, 516.

[49] Wolfram, Book X, 517.

[50] Wolfram, Book X, 519.

[51] Wolfram, Book X, 520.

[52] Wolfram, Book X, 521.

[53] Wolfram, Book X, 523.

[54] Wolfram, Book X, 523.

[55] Wolfram, Book X, 531.

[56] Wolfram, Book X, 547.

[57] Wolfram, Book X, 548.

[58] Wolfram, Book X, 516.

[59] Caitlin Matthews, *Elements of the Celtic Tradition,* 25–27.

[60] Alwyn Rees and Brinley Rees, *Celtic Heritage,* 74.

[61] Rees and Rees, 76.

[62] Rowland, 97.

[63] Rainer Maria Rilke, "Sonnets to Orpheus #7," in Robert Bly, trans., *Selected Poems of Rainer Maria Rilke,* 207.

CHAPTER SIX

"You Will Have to Force Your Horse to a Mighty Leap"

The Grail King Speaks

To liberate the healing balm
Of the Ones-Who-Watch-and-Wait —
Held captive by the deceiving power
Of appearances —
Stay shielded, Oh Speaker,
And find footing
In the bloody battle
With fear and desire.
Then, sacrifice all certainty.
Leap toward the Unknown,
So the inner Bride
And true Bridegroom
Will be returned to themselves
And to each other.

BOOK XI

Gawan has fallen into an exhausted sleep in the home of the fer-ryman, Plippalinot. He wakes early and, wanting to orient himself, get some air, and hear the birds, goes to the window that faces the castle he saw the night before. Again he notices about four hundred women sitting at the windows and marvels that they "had not grown tired of staying awake,"[1] for their position suggests they have not slept. He feels so tired, though, that he decides to "honor them by going back to sleep."[2]

When he awakens again, he finds the ferryman's daughter, Bene, sitting by his bed, watching over his sleep. He thanks her, accepts her adoring and respectful comments, and then, since she has said she would serve him in any way, asks her to tell him about the ladies in the castle. At this, she begins to weep loudly, insisting she must not tell him and imploring him not to question her. Her father comes in and thinks her upset comes from "tumbling" with Gawan in bed. He urges her not to cry, but then, when he hears Gawan's questions, he also expresses great anxiety and pleads, "For God's sake! Don't ask!"[3]

Gawan wants to know why they find his question so distressing. Plippalinot replies, "If you won't forego your questioning, you will presently want to go further," and that will place Gawan in peril and thus remove all joy from the hearts of the ferryman and his family who, he declares, were "born to serve you."[4] When Gawan persists, saying that he's going to find out some way, the ferryman regretfully tells him that he will lend him a shield and that Gawan must arm him-self for battle because he is in the Land of Wonders, with the Castle of Wonders and its perilous Wonder Bed right in front of him. All previous adventures, he warns, have been nothing compared to the one that now beckons.

Gawan, though concerned at his host's dismay, nonetheless feels obliged to investigate the plight of the women, whom he heard about before anyway, from Cundrie *la sorcière*, at Arthur's court. He requests the ferryman's advice in approaching the Castle of Won-ders and is told that the ladies there are "held hostage" since being "brought here by mighty enchantment."[5] If Gawan survives the tests, he will liberate them and become lord of the castle and the lands around it. He also learns that just the day before, Parzival has passed this way, searching for the Grail. He did not inquire about the castle and its captive ladies, so the ferryman did not tell him because of the "strong magic, sharp with terror,"[6] therein.

Gawan calls for his weapons and armor and, along with them, is given a large shield that hangs on the ferryman's wall. Plippalinot tells him about a rich trader in front of the castle with whom Gawan, after buying something, can safely leave his horse before entering the castle. He tells Gawan about the Wonder Bed and that, no matter what, Gawan must not let go of his shield and sword. "For when you think your troubles have come to an end, then you will just be beginning to fight."[7]

Gawan does as instructed, stopping at the trader's hut, which is filled with the wealth of a kingdom. The trader welcomes him, shows him his wares, offers to care for his horse and says that all his wares will belong to Gawan if he succeeds in liberating the Castle of Wonders. Gawan leaves his horse and enters the castle on foot.

The castle is mightily fortified on all sides, but Gawan enters without incident. He sees that the roof of the great hall is deeply colored like peacock's plumes and "of a color that neither rain nor snow could damage the roof's brilliance at all."[8] Inside, high arches with detailed and handsome adornments vault the ceiling, and the numerous divans are richly covered. A door stands open at one side of the great hall, and Gawan crosses the threshold into an inner chamber where the Wonder Bed stands waiting.

The chamber is empty except for the bed, and the floor pavement "shone bright and smooth as glass."[9] The Wonder Bed itself is a marvel of beauty and engineering. Each of its four posts has a wheel made of a ruby, and it rolls swifter than the wind on the glassy floor. Gawan can hardly keep his footing on the slippery floor, and every time he approaches the bed, it veers swiftly from him. The heavy shield greatly encumbers him, but he obeys Plippalinot's warning not to let go of it. Finally, in frustration, Gawan mentally speaks to the bed: "How am I going to catch you if you dodge me this way? I'll show you if I can jump on you!"[10]

With that, the bed stops squarely in front of him and he takes a flying leap into the middle. Immediately the bed begins racing across the floor, slamming into all four walls in its course, causing the fortress to resound with a thunderous noise — a din so loud that Gawan crawls under his shield for some relief. There is nothing he can do but pray.

Finally the din subsides and the handsomely colored bed stops abruptly in the middle of the room. But the stillness quickly ends, as Gawan now becomes the target for five hundred sling shots, pelting him so hard with small stones that, in some places, they penetrate the shield. Following this barrage, five hundred arrows are loosed from invisible bows. Some of these pierce the shield. Then silence comes again.

Already bruised and wounded, Gawan now confronts a stocky, scowling peasant clothed in fish skin and carrying a huge club. Gawan is irritated to be challenged by so poorly outfitted a warrior, but his preparations to fight are for naught. Once the thug sees Gawan is still alive, he simply tells him that he is sending in something that will certainly kill him. Gawan has barely had time to rake off the arrow shafts stuck in his shield and chain mail when a rumbling sound like twenty drums announces the sudden arrival of a huge hungry lion the size of a horse. The lion roars and attacks Gawan, slicing through the shield with his claws. Gawan manages to cut off its leg, leaving the lion spurting blood and hobbling on three legs. The blood gives Gawan firmer footing on the treacherous floor but by now he is badly wounded too. The lion lurches toward him repeatedly and tries to pull him down, but Gawan finally thrusts his sword up to its hilt into the beast's breast, killing it.

Dazed, Gawan stands in the blood-drenched room wondering what he should do next. He is exhausted but realizes the bed certainly promises no rest. He staggers from dizziness and finally collapses unconscious on his shield, his head supported by the lion's body. A young maiden who has witnessed this struggle from a balcony runs to tell Arnive, Arthur's mother, what has happened. At her command, two maidens descend to the chamber to see if the embattled knight still lives. His breath is so faint, they can detect it only by holding a piece of fur torn from his garments up to his froth-covered lips. It moves, so they know he is alive.

One maiden then forces her ring between his teeth so she can gently pour some water down his throat. When Gawan regains consciousness, he feels ashamed at the position they have found him in and asks them to tell no one. They assure him that, despite his position here on the floor, he has just won great renown. "The victory is yours today."[11]

When the maidens ask about his wounds, Gawan says that, if he is to live, he needs help from someone who knows about healing. But, if he is supposed to fight again, he tells them they should tie on his helmet and let him continue to fight for his life. They reassure him that his fighting is finished for now and then submit him to the care of Arnive who, already having prepared his bed, now has his armor removed in a manner respectful of his dignity. She applies ointments and salve to his fifty wounds, which were not fatal only because the shield protected him so well.

Arnive tells Gawan that she received her knowledge of medicines and healing from Cundrie, who comes to visit her frequently. The salve used on Gawan's wounds is the same one applied to Anfortas's wounds at the Grail castle. Gawan is inspired to hear that the Grail castle might be near, since that is where he thinks he is going, and thanks Arnive for her help. She gives him an herb for sleeping and makes sure he is not disturbed while he sleeps the rest of the day.

At nightfall, they remove the sleeping herb from his mouth, and he wakes and sits up in bed to receive the dinner Arnive has had prepared. He protests when the noble ladies attending him refuse his invitation either to sit down or to eat with him, but Arnive assures him that they are pleased to honor and serve him so. He looks among them eagerly to see if Orgeluse is there, but he cannot find her. After dinner, sleep again overtakes him.

Initiatory Themes

Led as always by the feeling in his heart — his concern for the plight of the women along with his passion for Orgeluse — and having the courage to remain true to that, Gawan has survived the tests in the Castle of Wonders and has become its king. The wicked magician Clinschor, whom we will hear more of but never actually meet in the story, has left the land, and the captive ladies are free. Among the hostages are Arthur's mother, her daughter, who is Gawan's mother, and Gawan's two sisters. All three phases of womanhood — maiden, mother and crone — have been released by Gawan from their imprisonment.

Like Parzival on his first visit to the Grail castle, Gawan comes unbidden to the Castle of Wonders. But there the similarity ends. The Castle Merveil is the mirror opposite of the Grail castle.[12] The Grail castle is located on a mountain, the Castle Merveil on a plain. At the Grail castle, Parzival is supposed to ask a question; Gawan is repeatedly begged not to ask any questions about the Castle Merveil. The Grail castle is hard to get into; the Castle Merveil is difficult to get out of. People are called to the Grail castle by their destiny; the ladies are brought to Merveil by enchantment. Parzival is given a sword; Gawan is given a shield. No one can prompt Parzival about what he is supposed to do; Gawan is provided with precise instructions. At the Grail castle Parzival has to heal Anfortas's wound; at Merveil, it is Gawan who is wounded and must await healing. At the Grail castle, women are honored as appointed carriers of the Grail; at Merveil, they are held hostage, sitting useless at the windows day and night. Anfortas, the wounded Grail King, inhabits his castle, where he help-lessly waits, being powerless in his land; Clinschor, lord of Merveil, has no open wound (though, we will learn later, he has been cas-trated) and is not physically present, yet his power permeates the cas-tle and land.

We never meet Clinschor in person, but we can discover his qual-ities in the castle he constructed. It is well fortified on the horizon-tal plain; its great hall, where the host would normally welcome guests, has a roof colored like a peacock, whose bright appearance is not altered by rain or fog. On the outside it calls attention to itself, but inside it is treacherous. One can attain a footing on Clinschor's polished, slippery surface only by standing in blood. There is great beauty and great violence here. The violence meets one just at the place where one would want to sleep, or become unconscious, and the attack has the fury of a hungry lion. In this castle, the feminine forces are immobilized. Like fairy tale dragons with their gold, Clin-schor hoards his women; he cannot really do anything with them or let them do anything.

With the feminine forces held so powerless, the sheer physicality of the Wonder Bed and the Lion focuses the activity in Clinschor's castle. Here unconscious impulses veer and buck and slam against the walls, and roaring desire perpetrates acts of violence — physical or verbal — to get what it wants. The Wonder Bed and Lion represent the antithesis of relatedness and responsiveness, and it is no acci-dent that neither "speak." All actions and words based in the Bed or the Lion have no speech in them, no gesture toward anything, only compulsion.

Gawan has come up against Clinschor, in the guise of his castle, because Gawan has asked questions, those acts of speech which, as we have seen before, bring us into relationship with others. He will survive that meeting only if his shield is strong and he does not let go of it. The shield could be described as his relatedness — his ability to honor, learn from, and help whatever confronts him. The enchantment created by Clinschor's terrible peacock pride is overcome by a person who can receive instruction from a common ferryman.

Repeatedly, Gawan demonstrates his ability to relate sensitively to diverse people, animals and even objects. The Wonder Bed only stops for him when he addresses it as if it were a person. When he sees his horse, Gringuljete, he greets him with the enthusiasm he would a valued friend. This relatedness to the world manifests in his numerous aptitudes, which even scornful Orgeluse has noticed. He is a knight, a lover, a healer, an owner of a trader's booth, and will soon become a negotiator and mediator. He possesses many of the skills required to live successfully in the everyday, material world — those of fighting, loving, healing, trading, and negotiating.

Gawan's capacity for relatedness is what truly frees the hostages in the Castle of Wonders. No august Grail procession welcomes the new king here, but, instead, a simple ceremony of healing, dining and sleeping. The wounds suffered in Clinschor's realm can be healed only through the feminine forces that are empowered by his fight in their service. For Clinschor, the women are objects among other objects, collectibles. In Gawan's kingdom they regain their status as individual persons, each due her recognition and respect, no matter how young or old, how beautiful or loathly.

It should be noted that Gawan does not lose himself in relating to others. He responds to what presents itself to him — almost always with understanding, kindness, appropriate words and deeds — but he does not forget who he is or where he is going. He adheres faithfully to the code of knighthood and to the direction he has chosen. He copes with the taunts and jeers, the false accusations, the violence, the petty feuds between lovers, even his own ambivalence, impulsiveness and emotional reactiveness and remains true to himself and his path. Throughout, his humility equals his perseverance and courage. Even when badly wounded and exhausted, he is troubled by the possible discomfort of the noble women who stand while he has dinner.

From the moment when Gawan encounters the wounded knight, the events in this realm show that Clinschor's reign depends on the power of appearances. He controls human beings by the powerful "magic" of making things, people and situations appear desirable or repulsive, needy, fearsome or sheltering. Gawan always seeks to know what lies *behind* the appearances of things. When he sees Parzival entranced with the blood on the snow, when he sees the two armies approaching Bearosche, when he looks at the Castle Merveil, he asks questions and considers what to do. In particular, he sees something behind Orgeluse's intimidating mask, more than she exhibits on the surface. In mastering Clinschor's slippery and illusory surface, Gawan will gain access to greatly enhanced abilities to perceive with his senses.

To refine the senses can feel risky and requires concentrated effort. The test of the Wonder Bed, unconsciousness and desire, and the test of the Lion, fear and anger, must first be passed. Paradoxically, Clinschor himself supplies the tests through which Gawan and the initiate-speaker may wrest themselves from the thrall of his illusions. To undertake and succeed in the battle with the perilous Wonder Bed requires that one ride and tame one's own unconscious, desirous impulsiveness. Instead of continuing to lunge after the bed, Gawan stops and speaks to it. Then, once mounted, "Gawan had to stay awake though he was lying in bed,"[13] which is to say, he has to maintain mindfulness even in the grip of the most powerful passions. In fighting the Lion, one must overcome one's own mad hunger for comfort and certainty, often called "security."[14] Not to be driven by this hungering for security leads to a pitched battle with oneself (and sometimes others) yet, again, paradoxically, it is in the blood of that sacrifice of certainty that one finds surer footing in Clinschor's realm.

From this perspective, the crushing, bloody tests of the Bed and the Lion suggest the epistemological chaos that can be experienced as the initiate-speaker relinquishes programmed judgments about people and the world. Custom, dogma, mores, rules and regulations — all the "shoulds" of life provided from the outside — actually form a secure container, a kind of protection from the kind of battles Gawan and any initiate must fight. As a matter of fact, because those traditional forms are disintegrating in the twentieth century, people in general have less and less option to rest unquestioningly within such forms and therefore must contend with battles similar to Gawan's whether they choose to or not.

Our uncertain society differs markedly from non- or pre-scientific societies, where, as in medieval times, the world view is self-contained and complete. The predominant mode of awareness in such places and times, says cultural historian Morris Berman, is "participating consciousness", which he defines as learning or knowing that comes through "merger or identification with one's surroundings."[15] The worldview that such participating consciousness inspires is "at root, visceral/mimetic/sensuous,"[16] because

> Man is at the center of a universe that is bounded at its outermost sphere by God, the Unmoved Mover. . . . Everything moves and exists in accordance with divine purpose. All of nature, rocks as well as trees, is organic and repeats itself in eternal cycles of generation and corruption. As a result this world is ultimately changeless, but being riddled with purpose, is an exceptionally meaningful one. Fact and value, epistemology and ethics, are identical. "What do I know" and "How should I live" are in fact the same question.[17]

Berman argues that radical moral relativism "was *born* with the scientific method; it does not exist in any nonscientific culture or context."[18] He describes the quandary for us in the twentieth century who are

> brought face to face with an unsettling question: Is reality nothing more than a cultural artifact? . . . There is then no Truth, but merely your truth, my truth, the truth of this time or that place. . . . The distinction between knowledge and opinion, between science and ideology, crumbles, and what is right becomes a matter of majority rule or "mob psychology." Modern science, astrology, witchcraft, Aristotelianism, Marxism, whatever — all become equally true in the absence of objective knowledge and the concept of a fixed, underlying reality.[19]

Berman turns to a range of twentieth century thinkers (psychiatrists C.G. Jung and Wilhelm Reich, scientist Michael Polanyi, linguistic thinker Owen Barfield, and anthropologist Gregory Bateson) to find direction toward a new kind of participatory consciousness. Wolfram's Gawan offers us his own example. Amidst the din and chaos at the Castle Merveil, relational knowing prevails in Gawan's approach to the world even when he is weakened and wounded. Preserving this relational mode against all temptation to do otherwise not only assures his own survival but also rescues the feminine forces, whose most fundamental essence is relatedness.

Relatedness does not defeat Clinschor himself; that is not possible on the horizontal plane. But he can be displaced; a certain part of his realm can be claimed by each human being who successfully undertakes the tests of the Bed and the Lion. The struggle and suffering in those tests are inevitable, as the etymology of the words "relate" and "suffer" indicates. In Latin, "relate" comes from *refero* and "suffer" from *suffero;* both share the root *fero,* which includes among its meanings "to bear," "to carry," "to endure," "to put up with."[20]

These meanings evoke the image of a witness, one who sees and wakefully bears the truth of what she or he sees without looking away. We can think of Mary at the foot of the Cross or the grandmothers of the "disappeared ones" in 1970's Argentina who brought down an oppressive government through the power of their courageous, silent witnessing. The ladies constantly awake at the windows of the Castle Merveil may represent, therefore, the soul of the world,[21] who watches, suffers and waits until one (or more) who embodies relatedness releases some part of the world from the blind violence of those compulsively in pursuit of Clinschor's illusory promise of security and power.

If the shield, a weapon of defense, represents consistent relatedness, what, we might ask, empowers Gawan and the initiate-speaker to hold on to it? We can only assume that the strength to stay shielded has come from previous events. Of these, recognizing one's own imperfection, one's own errors and evil, constitutes a protection in the battles with the Prince of This World, who, in Wolfram's epic, is named Clinschor. As Jungian analyst Marie Louise von Franz bluntly explains:

> . . . In general, as you know, looking at one's own shadow is not only disagreeable, it is no fun and the results are not very amusing, but it has one great advantage: the more one knows about one's own wickedness, the more one is able to protect oneself against other people. In some sense the evil within oneself recognizes evil outside. . . . One can thus avoid evil, but only by knowing how evil one is oneself, for only then has one an immediate, instinctive awareness and recognition. The idealistic fool who gets cheated by everybody and always has bad tricks played on him cannot be helped by pity,

but only by being led to his own shadow. Awareness of his own evil will enable him to defend himself better.[22]

Gawan, Parzival and the initiate-speaker, growing "slowly wise," as Wolfram promised at the beginning, are quite well along their way to a new understanding of "imperfection." They are much closer to being able to appreciate, if not actually love, the black-and-white mix of their natures. The question then becomes how to structure that understanding so that "What I know" about myself and the world can be reunited with "How should I live?"

At this juncture, Gawan is too weak to do anything but rest and regain his strength. He has been severely wounded in the battles, surviving only because he could accept help from a lowly person, the ferryman, and from the highest God. Yet, his wounds are of this world, and they can be cured — as Anfortas's cannot — by the medicines of this world. Arnive, the grandmother, has learned her healing skills from Cundrie *la sorcière,* who brings the ointment from the Grail castle. Gawan is saved again through the Grail company — as he was when Vergulaht transferred to him the oath to get the Grail. Though Gawan's tasks are to "straighten out" the warped world on the horizontal plane, he succeeds because of his intimate connection with the Grail castle and the vertical plane. A few more trials await him, but, because of all he has accomplished already, the predominant themes in the remaining episodes will be return and reunification.

Toward Speech of the Grail

Two moments of Gawan's speaking provide clues to the phase the initiate-speaker has reached with this episode. The first is when Bene and her father despair at Gawan's insistence on asking questions about the Castle Merveil. They sense, rightly, that questioning some thing tends to lead one beyond the boundaries of what is known and accepted. These ordinary folk, who live their lives in Clinschor's land with little difficulty — and even profit! — cannot see the necessity of Gawan's questions. They represent the part of each initiate-speaker that does not want to ask, that would rather stay comfortable, safe and well-fed in the herd rather than pursue the solitary, difficult and sometimes dangerous path of the question.

The second moment is when Gawan speaks to the Wonder Bed. Gawan's relatedness, as we have seen, extends to everything — allowing him to be an excellent herbalist, for instance. Gawan speaks to the "being" in things as well as in people. He apparently regards the world, and everything in it, as "alive." When added to the skill Parzival developed in Trevrizent's cave — listening to the inner speech of things and events — this quality of perception endows metaphor with "life." The initiate-speaker, with Gawan as guide, decides, from the heart, to interact with the world "as if" she or he can see the living being within each creature or thing. In deeds as well as words, the initiate-speaker's practice is to grant reverent attention to each person, thing or event, even when folks of ordinary consciousness consider it unwise or unsafe.

Relatedness by itself, however, is not sufficient to evoke the speech in persons, things and events. Equally necessary is poesis — the process of imaginatively making, shaping, crafting one's perceptions, thoughts and experiences in the medium of words.[23] Not every initiate-speaker will become a poet, but every initiate-speaker will, in some way or another, arrive at poetry's threshold. The reason is that the "living being" within language also calls to be known through relationship. This appeal, Martin Heidegger would say, is made to every human being, and the means for seeing and listening "into" language is poetry:

> Man first speaks when, and only when, he responds to language by listening to its appeal. Among all the appeals that we human beings, on our part, may help to be voiced, language is the highest and everywhere the first. Language beckons us, at first and then again at the end, toward a thing's nature. But that is not to say, ever, that in any word-meaning picked up at will language supplies us, straight away and definitively, with the transparent nature of the matter as if it were an object ready for use. But the responding in which man authentically listens to the appeal of language is that which speaks in the element of poetry.[24]

If the trials of the Bed and the Lion represent the chaotic, painful turbulence that distress one who relinquishes judgmental attitudes or who experiences the "radical relativism" of times when secure forms of custom and dogma deteriorate, then the aftermath must involve the formation of a new containing structure. As the old shielding forms are riddled with holes, a new dwelling must be found, a dwelling that is not a thing but a way of inhabiting language and speech such that the world can feel like home again. "Poetry is what really lets us dwell," says Heidegger because "[p]oetic creation, which lets us dwell, is a kind of building."[25] American poet Denise Levertov expresses much the same idea, after a brief lament for a culture of more "noble simplicity":

> Our age appears to me a chaos and our environment lacks the qualities for which one could call it a culture. But by way of consolation we have this knowledge of power that perhaps no one in such a harmonious time had; what in the greatest poets is recognizable as Imagination, that breathing of life into the dust, is present in us all embryonically — manifests itself in the life of dream — and in that manifestation shows us the possibility; to permeate, to quicken, all of our life and the works we make. What joy to be reminded by truth in dream that the imagination does not arise from the environment but has the power to create it![26]

Times come in every life when one's worldview is not solid, when traditional mores and rules seem not to pertain. One feels awash, with no structure to guide one's actions. As young children, all of us are subject to the turbulent chaos of an adult world beyond our understanding. What children have traditionally been given to structure their relationship to life are fairy tales. A child's way of experiencing, as Gawan learned from Obilot, can augment an adult's, and the fairy tale best expresses this way of experiencing. Incredible as it might seem to the initiate-speaker, a child's book of fairy tales harbors a treasure. It is no coincidence that interest in fairy tales, and other traditional stories, burgeons now when so many adults feel divested of a secure worldview, when so many aspects of life merit questioning.

Shrouded by their antiquity, the origins of fairy tales, like language itself, are unknown. Fairy tales are perhaps the oldest form of "literature," although that term is inexact since they were originally transmitted orally, and still are most effective that way. Distilled over hundreds, even thousands, of years their images possess archetypal precision and their narrative structures are harmonious and artful.

True fairy tales do not teach anything *per se* but "show and tell" through concise portrayal, and well-defined actions. Furthermore, in a fairy tale, notes folklorist Max Luthi, "Everything can enter into relationship with everything else; that is the actual miracle and at the same time the simple foregone conclusion."[27] In other words, the fairy tale presents a holistic vision of reality.

"Every fairy tale," says Luthi, "is, in its own way, something of a dragon slayer."[28] While having the character of dream, fairy tales nonetheless convey a sense of "sheltering" order to tellers and listeners, giving not only pleasure but form and inspiration.[29] They are reassuring for adults as well as children, and there are many reports of their soothing, healing power for hospital patients of all ages. Fairy tales can form a shield against the chaos of the Wonder Bed and the Lion because of their ordered structure, because they show that real virtue is inevitably rewarded, and because, as Ursula Grahl explains, they gift teller and listeners with

> an unshakable faith in the power of metamorphosis. . . . Nothing is so hopelessly bewitched, either in fairy tale or in human life, but that somewhere there is a healing magic that can release it.[30]

Gawan's relatedness, his ability to honor the inner, living being of all he encounters, is the precursor to the greater powers of perception and of poesis which evolve further through the trials at the Castle Merveil. Gawan exemplifies Denise Levertov's reflection:

> All the thinking I do about poetry leads me back, always, to Reverence for Life as the ground for poetic activity; because it seems the ground for Attention. This is not to put the cart before the horse: some sense of identity, at which we wonder; an innocent self-regard, which we see in infants and in the humblest forms of life; these come first, a center out of which Attention reaches. Without Attention — to the world outside us, to the voices within us — what poems could possibly come into existence? Attention is the exercise of Reverence for the "other forms of life that want to live." The progression seems clear to me: from Reverence for Life to Attention to Life, from Attention to Life to a highly developed Seeing and Hearing, from Seeing and Hearing (faculties almost indistinguishable for the poet) to the Discovery and Revelation of Form, from Form to Song.[31]

For the ancient Greeks, poetic song was the province of the Muses, that host of feminine beings whom the poets called upon to grace their poetry and music with qualities of living presence. The Muses' favorite places are the springs that bubble forth, like the inspiration they bring, from the rocks and earthy ground. It is the Muses, nourishers of poetry, whom Gawan has released for the initiate-speaker by undergoing his trials at the Castle Merveil.

Language and speech can appear to be very much in Clinschor's service. They can hypnotize and enthrall as often as awaken and release. Wrestling with one's unconscious, impulsive speech habits can feel as exhausting and perilous as trying to tame the bucking Bed on the slippery floor or overcoming the impetuous Lion, ever-threatening to leap from one's tongue. However, if the tests are passed, then the initiate-speaker, like Gawan, liberates the goddesses who confer poetic grace upon the words. The speech of the initiate-speaker will thus become more poetic. Living metaphor, rhythmic timing and sound begin to dance with each other in one's speaking, along with restraint, where just enough is said but not too much. Words without these goddesses are mere pawns in power plays, however subtle the aggression or manipulation might be.

With the help of the Muses, and having learned from fairy tales, the initiate-speaker can now begin to respond to language's calling to build a dwelling out of the substance of language — that is, meaning-filled words. The initiate-speaker finds a "story" in each person or situation, perceives how that story could be connected to a larger traditional story and to his or her own life, and then formulates the connection with rhythmic, resonant images. Such poesis constructs an oral architecture of experience,[32] with tradition as its foundation, which enfolds and unfolds a worldview. The dwelling exists during the speaking, and, like music, which exists only when it is played, never stands once and for all but must be constantly re-created. From this point on, things can come together again for the initiate-speaker, instead of falling apart, and the initiate-speaker will experience what William Stafford describes in his poem "When I Met My Muse."

> I glanced at her and took my glasses
> off — they were still singing. They buzzed
> like a locust on the coffee table and then

ceased. Her voice belled forth, and the
sunlight bent. I felt the ceiling arch, and
knew that nails up there took a new grip
on whatever they touched. "I am your own
way of looking at things," she said. "When
you allow me to live with you, every
glance at the world around you will be
a sort of salvation." And I took her hand.[33]

Gawan, like Parzival now, knows his salvation. He has no doubt
that it is in taking the hand of his Muse, his own Lady-at-the-Spring,
Orgeluse.[34] Her allure has brought him to the Castle Merveil, and his
yearning for her has not diminished, but only increased, during his
struggles there. Now the time has come to make the leap that will
assure that union.

BOOK XII

All the torments Gawan and other brave warriors have endured
are nothing compared to the intense longing for Orgeluse that dis-
turbs Gawan's sleep, causing him to toss and turn in his bed, tearing
loose his bandages. Finally, Gawan arises, in blood-stained clothes,
and finds fresh ones at his bedside. Then he wanders through the castle that now belongs to him.

At one end of the great hall, a narrow, winding staircase leads up
into a slim tower, which rises high above the castle roof. In the middle of the tower room is a shining circular pillar. The tower itself is
encrusted with precious jewels of every kind, but the column in the
middle outshines them all. It was brought by Clinschor from the East
where it had been "wrought by sorcery."[35] When Gawan approaches
the pillar, he sees in it all the lands surrounding the Castle Merveil
and sits down to observe the panorama of landscape and people at
their various occupations. The panorama moves, seeming to circle in
the column.

Just then, Arnive, the grandmother, comes in with her daughter,
Sangive, and her two granddaughters, Itonje and Cundrie. Gawan
jumps to his feet to greet her and thank her for saving his life. After
satisfying her request that he also greet Sangive and her two daughters, he asks about the pillar. Arnive explains that it was stolen from
Queen Secundille and is made from a stone that lights up both day

and night and thus shows all that is happening within a six-mile radius of the castle.

Gawan suddenly sees in the pillar that Orgeluse is riding up to the river quay in the company of a knight, a Turkoite. Arnive tries unsuccessfully to dissuade him from going out to face the knight, who has his spear raised for battle, which signals a hostile challenge to Gawan and the castle. Gawan feels conflicted for a moment by the ladies' distress, for they fear he will reopen his wounds and bleed to death, leaving them captives again. However, Orgeluse and his own honor prove to be stronger for him, and he calls for his horse and armor. The women help him so quietly that no one but the chamberlain knows of his departure.

Terribly weakened from his wounds, Gawan can barely carry his shield, which is riddled with holes. He rides over to the ferryman who provides him with a spear and, as he ferries him across, some information about the Turkoite knight. Plippalinot tells Gawan that this knight has sworn an oath that he will fall by spear only; anyone who knocks him from his horse will win, for he will fight no further with sword. Gawan pledges that the ferryman will win whatever the loser loses in this battle and goes to meet the knight. They gallop toward each other, and Gawan manages to knock the knight off his horse, though not before taking a blow himself. The Turkoite surrenders, and Gawan sends him up to the castle after a brief exchange with Orgeluse.

Orgeluse remains unimpressed. She knows of his battles with the Bed and Lion, yet she ridicules Gawan's damaged shield and says he is obviously too weak to go into the combat to which she would send him. "I thumb my nose at you," she says.[36] He replies that just seeing her has helped him grow stronger and that indeed he will go and fight for her. She accepts and they ride off, even as the ladies in the castle weep for him.

To win her praise, Orgeluse tells Gawan, he must get a wreath for her from the branch of a tree in Clinschor's forest. If he does this, she says, he may ask for her love. The tree is in a ravine and is guarded by "a man who robbed me of my joy."[37] When they reach the ravine, Orgeluse points to a tree on the other side and tells Gawan he must make his horse jump across the perilous waterfall that has formed the ravine. "May God watch over your fortunes,"[38] she adds and then waits to see how he accomplishes the task she has given him.

Gawan rides to the ravine and urges his horse to jump Li gweiz prelljus. Gringuljete only manages to get two feet on the opposite rim, so horse and rider fall into the thundering water. At this, Orgeluse bursts into tears. Still holding onto his spear but sinking under the weight of his armor, Gawan struggles in the water until he finally grabs a tree branch and pulls himself ashore. Gringuljete has a harder time of it and is being swept downstream. Though hampered by heavy armor and his many unhealed wounds, Gawan is yet able to help the horse, thanks to a whirlpool and a split in the shore which allows him to use his spear to guide Gringuljete close enough that he can catch the bridle.

Remounted and arriving finally at the designated tree, Gawan plucks the wreath from the branch and sets it on his helmet. Just then a knight approaches. It is Gramoflanz, a knight so bold that he has vowed never to fight just one man; there must always be at least two. He announces this to Gawan along with his refusal to renounce his claim to the wreath. Gramoflanz wears a hat of peacock plumes and is unarmed, carrying only a falcon on his hand — a bird that has been sent to him by Itonje, Gawan's sister.

Gramoflanz notices the condition of Gawan's shield and deduces that he has endured the trial of the Wonder Bed. He tells Gawan that might have been his own fate, were he not favored by Clinschor. As it is, he is at war with Orgeluse, whose husband he killed. Gramoflanz then held Orgeluse prisoner for a year, but she continued to refuse him her love. Now his heart longs for another. Although he has never seen Itonje, Gramoflanz yearns for her and asks Gawan to take her a small gold ring. He repeats that if Gawan were in the company of another, he would have to fight him, but to fight him alone would be a disgrace.

Gawan says that there is no great honor for him either in taking the wreath from an unarmed man. He agrees to carry Gramoflanz's message of love to Itonje and to give her the ring. He then asks Gramoflanz to identify himself.

Gramoflanz introduces himself and his lineage, saying that he has vowed never to fight only one man unless that man happens to bear the name of Gawan. This is because Gawan's father, Lot, slew his father and he wants revenge. Gawan responds, with some irony, that Gramoflanz's petition to Itonje will not go easily since he slanders her father and seeks to kill her brother. Then he tells Gramoflanz his name and says he is ready to defend both himself and his father's name.

Instead, Gramoflanz proposes that they joust in sixteen days and says that he himself will bring fifteen hundred ladies to watch. After all, it is an honor for Gawan that he, Gramoflanz, deigns to fight with him alone, and he reminds Gawan that his audience can be the company from the Castle of Wonders as well as Arthur's court, if he sends for them. As they prepare to part, he suggests that Gawan ride with him to a town downstream where he can cross the river by bridge, but Gawan prefers to "go back the way I came"[39] and this time Gringuljete, spurred on by Gawan with the wreath on his helmet, clears the jump with no difficulty.

Once he is back, Orgeluse throws herself gratefully at his feet, declaring, "Your peril and distress do indeed cause me such anguish of heart as a loving woman must feel for her beloved lover."[40] Gawan accepts her prostrations, offers her the wreath and enjoins her never again to "use your shining beauty to bring such dishonor on any knight. If I must endure your mockery, I would rather be without love."[41] Weeping, she then tells him her story; how her beloved husband, Cidegast, was killed and what an honorable person he was. "My words did wound you," she explains, "but they were simply meant to test you. . . . I would compare you with gold. As it is refined in the glowing fire, so your courage has been refined."[42] Then she asks his forgiveness.

Gawan says that he has forgiven her and that, even more, he has agreed to meet Gramoflanz, her husband's slayer, in battle. He is so overjoyed at her change of heart that he asks her to grant him her favor there and then. "You see there is no one here but us."[43] She responds, "In an ironclad arm I have seldom gotten warm,"[44] but says that if he will wait for some other time to request her reward for his service, then she certainly will not resist.

He pulls her up with him on his horse, holding her close, and they ride to the Castle of Wonders. She is weeping so much that he too grows sad and asks her the cause of her sorrow. She relates the rest of her story, telling him that, after Cidegast's death, she sought to have Gramoflanz killed, no matter what the cost. She sought the service of many knights and finally even won the heart of Anfortas. It was he who gave her the rich trader's booth standing near the entrance to the Castle of Wonders. However, while serving her, Anfortas was grievously wounded, and this doubled her anguish, since Anfortas still lies so helpless on account of her.

Meanwhile, Clinschor coveted the wealth of the trader's booth. To appease him and avoid his black magic, Orgeluse gave it to him, on the condition that if any knight withstood the adventure in the Castle

Merveil, thus winning both castle and treasure, she was to seek that knight's love. If he refused her, then the treasure would be hers again. Thus, the treasure now belongs to them both.

It happened that every day of the year she managed to send some knight to look for Gramoflanz and never was he defeated. Some served her for pay, but others, already wealthy, served her for love, though she did not promise them any reward. Only one had come who had refused her offer of love. A knight named Parzival, dressed all in red armor, defeated five of her knights but, when she offered herself to him, he declined, saying he already had a beautiful wife whom he loved dearly. "The Grail causes me grief enough," he had said.[45]

Orgeluse asks if Gawan thinks less of her for offering herself to Parzival. Gawan assures her that he knows Parzival well and that certainly he does not think less of her. Then he asks her to keep his own identity a secret at the castle, and she agrees.

An armed host rides out to meet them from the castle, and Gawan wonders if they are going to attack. Orgeluse reassures him that these are Clinschor's former knights coming to welcome him. At the river, the ferryman and his daughter are waiting. During the crossing, the two lovers feast on larks and bread, gazing at one another all the while. Gawan's heart soars with joy.

At Orgeluse's request, Gawan ransoms the Turkoite and the other knight, Lischois, from the ferryman, and frees them. In exchange, the ferryman requests and is granted a harp that Anfortas had received from Queen Secundille and given to Orgeluse. At the castle, Gawan has his wounds tended and then, swearing a squire to secrecy, sends a letter to Arthur inviting him to the joust in sixteen days. He orders the squire not to tell anyone that Gawan is at the Castle of Wonders. Arnive intercepts the squire as he is leaving the castle and tries to find out his destination and mission, but the squire keeps his oath and departs for Arthur's court.

Initiatory Themes

Two vertical images form mileposts in this phase of Gawan's journey. The "seeing" pillar in the Castle of Wonders extends Gawan's powers of perception; in possession of it, he will, from now on, always have a much broader view than was possible in the past. It belonged to Queen Secundille and was fashioned by sorcerers, yet, for all its marvelous attributes, the pillar has earthly origins. It cannot compare in significance with the other vertical image, the tree, whose divine origins are celebrated in myths from many places. This tree, with its ever-blooming wreath,[46] also belongs to a queen: to Orgeluse, Queen of Life. In leaping across the raging waters, Gawan has returned the goddess to the tree that once belonged to her in that first Garden.[47] He has, in other words, reunited the horizontal plane of the earthly world with the vertical plane of the heavenly realm. From this point on, Gawan's work becomes reunification of all those who have been painfully separated.

Uniting the horizontal and vertical dimensions, marrying female and male, entails a perilous leap. The person who dares it must be prepared for a heart-wrenching plunge into the depths. Earlier, Gawan would not have succeeded, as indicated by the incident when the Grail templar accosts Parzival and the horse he won at Bearosche, which was Gawan's, plummets into a ravine and is killed. Now, in the leap across Li gweiz prelljus, Gawan is strong enough to save both himself and his horse. The leap is not picture-perfect, letting us know once again that Wolfram is imagining no perfect hero. Nonetheless, Gawan stays loyal to his intention — to love and serve Orgeluse by retrieving the wreath — and keeps going despite arduous difficulties.

Once he has made the connection with the tree, thereby linking the horizontal and vertical planes, he makes the leap back across the ravine with more ease. Gawan can see beyond his immediate desire now. He is able, as James Hillman puts it, "to desire and to see through desire (which) is the courage the heart requires."[48]

This tempered courage comes through honoring the heart, not through possessing the persons or objects that claim its desires. When desire and its object are indistinguishable, one "burns" and therefore obliterates the gentle pulse that is the heart's true way. The quality of the heart is not rock solid nor mechanically incessant, but pliably soft and reassuringly rhythmic. Robert Sardello comments that the heart hesitates briefly before the next beat; it stops for a split second before going on because with "a mind of its own"[49] it knows that "the key to regeneration lies in the moment of uncertainty," in that "ever-present gap"[50] which remains open to the unknown even as it is bridged by every next beat.

What Gawan and the initiate-speaker have strengthened in themselves by listening to the heart ("the only organ that can be

continually heard"!⁵¹) is the ability to make the leap which it makes
— that leap which is the essence of any truly creative, and therefore
any truly erotic, act. And it is not only humans but gods also who
leap, thereby creating and rejuvenating the earth. In ancient Crete,
the Kouretes, male youths leaping in ceremonial dance, called out
to their god: "To us also leap for full jars, and leap for fleecy flocks,
and leap for fields of fruit, and for hives to bring increase."⁵² H.G.
Baynes claims that, not much later, the Greeks perceived in mischie-
vous Eros and his arrows

> . . . the divine (i.e. creative) shaft which leaps across the guarded
> frontier of the subject in order to reach the object. The creative shaft
> is the impregnating phallus, the impressive, fertilizing image, the
> creative word, the idea which gets home, the divine leap by which
> the individual subject is able to transcend his own subjectivity and
> take an effective part in the work of creation. This is Eros, the god
> which bringeth twain together in the service of life.⁵³

As we have seen, Gawan is no stranger to Eros and serves the
Queen of Life. His leap and retrieval of the wreath mark a turning
point when many things will start to come full circle. When he
returns, Gawan carries two circles; he bears the wreath for Orgeluse
and a ring for Itonje, given to him by Gramoflanz who, in the topsy-
turvy world of Clinschor's forest, both challenges Gawan to deadly
battle and asks him to convey his sentiments to his lady love.

When he meets Gawan, Gramoflanz wears the peacock's feathers
on his hat and bears a falcon, a gift from Itonje, on his wrist. The peacock's feathers show him to be connected to Clinschor, for the roof at
Clinschor's castle radiates the bright hues of this bird's prideful display. Gramoflanz admits that he too would have had to bear the tur-
moil of the perilous bed if Clinschor was not so friendly to him. In
fact, Gramoflanz has been serving Clinschor, maybe unawares, by
keeping Orgeluse from her wreath and her tree and tormenting her
with his seeming invincibility. (We might remember that Anfortas's
hat sports peacock's feathers when Parzival first meets him at the
lake. This implies that Anfortas, too, was closer to Clinschor than to
the Grail. He and Gramoflanz, then, are both "false" kings: kings in
appearance — and title — but not in action and presence.)

The first result we notice, after Gawan's return with the wreath, is that Orgeluse has "returned" — to herself. No longer a mocking shrew, she presents herself gratefully to Gawan and professes her love for him. He is changed also. No longer a lovesick knight, he regains his dignity and, while forgiving her, declares he would forego her love rather than endure any further mockery. (He has, however, lost none of his spontaneity, proposing delightedly that they consummate their love then and there.)

But Gawan's time for full self-disclosure has not yet arrived. He asks Orgeluse to help keep his identity secret, even as her own is becoming less hidden. Like Herzeloyde, Belacane, Sigune and others, Orgeluse is a grieving widow. The growing warmth of her trust, which Gawan has won, evaporates her rage, and now the grief underlying it is revealed.

Who is this sorrowing widow who appears so often in this story, though in the guise of different women characters with various names? The ancient Egyptians called her Isis, though they knew she was the Goddess of Many Names.[54] This widow wanders through the world or retreats from it, both being strategies to survive the loss of someone who has meant almost more to her than life itself. In every case, her grief is only assuaged by a spirited man who yearns for the heights and has courage and skill enough to risk the depths to follow that yearning. The mystery, of course, is that this man — as many myths tell us — is always intimately related to her; her brother or her son is also her beloved, the one who is killed and also the one who reappears. The challenge for her is to maintain faith that the one who belongs to her will return.

Like Parzival, Orgeluse lost her faith. She then sought to force her way back to a sense of connection through revenge. Fierce in rage but weak in faith, she used her "shining beauty" to entrap knights into her service, and it was thus that Anfortas was wounded and the whole Grail world thrown into mourning. For this, she has suffered, even as she caused suffering. In pursuing her despite her mockery, in refusing to be intimidated by her loathsomeness, Gawan has freed her as fully as he has freed the other queens at the Castle of Wonders. Now he serves as her confessor, as Trevrizent did for Parzival, forgiving her and, at the same time, admonishing her to change her ways.

Only once had Orgeluse offered her love to anyone and that was to Parzival, who refused it. Parzival knew that love without faith, like a search for the Grail without faith, is futile and full of grief, and he said he already had enough of that. Besides, he had given his pledge to Condwiramurs. It takes Gawan and his ability to withstand all her tests to return Orgeluse to faith and faithfulness. He has accomplished this with the "leap of faith" — being faithful to himself, to her, and to God. The abandoned widow has become again a cherished beloved, so Gawan's work for Parzival must almost be complete.

Toward Speech of the Grail

The previous phase of the journey had the initiate-speaker practicing participatory poesis, restructuring a worldview through story. Now it seems that one must leap off into space, leave the careful crafting of an oral architecture and risk sinking in uncertainty. William Irwin Thompson reminds us though that "Any system, to be a living system, has to be a balance between the fixed and the fluid."[55] A living system of speech would be subject to the same principle: as soon as anything is "established," is habitual, the initiate-speaker must leap away from it — or life, and liveliness, will be left a widow. Rudolf Steiner therefore advised public speakers to avoid memorization (and storytellers can use the same advice):

> The worst thing you can do is select a theme, master the material by memorizing every word, and then give several speeches a week ... repeating the same speech over and over again. That is the worst method you can select. One can only cultivate the right sense of responsibility towards that which is carried in one's speaking when every address, subjectively speaking, is personally experienced as something new. Even if the same theme is treated thirty times, it is necessary that for the speaker there is always something new.[56]

Like Gawan, the initiate-speaker has to leap in two directions, and both leaps are a kind of listening. The speaker, like language, stands at the intersection of the manifest and unmanifest worlds, whether "unmanifest" refers to the unconscious, the spiritual domain or just to the unknown. If preconceptions, assumptions and the tendency to be judgmental have been sufficiently released, the initiate-speaker stands mostly in "not knowing." One can then listen into what wants to be said, for which one must leap toward the unmanifest, and into what can or must be said, for which one must leap toward the manifest, the social context. Both are difficult leaps, but, if accomplished, the speaker allows those two worlds to touch in and through the words. When this occurs, the sorrowing widow in both speaker and listeners smiles again, her faith revived.

But where does the initiate-speaker learn such leaping? What can strengthen and sharpen the imaginative, intuitive abilities that such leaping entails? One of the best places to practice is with mythology. If the fairy tale fosters a sense of harmonious containment, encouraging the ordering poesis of the initiate-speaker, myth proffers riddles, paradox, disorder — at least when viewed from a logical standpoint — and endless multiplicity. James Hillman says:

> Myth moves into meaning merely by taking one out of literal objectivities, and the place to which myth carries one is not even a central meaning, or the center of meaning where things are supposed to feel certain. Instead, we hover in puzzlement at the border where the true depths are. Rather than an increase of certainty there is a spread of mystery which is both the precondition and the consequence of revelation.[57]

If the fairy tale presents an orderly world where everything is related to everything else, myth presents a jumbled world where everything seems to be happening at once.[58] If the fairy tale reassures, myth shakes us up, asks us to reorganize. If the fairy tale seems moral, myth seems amoral or premoral. The gods do not play by human rules. And, very often, a mythology includes a Trickster who does not even play, consistently, by the gods' rules.

Playing by the rules, human or divine, evokes the image of play, and, in general, myth often evidences a playful quality not found in the more somber fairy tale. Play and playfulness call for leaping. So it is understandable that Gawan becomes quite playful at this juncture in the story, beginning games of hide-and-seek with Arnive and Arthur. Leaping makes one more playful; playfulness requires leaping.

After examining numerous ethnographic accounts, cultural historian Johan Huizinga, in his seminal study of play in culture, doubted that the great ritual enactments of myth in tribal societies were performed with a completely literal understanding.[59] Even among traditional peoples celebrating their most sacred stories, an "as if" quality suffuses their participation, resulting in a "lightness" and sense of humor often lacking in the ceremonies of more "advanced" religions. The initiate-speaker meeting mythology in the late twentieth century leaps into the world of myth with the same "as if" attitude that children exemplify in their games, although for Western speakers this may be easier if the mythology is, at first, not Judeo-Christian.

Myths are sacred stories revealing, through their images and motifs, the way our ancestors, in a particular time and place, expressed their experience of the spiritual world. To learn anything from myth, one has to be willing to encounter myth on these terms. As Mircea Eliade declares, "Myths are the most general and effective means of awakening and maintaining consciousness of another world, a beyond, whether it be the divine world or the world of the Ancestors."[60] If one is willing to enter the mythic narrative "as if" one believes there is value in what it has to say, then one can experience the myth's way of telling. When one has seen and heard what the myth has to show and tell, one can return with the life-giving images just as Gawan returns with the wreath.

The initiate-speaker returns with even more, however. In the leaping — that is, acting-as-if one believes — faith is renewed. The proof is the transformation of Orgeluse. David Miller tells us:

> The point is simple, as simple as the wisdom of a playful child. Faith is being gripped by a story, by a vision, by a ritual (game). It is being seized, being gripped by a pattern of meaning, a pattern of meaning that affects one's life-pattern, that becomes a paradigm for the way one sees the world. It is not belief. These kids do not believe in this business, at least they do not believe in thoughtful reflection when the mind's light is on. . . . Belief is beside the point. Faith is not belief. It is not intellectual assent. It is not some ritual played *so that* something will happen. Faith is being turned on by an incredible vision. It is make believe.[61]

It is impossible to play seriously with a sacred story and not have it change one's life, change one's seeing, listening, experiencing and understanding. Spiritual teachers have long known this and have instructed their disciples through highly refined narratives that demand leaping to new ways of seeing and listening, of imagining and intuiting. Sufi, Zen and Hasidic masters employ these succinct stories for their students to contemplate and chew on until they can leap beyond ordinary thinking to a deeper, intuitive understanding of spiritual principles. Here the harvest is not specific images but intuitive understanding. The initiate-speaker can learn much in and from these teaching stories as well.

Playing in myth and story, the initiate-speaker learns a mode of mythic imagining that requires "leaps." Robert Bly has explored this idea and notices that leaping in language is

> . . . the ability to associate fast. In a great ancient or modern poem the considerable distance between associations, the distance the spark has to leap, gives the lines their bottomless feeling, their space, and the speed of association increases the excitement of the poetry.[62]

To be able to make such leaps, initiate-speakers will have to be strengthened, like Gawan, in their courage to confront uncertainty, to tolerate that bottomless feeling. Evidence of this courage will be an increasing willingness to speak out of the unknown, extemporaneously, and to speak more from one's questions than one's always provisional answers. "Not knowing is an Eros moment," says Russell Lockhart[63] and, as we have seen, when that god is present, arrows begin to fly, leaps are made. Facts and information become, for the initiate-speaker, only fuel for speech. The fire comes from the leaping forth, the daring to leave one's sure footing in facts and reach for the ever-blooming wreath on the Tree of Life across the abyss of the unknown.[64]

The word "tree" has the same etymological root as "truth,"[65] and, of course, this is what the initiate-speaker is reaching and leaping toward. But truth here is not fact or thing. It is closer to what is meant by the Greek word *aleithia,* "unhiddenness." As we have learned from our own hearts, sustaining the leaping beat and keeping it rhythmical includes uncertainty, the moment of bottomless space in between. Therefore unhiddenness, "truthing," will never be complete or finished. New levels and depths are always being disclosed by new leaps. We see in Gawan, Orgeluse and Gramoflanz

increasing clarity, or unhiddenness, in who they are. Gawan's leaping allows more and more of them to be revealed, and this unveiling
theme continues in the next episode.

Skillful now in "leaping" — speaking and disclosing truth
through playful, poetic and mythically imagined metaphors — the
initiate-speaker has traversed many of the phases in the initiation.
One's speech is becoming more beautiful and more compelling, and
thus it is increasingly necessary for one to guard against any temptation to use the shining beauty of such speech to entrap or manipulate others. Wounds caused by speech used for personal ends, for
seduction or power, no matter how subtle, will be long lasting and
difficult to heal. Georg Kühlewind points out that

> Nearly all the myths and popular traditions on earth tell of the heav-
> enly, divine origin of language. . . . To talk nonsense — speaking to
> kill time or to say something worthless — is just as unnatural, from
> this perspective, as speaking in order to lie, in order to hide one's
> own intentions, or in order to mislead others. Man causes most of
> the evil in the world, even when it hurts his human dignity, by
> means of language. It is a deep truth that when language is deca-
> dent, mankind is in danger.
>
> It should come as no surprise, then, that *right speech* is seen as
> one of the fundamental measures in the health of the soul. Unright
> speech mostly harms the person who uses it, not his interlocutor."[66]

This means that the initiate-speaker's sense of responsibility in
speaking must be refined to the same degree as his or her ability to
speak. There is no exact list of rules or code of ethics to define such
responsibility. It emerges from an exquisite and disciplined honesty
about oneself and an attentive attunement to the effect of one's speaking on whoever is spoken to. Rudolf Steiner surmised that an indication a speaker is on the right track is a certain reluctance to speak,
even a distaste for one's own speaking.[67]

Responsible speaking, though often metaphoric and sometimes
even poetic, will tend to be plain, rather than fancy, thought-pro-
voking rather than inspiring. The intention is not to inflame the listener's emotions through sentimentality or grandiosity but to open a
space, to dispel the sorcery of ignorance, disease, despair, vengeance
or victimization. The initiate-speaker invites the captives to walk
out of such prisons and take a new path. The speech that heals is

the speech that frees. The leap is made to help others return to themselves and then to make their own leaps, without defining what kind of leap should be made or where or when.

Wolfram enlists another bird to show that Gawan and the initiate-speaker are guarding against any tendency to misuse the poetical, leaping powers that are now theirs. It appears in the image of the harp that Anfortas gave Orgeluse, which the ferryman requests in exchange for Orgeluse's two knights. The German word for this harp is *swalwe* which means both "harp" and "swallow."[68] In the later German legend of Tristan and Isolde, a harp called "the swallow" helps Tristan find Isolde, after a swallow has borne one of her golden hairs to his uncle's court. Since that legend refers to Gawan as a friend of Tristan's, Walter Johannes Stein contends that Orgeluse's harp must be the one which eventually belongs to Tristan, who "possessed linguistic and musical talents to an unusual degree and familiarized himself with musicality of every kind — language, song, stringed music."[69]

Tristan's gifts of poetic song are a kind of flight that bridges the worlds, and his instrument, in the shape of a swallow's wing, has the same name as the sacred bird whose name in Hebrew derives from a root meaning "to release." Thought to be divine in the ancient Mediterranean world, swallows were allowed to fly unharmed in the temples. Those sources reported as well that the swallow, "unlike many other songbirds, does not thrive in captivity."[70] The *Egyptian Book of the Dead* follows suit by advising the soul of the deceased to transform into a swallow; once transformed, the soul joyfully sings "I have gained the mastery over my footsteps before the God of Light."[71]

With its subtle persuasive voice, the harp, like human speech, can release the human heart from heavy care to the swallow's hallowed flight. It all depends, however, on whom the harp or speech serves. Orgeluse and Gawan place this powerful instrument in the hands of the humble ferryman, who has already pledged that he and his daughter were born to serve Gawan. Therefore, the harp does not serve either the personal pleasure or purposes of Gawan — or the initiate-speaker — but instead is given over to its own highest purpose, which is to set free the captured knights. Not known for leaping into wild escapades, the ferryman patiently rows from shore to shore, and yet, in his possession, the harp soars to its truest song.

The choice to give the harp to the ferryman is the first that Gawan and Orgeluse make together, and it foreshadows the gift which their union is for the world. In their coming together, they free others to come together, and the formation of all these circles is what will call Parzival back to Arthur's court.

NOTES

[1] Wolfram, Book XI, 553.

[2] Wolfram, Book XI, 553.

[3] Wolfram, Book XI, 556.

[4] Wolfram, Book XI, 556.

[5] Wolfram, Book XI, 558.

[6] Wolfram, Book XI, 559.

[7] Wolfram, Book XI, 562.

[8] Wolfram, Book XI, 565.

[9] Wolfram, Book XI, 566.

[10] Wolfram, Book XI, 567.

[11] Wolfram, Book XI, 577.

[12] Walter Johannes Stein (*The Ninth Century and the Holy Grail,* 123) suggests this idea but does not detail the contrasts.

[13] Wolfram, Book XI, 567.

[14] For another interpretation of the Wonder Bed and the Lion, see Stein, *The Ninth Century and the Holy Grail,* 177–80. Stein determines, from his knowledge of alchemical writings, that Gawan should have mounted the Lion. Since he killed it, he himself is injured almost to the point of death.

[15] Morris Berman, *The Reenchantment of the World,* 2.

[16] Berman, 146.

[17] Berman, 38.

[18] Berman, 144.

[19] Berman, 55.

[20] Russell Lockhart, *Words as Eggs: Psyche in Language and Clinic,* 116.

[21] According to Robert Sardello in *Facing the World with Soul*, "All of these women form repetitive images of Sophia — mother, lover, bride of the world. . . . This story informs us that the point of seeking the soul of the world is in the seeking, in paying attention to what is abandoned" (18).

[22] Marie-Louise von Franz, *The Feminine in Fairy Tales*, 182–83. I also refer the reader to Robert Bly's piquant study *A Little Book on the Human Shadow*.

[23] James Hillman, *Healing Fiction*, 4.

[24] Martin Heidegger, *Poetry, Language, Thought*, 216.

[25] Heidegger, 215.

[26] Denise Levertov, *The Poet in the World*, 205.

[27] Max Luthi, *Once Upon a Time: On the Nature of Fairy Tales*, 76.

[28] Luthi, 52.

[29] Luthi, 94.

[30] Ursula Grahl, *The Wisdom in Fairy Tales*, 32.

[31] Levertov, 54–55.

[32] Rilke puts it this way, toward the end of No. 1 of "Sonnets to Orpheus," quoted in Robert Bly, *Selected Poems of Rainer Maria Rilke*, 195:

> Growling, yelping, grunting now
> seemed all nonsense to them. And where before
> there was hardly a shed where this listening could go,
> a rough shelter put up out of brushy longings,
> with an entrance gate whose poles were wobbly,
> you created a temple for them deep inside their ears.

[33] William Stafford, *An Oregon Message*, 79.

[34] The comparison can be substantiated. One of the "continuations" of Chrétien de Troyes's unfinished *Perceval*, entitled "The Elucidation" (possibly written about 1230 A.D.) was written to be an explanatory preface to Chrétien's Grail poem. "The Elucidation" reports that the Grail country was devastated because the maidens who were the voices and beings of the wells had been raped and their golden goblets (from which they nourished all travelers) stolen by the king and his knights who were supposed to protect them. Now the withered land can be made fruitful again only by the Knights of the Round Table finding the Court of the Rich Fisherman, who is a shapeshifter, and asking the right questions. For the full story, see Caitlin Matthews, *Arthur and the Sovereignty of Britain*, 250–51. Additionally, Joseph Campbell in *The Masks of God* says: "For psychologically, as well

as mythologically, the sense of such a female by a spring is of an apparition of the abyss: psychologically, the unconscious; mythologically, the Land below Waves, Hell, Purgatory or Heaven. She is a portion of oneself, one's destiny, or, as Schopenhauer states in his meditation on Fate, one's secret intention for oneself" (489).

[35] Wolfram, Book XII, 589

[36] Wolfram, Book XII, 599.

[37] Wolfram, Book XII, 601

[38] Wolfram, Book XII, 602.

[39] Wolfram, Book XII, 610.

[40] Wolfram, Book XII, 611.

[41] Wolfram, Book XII, 612.

[42] Wolfram, Book XII, 614.

[43] Wolfram, Book XII, 615.

44 Wolfram, Book XII, 615.

45 Wolfram, Book XII, 619.

[46] It seems that when one wreath is taken, another replaces it. In Book XIV, Parzival reappears with a wreath on his helmet that is the same as the one Gawan retrieved, causing Gawan to mistake him for Gramoflanz.

[47] Kim Chernin, in *Reinventing Eve*, verifies that the goddess and the tree originally belong together in many traditions: "In other mythic traditions from the ancient world the apple tree in the garden belongs to a goddess. In Avalon, 'apple-land,' the Celtic queen of the dead was kept busy handing out apples to Irish kings. . . . Idun, goddess of apple-land in Norse mythology, fed the gods her magic apples to keep them from dying. Gaea, the earth goddess of the Greeks brought a tree bearing golden apples to the wedding of Hera and Zeus. The tree was planted in the garden of the Hesperides and guarded by Ladon, the watchful dragon" (xviii). I would include Inanna, the ancient Sumerian goddess, and her "huluppu" tree (see Diane Wolkstein and Stanley Noah Kramer, *Inanna: Queen of Heaven and Earth*, 4–9) and the Egyptian Isis, who finds her brother-husband, Osiris, encased in a tree in Byblos.

[48] James Hillman, "The Thought of the Heart," *Eranos Lectures* 2, 9.

[49] Sardello, *Facing the World with Soul*: "While the rhythm of the heart requires stimulation, it does not rely on the brain. The wave that starts and

keeps the heart beating comes from a tiny bundle of tissue in the right atrium, the sinoatrial node, the pacemaker of the heart. The heart has a mind of its own; it knows what to do without orders from above, just as someone who knows what is in her heart does not require directions concerning what to do and how to act" (76).

[50] Sardello, 79.

[51] Sardello, 77.

[52] Jessie Weston, *From Ritual to Romance*, 87–88.

[53] H.G. Baynes, *Mythology of the Soul*, 132, quoted in Russell A. Lockhart, *Psyche Speaks*, 22.

[54] Diane Wolkstein, *The First Love Stories*, 24.

[55] David Spangler and William Irwin Thompson, *Reimagination of the World: A Critique of the New Age, Science and Popular Culture*, 169.

[56] Werner Glas, *An Analytical Study of the Rhetorical Thought of Rudolf Steiner with Some Implications for the Teaching of Speech*, 173.

[57] James Hillman, *Re-Visioning Psychology*, 142. The interpretations of myth are multiple too. Each interpreter utilizes a different mode (e.g., psychological, anthropological, literary, etc., and there are even "schools" within each of these) and constructs a different coherence from the pieces of myth that come to us from antiquity. Marie-Louise von Franz suggests that "we interpret for the same reason as that for which fairy tales and myths were told: because it has a vivifying effect and gives a satisfactory reaction and brings one into peace with one's unconscious instinctive substratum, just as fairy tales always did. Psychological interpretation is our way of telling stories" (*The Interpretation of Fairy Tales*, 32).

[58] We mostly inherit "pieces" of myths; the few complete narratives have been pieced together from ancient oral sources and we lack the original rites of enactment, the cultus, in which myth was embedded and from which it drew its "life."

[59] Johan Huizinga, *Homo Ludens: A Study of the Play Element in Culture*, 22.

[60] Wendell C. Beane and William G. Doty, *Myths, Rites, Symbols: A Mircea Eliade Reader*, 7.

[61] David Miller, *Gods and Games: Toward a Theology of Play*, 168.

[62] Robert Bly, *Leaping Poetry: An Idea with Poems and Translations*, 4.

[63] Lockhart, *Psyche Speaks*, 45.

64 What is ever-blooming on that Tree of Life, as Jewish Kabbalists knew, is the alphabet. See Anna Morduch, *The Sovereign Adventure:* "The tree of life is built upon a system of one, three and ten. It consists of three triangles and three pillars connecting the ten *sephirot* or lights, which again are interconnected by crossing lines which are called paths and correspond with the letters of the alphabet"(80–83).

65 Lockhart, *Psyche Speaks,* 18.

66 Georg Kühlewind, *From Normal to Healthy: Paths to the Liberation of Consciousness,* 100.

67 Glas quotes Steiner: "A good speaker really always has to endure a certain reluctance when he is to speak. He must clearly feel this reluctance. Above all, he should much prefer listening to another speaker, even the worst, to speaking himself. . . . It is really through listening that one becomes a speaker, not through love of speaking oneself. . . . [O]ne acquires a strong feeling of distaste for one's own speaking. And this distaste for one's own speaking is actually what enables one in fact to speak adequately" (179).

68 Wolfram, Mustard and Passage, translation, 328.

69 Walter Johannes Stein, *The Death of Merlin: Arthurian Myth and Alchemy,* 200.

70 Beryl Rowland, *Birds with Human Souls,* 164.

71 Stein, *The Death of Merlin,* 214.

CHAPTER SEVEN

"See How Rich I Am . . .
It Is Myself I Have Vanquished"

The Grail King Speaks

Let those within speak
And dance with each other.
Play at performance,
Aspiring to transparency.
And, if Pride appears,
Sort him out,
Appreciate his distinction,
Then marry him to heart's discipline
Which serves the speaking Presence
Who returns the listening Speaker
To the community
In true form.

BOOK XIII

After returning with Orgeluse to the Castle of Wonders and sending the messenger to Arthur, Gawan sleeps until evening. He awakens in time for the great feast that has been prepared, taking care to see that Orgeluse's two knights, Lischois and the Turkoite, are as richly dressed for the occasion as he. The three then go to meet Orgeluse, the four queens (Arnive, Sangive, Itonje and Cundrie) and the hundreds of knights and ladies of the castle.

At Gawan's request, Bene, the ferryman's daughter, points out Itonje, whom Bene lovingly serves by taking her tokens and messages to Gramoflanz. Gawan sits with his young sister, who does not know she speaks with her own brother, to find out if she does indeed love Gramoflanz. Blushing, she responds to his courteous inquiries, and confesses she loves the knight and gave him the ring which Gawan holds in his hand. She admits she feels like a traitor to Gramoflanz, sitting here with Orgeluse, Lischois, and the Turkoite, and yet begs Gawan not to tell her secret to anyone. She also asks him to help her and Gramoflanz.

Hundreds of knights and ladies enter the great hall and take their places for the feast — men on one side and ladies on the other. Lavish food is served with ceremony, but the greatest happiness is that now the knights and ladies may speak with one another.

> Clinschor's power had overcome them with his arts, they had remained unknown to each other, though a single gate closed them in, and had never exchanged a word with each other, the ladies and the men. My lord Gawan gave the order that this company should meet, and they were very pleased. . . .[1]

When the food is cleared away, Gawan calls for fiddlers, and the knights mingle among the ladies. At first reserved and shy, but with increasing ease and joy, couples form and begin to dance. Gawan and Orgeluse hold hands and watch the gladness spread through the room. Arnive reminds Gawan that he is still recuperating and asks if Orgeluse will watch over him as he sleeps. He replies, "Ask her," and Orgeluse answers that of course she will.

After Gawan has called for the drink that culminates the evening, he and Orgeluse retire to their chamber. Finally, the moment has arrived for which Gawan has been waiting. Via some elaborate indirection, Wolfram tells us that Gawan "found the proper herb"[2] for his healing, exchanging "bitter need for sweet delight"[3] during that night with Orgeluse, which greatly quickened his recovery. In the medieval world, where the consummation often preceded the official ceremony, this means they are now married.

Meanwhile, Gawan's squire has reached Arthur's court. Having first told Ginover of his mission, he is instructed by her how to bring the message to the court, as if he had not spoken to her first. She tells the squire it has been four-and-one-half years and six weeks since "the Table Round was broken with angry words"[4] of Cundrie *la sorcière* and Gawan and Parzival departed. Arthur is overjoyed to hear from Gawan but also outraged that Gramoflanz has charged Gawan's father with murder. He agrees at once to bring the knights to witness Gawan's joust and asks Ginover to prevail upon the ladies to join them. Keie, the irritable seneschal, grumbles about their having to inconvenience themselves to chase around after Gawan.

Meanwhile, Arnive is angry that neither the squire sent to Arthur as Gawan's messenger nor Orgeluse have satisfied her questions about Gawan. Even though detained by the watchman she posted to tell her of his return, the squire again refuses to answer her questions and then goes to Gawan who is pleased to hear Arthur's reply.

Some days later, Gawan sits with Arnive, whom he calls Lady of Healing, and asks her to tell him more about Clinschor. She explains that Clinschor was renowned in his land, Italy, until he had an affair with a woman whose husband found them in bed and castrated Clinschor on the spot. Because he was "smooth between the legs," Clinschor "became a mock of the world."[5] Gawan laughs aloud at this report and then hears how Clinschor became so bitter that he could only find pleasure in robbing people of their joy, particularly people who are honored and respected.

For all its splendor, the Castle of Wonders is small compared with Clinschor's holdings in many other lands, Arnive says. A local king gave him the site in exchange for Clinschor's promise to leave him in peace. The Castle is well enough supplied to hold out for thirty years if besieged, and all the spirits of the place are commanded by Clinschor, except those protected by God. However, Clinschor —"a man of his word"[6] — declared that any knight who withstood the perils would win the Castle, its inhabitants and the surrounding lands and that he, Clinschor, would trouble them no further.

Arnive tells Gawan that many Christian and heathen people have been held captive here and urges him to release them. She also refers obliquely to her own identity as a queen and avers that she has never mistreated anyone, yet she has been held captive here. Gawan promises her she will soon be happy once more.

That day Arthur's army arrives, prompting grateful tears of relief to spurt from Gawan's eyes. Arnive counsels him not to be perturbed but glad, for this is not an invading army but rather Orgeluse's company. Gawan does not let on that he knows very well whose army it is and what they have come for. He tells the ferryman, through Bene, to tie the boats on the castle side of the river so no one from Arthur's court can cross the river yet. He asks the castle inhabitants to swear that they will fight with him if this army attacks them, and, when they agree, he showers them with gifts, as if he were about to die. Orgeluse, meanwhile, realizes that this cannot be her army but that it must have fought her army on the way, which Arthur later confirms.

Gawan could clear up all this confusion by announcing it is Arthur's army, whom he has sent for. Instead, he oversees preparations for an elaborate parade so he can show everyone "how rich I am."[7] Now, the ferryman busily conveys people and equipment across the river, and Gawan's luxurious tent — formerly belonging to Clinschor — is set up. Finally, Gawan, Orgeluse, the queens, and all the knights and ladies parade through Arthur's circle of tents, forming at last a large circle around the whole camp. Then, mounted on his charger, Arthur rides all around the ring of ladies with knights beside them.

When Gawan, Orgeluse and the four queens are finally seated in Arthur's tent, Arthur asks Gawan to introduce him to the ladies. Gawan courteously presents Arnive, Arthur's mother, and Sangive, his own mother, and his two sisters. When Gawan introduces Orgeluse, Arthur tells about the losses he incurred when they met her army and about the captives still held there. Gawan speaks accurately when he comments that Arthur "could be a kind of widow yourself,"[8] because numerous knights died in the fighting.

With Arthur's agreement, Orgeluse's army is summoned to join the company already on the plain, composing an impressive assembly. Keie, the seneschal, complains that Gawan seems to be trying to "shame us" by setting up so splendid a camp apart from the court and makes some sarcastic comments about Gawan's failure to avenge Parzival's breaking his arm those many years ago. But none of his criticism diminishes the excitement attending the arrival of Orgeluse's army, and Gawan goes to greet personally each of the knights from many lands who have fought in her service.

Meanwhile, Arthur has sent a message to Gramoflanz notifying him about the gathering on the plain and informing him that they are ready if he still desires a joust with Gawan. Gawan secrets himself in his room to prepare his arms and to see if his wounds are bound well enough. Then he rides out away from the army, giving Gringuljete free rein while he loosens up and practices for the joust ahead. It comes sooner than he thinks, for there on the river bank, out of sight of the armies, he meets a well armed knight set for battle.

Initiatory Themes

Preparations for the great joust that never happens occupy most of two episodes. Yet, all the while that the upcoming fight has the court's attention, marriage and reunification are the actual events. Gawan is now king of this realm, but being on the horizontal plane of *this* world where Clinschor has established his rule, slippery appearances still make it difficult to determine who is who and what is actually happening.

The first of the two episodes abounds with circles, and circles within circles. Gawan transports the ring to Itonje; Ginover rejoices over the mending of the circle of the Round Table, which had been broken almost five years before; and Arnive, Sangive and Sangive's daughters are returned to the circle of their family. The knights and ladies circle on the dance floor at the Castle of Wonders, then they all form a circle around the circle of Arthur's encampment and are, in turn, circled by Arthur mounted on his charger. Notice that the circles within circles are no longer inner and outer armies poised for combat — as in earlier episodes — but now are men and women, partnered like dancers circling up for an elegant waltz.

Circuitous secrecy also characterizes this episode. Gawan becomes more deeply enmeshed in Itonje's romance with Gramoflanz, and she begs him not to tell anyone. He, meanwhile, has not yet revealed his identity to the people at the Castle of Wonders and does not let them know that the army gathered on the plain outside is Arthur's. The indirection also infects his messenger, who goes first to Ginover and then is instructed to bear Gawan's message to the court as if he had not come to her first.

The marriage of Gawan and Orgeluse reassembles the sociocultural world, which, in Wolfram's story, is the court of Arthur and

Ginover and, in the initiate-speaker, is the conscious personality. Neither the court, nor one's personality, will come back together as it was before the dispersion; it will be altered by Gawan's new sovereignty and by the different personages he brings to the court.

True to his nature, Gawan, the "Hawk of May," is circling. He is not one who pierces right through the middle, like Parzival, but Parzival needs this containing circling, this framing of a target, so that he has a middle to pierce through. Without really knowing it, Gawan is preparing the court for Parzival's re-entry into the story. Like a swooping hawk, Gawan will know just the moment to "make an appearance." He keeps his behind-the-scenes secrets and prepares for a grand display of himself and his triumph. He conceals his old, familiar identity in order to reveal himself in his new identity, wanting others to see "how rich I am." He wants to show them the new powers that permit him to manage appearances now rather than just be subject to them.

Gawan's sovereignty, and the initiate-speaker's, manifests in the choice to create a ceremonial performance, a playful display of his new, rich self. Theater professor Richard Schechner confirms that Gawan has followed a time-honored pattern for reintegrating himself into his community:

> [T]he basic human plot is the same: someone begins to move to a new place in the social order; this move is accomplished through ritual, or blocked; in either case a crisis arises because any change in status involves a readjustment of the entire scheme; this readjustment is effected ceremonially — that is, by means of theater.[9]

How did Gawan know to do it this way? Why did he make this choice? Marie-Louise von Franz, out of her lifelong study of fairy tales, concludes that fairy-tale heroes always seem to know the "right" thing to do. Some of them "may just sit over the stove and yawn and apparently achieve nothing,"[10] but still wind up with the princess, while other heroes have to overcome giants, brigands, witches and all kinds of ordeals. No matter what the hero's path, the listeners participating with their feeling identify with it and intuitively learn that for any particular story, its hero's way was the right way to do it and that "this is the secret way in which to meet life."

This "rightness" could perhaps be better defined as being in complete accordance with the wholeness of the situation. . . . Thus no recipe is possible. You can only say that in this story it is obvious from the outcome that the hero did the right thing, though no one could have guessed what he had to do next, for what the hero does is always a surprise. Therefore this kind of getting at the right possibility is something much more primitive than an intellectually right attitude; it comes from the depths of the personality and is in accordance with the Self.[11]

The ceremonial performance Gawan orchestrates is not just empty, egotistical display. Anthropologist Victor Turner proposes, "If man is a sapient animal, a tool-making animal, a self-making animal, a symbol-using animal, he is, no less, a performing animal."[12] Thus performance is a kind of speaking and, like all uses of language, Turner would say, is "reflexive," which means that performance reveals the performers to themselves as well as to others.

In the ceremonial encircling, Gawan and the initiate-speaker are performing reflexively in both ways. Gawan experiences himself exercising new sovereignty and the community gets to know how it has been changed — quite literally expanded — through his efforts. Gawan returns to the court transformed, and his new attributes will be placed in the service of his community — for whom, in large part, he journeyed forth in the first place. (The knightly code he lives by guarantees, after all, the social cohesion of Arthur's kingdom.)

The circle Gawan forms offers the court an opportunity to see itself in a new context. His victory has opened the possibility for a new world but does not assure it. For that Gawan needs the participation of others, of those in the court — just as *they* need him to venture forth and return. "In this capacity of bringing forth a world, we are utterly incapable of doing it alone, for it requires others to enable us to be ourselves," William Irwin Thompson reminds us. A particularly relevant proof is that, though our language ability may be innate, human beings cannot bring forth language without others speaking it to them during infancy and young childhood.[13]

There are costs for Gawan's attempt to enlarge the context of his community. Arnive feels perplexed, irritable and anxious about her fate at the hands of this extraordinary but mysterious knight. And the losses incurred in the battle with Orgeluse's army leave Arthur something of a "widow." Since Gawan must have known the price in advance, he apparently thinks the reunion he intends is worth it.

"Both myth and science seem to agree on an ontology in which the universe is catastrophically transformative," William Irwin Thompson points out.[14] For something new to be born, a space must be opened — in the court and in the conscious personality of the initiate-speaker. This opening, felt initially as uncertainty or loss, is brought about here by the newest aspect of Gawan's enriched identity — his marriage with Orgeluse. First it is Orgeluse's army, the forces of the Goddess of Life, that has wreaked the damage on Arthur's army. Then it is Orgeluse's forces who are summoned to join Arthur's, augmenting the community which, just before, was beset by a sense of loss. (Maybe this is why the messenger has to go first to Ginover to announce Gawan's return. Since Gawan's Queen will enhance Arthur's realm, the Queen of Arthur's realm is the first one made aware of Gawan's return.)

Meanwhile, Gawan appears joyful, even jocular, as he circuitously circles homeward. Some people, including the initiate-speaker, may feel put off by his ostentatious display. Their objections are heard in Keie's grumbling about the attention Gawan receives and then about the separateness he is sure Gawan's display implies between Gawan and his old cronies. Such reactions always come from those who have forgotten the "play" in display. Having long ago abandoned the feathers and plumes of ceremonial tribal dances and the coats of arms and finely wrought armor of equally ceremonial jousts, we moderns reserve the role of display largely for the military, which parades its battle machinery in stiff, sober array, or for the Olympics, where play has been constrained into very serious sport.

Both play and display create new forms — sometimes to supplant the old ones. Display can be revolutionary, which is why the privileged and powerful prefer to control its expression. When those young African-American athletes raised their fists on the victory stand at the Mexico City Olympics, it was the display more than the gesture itself that provoked those who consider it their prerogative to determine who displays what, and how and when.

Keie is right. The court, and the initiate-speaker's conscious personality, are going to have to "move," to accommodate a new Gawan. Having achieved sovereignty in Clinschor's realm, he now has it to give, as empowerment, to Arthur's court — to the community of the initiate's conscious personality. The result will be a greater sense of differentiation within the community and within the initiate-speaker's conscious personality. Those who feel more comfortable without such differentiation will feel inconvenienced, even threatened, by a sense of separation.

Gawan and the initiate-speaker have taken pains — and risked causing pain — to create this performance because they are trying to bring forth a new world. The old world must be awakened from its lethargy, "moved" to a new place, and then apprised of what has changed in a way that allows it to maintain its self-respect — its integrity and coherence — at the same time that it is integrating the changes. Humor, playfulness and ritual performance offer means by which human beings encourage each other to be reflexive and, thereby, to change without undergoing destructive conflict. The more inclusive world that Gawan is building, with the participation of Arthur's court, is a world to which the "new" Parzival can also return. But, even more, it is a world that can contemplate utter strangeness and remain welcoming. Feirefiz, too, draws near.

Toward Speech of the Grail

Making an appearance, as Gawan does in creating his display, propels the initiate-speaker across the threshold of performance into a domain replete with questions. What part does performance play in speaking in a way that heals and transforms? What kind of performance helps and what kind hinders transmission of sovereignty to one's listeners? What performances entrain the audience to be passive observers, insulated from any meaningful relationship to what they are experiencing, and what kind invite the audience to become active co-creators of an experience that contributes to everyone's freedom and growth? How can performances be cleansed of their tendency to manipulate the sentimentalities of the listeners rather than truly educate the discerning power of the feeling heart? What is the interplay between performance and humility? When is performance just empty, deadening display, and when does it possess real awakening power?

Wolfram offers some hints regarding these puzzles in the events preceding the performance. Gawan's adventure at the Castle of

Wonders has not just released the women captives. Knights too were held hostage by Clinschor, though they have apparently been able to leave the castle to defend it. All the while, they and the ladies have been prevented from speaking with each other. Gawan's victory changes all that. Shyly, they move toward one another in the great hall, speak for the first time to one another, then dance the evening away. After this great festival, Gawan and Orgeluse consummate their marriage in the privacy of their chambers. Then, and only then, is the Round Table mended as Gawan encircles Arthur's camp with the couples formed in the previous night's revelry.

The events suggest that performance is powerfully transformative when the masculine and feminine forces in the speaker are reconnected, are able to speak with one another, are wed. Ancient peoples recognized that the marriage of the king and queen was sacred because it connected the earthly and spiritual worlds and thereby fructified the kingdom and all its inhabitants.

Christ proffers a different image. He does not refer to "masculine" and "feminine," but He does say that there must be at least two, and they must be "gathered" in His name for His divine presence to be in attendance. Having chosen to gather with one another, all the while listening to a sounding "name" that transcends their choosing, the two or more become connected like the king and queen in sacred marriage — a union of sovereign surrender. At such moments, Christ promises He will be present. Even more, He seems to say that He *must* be present, that these conditions constitute a call which He cannot refuse.

The two or more who are gathered in the initiate-speaker preparing for a performance — whether that performance be a lecture, a psychotherapeutic session, a sermon, a workshop, a serious conversation — can be called by many names, among them "masculine" and "feminine." The two may be "the active one" and "the receptive one" or "the one who wants to do" and "the one who wants to be" or "the one who wants to speak" and "the one who wants to be silent" or "the one who wants to shape thoughts into words" and "the one who waits to listen to what wants to be said." Whatever their names, these two or more represent the "king" and "queen" within the initiate-speaker whose marriage fosters performance of inspired speech.

The initiate-speaker's sovereign choice to serve a wider spiritual context brings the inner king and queen together in marriage. Like Gawan, many initiate-speakers will have a larger context (communal and spiritual) to rejoin with new sovereignty. For them, as well as others who have not as yet found a spiritual "home," study of the spiritual nature of language and the alphabet ignites wonder and awakens awareness of the unique calling extended to every bearer of the spoken word — that is, every human being. Such study engenders the recognition that speaking is a spiritual practice, a door to the deepest and highest knowledge of what it means to be human.[15]

The trouble is that all this spiritual surrender and lofty intentionality can become very heavy, overly somber and full of itself. Here is where the dis*play* aspect of performance comes in. Gawan does not just "hang out" in his sacred marriage. He "finds the proper herb" with Orgeluse (to use Wolfram's playful euphemism) and then promptly devises a performance. Shaping a performance, managing appearances through an artistically structured event, creates a ceremony of reunification. The initiate-speaker's task is the same; given the inner marriage, the two or more within gathered in spiritual service, the initiate-speaker must play in language, thereby bringing others into the circle of connection.

For making playful connections, the ancient Greek world knew no one could compare with Hermes, quicksilver messenger and trickster of the Greek pantheon. As soon as he was born, he played a trick on elder brother Apollo and then, when he lied about it, caused mighty Zeus to laugh and forgive. Light-footed Hermes never gets weighed down defending his dignity. While the other gods shrink from the ridicule Ares receives when he and Aphrodite are caught in adulterous intimacy by the golden net of her husband, Hephaistos, Hermes wishes aloud that he had the opportunity to be so ensnared. He is god of communication (that which occurs by means of indirection, lies and humor as well as straight talk) and of the boundaries, the "between," where all communication transpires. Hermes has access to all the worlds; playing with the gods on Olympus, guiding souls to the Underworld, appearing at crossroads on earth. With Hermes, there is never just one way; his paths are multiple, says Ginette Paris:

> He is comfortable somewhere between the explicit and the implicit and never tires of inventing nuances of voice, tone or gesture to

place his message in the right context. . . . [C]ommunication under the sign of Hermes borrows from twisted pathways, shortcuts and parallel routes; it makes many round trips and ends up sometimes in meaningful dead ends.[16]

In other words, Hermes' circling inscribes a labyrinth. Ancient astronomers saw his characteristic movement in the fast-moving planet Mercury (Roman name for Hermes), which, viewed from earth, appears to go first one direction then another in its orbit, both direct and indirect. The pattern formed out of the movements is the "classical seven-circuit labyrinth" found in stone circles, hedge mazes and rock carvings around the globe.[17]

Hermes and his ways lighten performance, helping the initiate-speaker to avoid the possible over-seriousness attending the responsibility that goes with creating performance-as-ceremony. And Eros, as we have seen, contributes the leaping, the fast and unusual associations that aerate too much density in speech, opening a space for imagination's flight.

However, something or someone is still missing, and, again, the festivities that precede Gawan's display for Arthur provide a clue. The knights and ladies flirt and dance, the sparkle of seduction suffuses the room in golden light, and, afterwards, Gawan and Orgeluse celebrate in each other's arms. Ancient Greeks saw a goddess behind all these events. Is it perhaps Aphrodite who can bring love-play into one's speaking?

In the Homeric Hymns and elsewhere, the preferred epithets for Aphrodite are "beautiful," "golden," "sweet smiling" and "lover of laughter." After Titans cast her father's penis into the sea, Aphrodite arises there and is borne, unashamedly naked, to shore on the sea foam. She was the only Olympian Goddess whom sculptors normally portrayed nude. Mythologist Christine Downing asserts that Aphrodite's "willingness to be seen unclothed also suggests that seeing and being seen are aspects of [her] divinity."[18] Her temples tend to be located on exposed promontories above the sea, where she serves to connect sky and sea and land.[19] She, like Hermes, serves to connect, but her mode of connection is not the turn of phrase but the tumbling of forms. The laughter she loves bubbles as lacy foam on the waves of sensual, sexual pleasure.

Aphrodite's beauteous presence suffuses things, people and

events, attracting the initiate-speaker to see and caress them with speech.[20] Gawan's choice to serve and to marry the formerly ill-tempered Orgeluse enables the initiate-speaker to partake of the "depth aesthetics" that James Hillman declares must be the starting point for any "depth psychology"[21] and, I would add, for speech of any depth.

According to Hillman, the Greek word *aisthesis* is usually given the pale rendition of "sense perception," which obscures its deeper sense of "taking in," "breathing in," a "gasp."[22] The beauty perceived by depth aesthetics is neither skin-deep, sentimentalized nor pornographized. Hillman advises:

> We must press beyond our usual ideas of beauty that have held the imagination captive to heavenly notions only . . . and away from the world of sense in which Aphrodite was always immanent. . . .
>
> . . . Beauty is the manifest anima mundi — and do notice here it is neither transcendent to the manifest or hiddenly immanent within, but refers to appearances as such, created as they are, in forms with which they are given, sense data, bare facts. . . . Aphrodite's beauty refers to the luster of each particular event; its clarity, its particular brightness; that particular things appear at all and in the form in which they appear. . . . Beauty is thus the very sensibility of the cosmos, that it has textures, tones, tastes, that it is attractive. . . . All things as they display their innate nature present Aphrodite's goldenness; they shine forth and as such are aesthetic.[23]

What makes for an aesthetic performance, then, rather than a vacuous display, is the revelation of beauty — in Hillman's sense of the word. If one can see the beauty of Aphrodite in the things, persons and events of the world, then the beauty of Aphrodite will begin to grace one's speech. To see in this way requires the potency of the heart's imagining — the ability to take things into oneself and to be "taken in" so that one "gasps" in wonder, and so that perceiving is as close and internalized as breathing. This is, as we have seen, precisely Gawan's strength. Gawan has shown us that to bring out the beauty in someone or something that may not seem beautiful at first often demands exertion.[24] From the resulting transformation, we can see that the rewards are worth the effort.

In addition, we have learned that speech and performance are reflexive. This means that the performance must not only reveal the beauty of something or someone else; the performance must also reveal the beauty of the initiate-speaker. One must have come to appreciate and love one's own Aphroditic beauty. In a performance that partakes of depth aesthetics one does not use performing or any of its components — words, movements, gestures, inflection, tone, etc. — to hide or cover oneself. Like Aphrodite, the initiate-speaker is unashamed in nakedness.

To be present nakedly in a skillfully crafted performance is a very subtle art, not easily described and only rarely experienced. When achieved, a kind of "transparency" results. Through seeing, imagining and speaking the beauty of things, just as they appear, and all the while appearing just as she or he is, the initiate-speaker transports self and listeners behind and beyond appearances. That is when the worlds touch, sensuously interpenetrating in Aphrodite's laughing embrace.

Surprisingly enough, though sexually playful with many of the gods, Aphrodite finds her husband in the crippled divine craftsman Hephaistos. This implies that the beauty in the world is best espoused by craft and those who practice a craft.[25] The initiate-speaker is such a spouse. All the previous skills that the initiate-speaker has developed will be the raw materials out of which the ceremonial performance is crafted and by which it is structured: envisioning, memory, metaphoric imagining, rhythm, timing, poetry, praise, storytelling, "leaping" associations, spiritual surrender, humor, etc. These will all be brought together and displayed with the lightest of touch, the whisper of a brush stroke in a Chinese watercolor.

One finds this light touch in the teachings of spiritual adepts such as Rumi, or Lao-Tzu, or Meister Eckhart. Speech that is inordinately loud, oppressive, or overly concretized, and therefore confining, only admits that the initiate-speaker has fallen under Clinschor's command. A profound spaciousness and lightness of touch grace the speech of spiritual masters. Their words rise barely above a whisper and yet command our attention for centuries.

When the initiate-speaker has developed a sovereign "king" and "queen" within, when their marriage invites the blessing of Hermes, Eros and Aphrodite, then, and only then, can someone new appear. Gawan and Orgeluse and the Arthurian world they have reunited now form a vessel for the reappearance of Parzival. His re-entry could not be more different from Gawan's. He reappears by the river bank at the very end of this episode, riding back into the story unannounced and unrecognized. But this is a new Parzival. As we shall see, he, like Gawan, bears the wreath from the Life Goddess's tree, and he also is not far from coming full circle. Wolfram tells us his story is now also circling back "to its main stalk."[26]

BOOK XIV

Having left the encampment at dawn to practice for the joust with Gramoflanz, Gawan sees a knight in glowing red armor by the river, his helmet down and upon it a wreath like the one Gawan retrieved for Orgeluse. The knight appears to be Gramoflanz and, since he seems ready for battle, Gawan decides it would be shameful if he did not respond — even though there is no lady present to witness the contest. Riding powerful Grail chargers, both knights attack at full gallop and knock each other down, horses and all. Then they continue battling with swords, hacking at each other ferociously.

Meanwhile, messengers have carried Arthur's message to Gramoflanz, advising him to come forth if he still wants this joust. Gramoflanz says that indeed he does and that he is glad Itonje will be watching, even though he has never before deigned to fight with just one man. Several allies and their armies have joined him, and present as well is Bene, the ferryman's daughter, who has delivered Itonje's ring to him. Gramoflanz rides toward Arthur's camp in rich array under a canopy borne by twelve maidens, with two maidens on either side to support his arms.

Arthur's messengers gallop ahead of this procession and, before long, come to the scene of Gawan's battle with the lone knight. It is not going well for Gawan, and the messengers, in their distress, call out his name. Hearing it, the unknown knight casts down his sword and curses himself for fighting with Gawan.

> "Accursed and dishonored am I," cried the stranger, and wept. "Fortune completely deserted me when my degraded hand engaged in this combat. Too great was this sacrilege for her. I own myself guilty. . . . Alas that I fought with Gawan! It is myself I have vanquished, and misfortune met me here."[27]

Surprised by this lamentation, Gawan asks the knight's identity, knowing he will have to fight him again if he is to regain the honor he was on the verge of losing. The knight replies, "Kinsman, I shall tell you who I am and shall be at your service now and ever more. I am your kinsman Parzival."[28] Gawan responds to the revelation by commenting on the accurate aim of "Folly," who has gone "straight to her mark" in getting two "simple hearts" to do violence to one another in hatred. He then addresses Parzival directly and says, "Your hand gained the victory over us both, now may you grieve for the sake of us both. It is yourself you have vanquished — if your heart knows true faith."[29]

Then, weakness from his old and recent wounds forces Gawan to the grass in a near faint. One of the messengers removes Gawan's helmet and fans him with a hat of white peacock feathers, just as Arthur's and Gramoflanz's armies amass on either side of the battleground in preparation for the joust. When events have been explained and it is obvious that Gawan is too weak to fight again right away, Gramoflanz agrees to wait until the following day. Parzival, as Gawan's kinsman, offers to fight in his place, but Gramoflanz declines.

Bene, who has just now realized Gawan's identity as Itonje's brother, shouts angrily at Gramoflanz, "Your heart is in the hand of the man whom your heart hates,"[30] implying that his suit for Itonje's love is doomed if he pursues this course. Gramoflanz is not dissuaded but pleads with her to carry a message to Itonje. Bene only curses him and commands him to leave, as she sobs, helpless to prevent this forthcoming duel between her lord Gawan and her own lady's beloved.

At Arthur's camp, Parzival receives a warm welcome and praise for all the battles he has won. He still feels ashamed to be among them, but Gawan insists he join them and be given rich clothes and heartfelt greetings. Orgeluse feels reluctant to kiss Parzival, the knight who shamed her by refusing her love, and later, hesitates in following Gawan's request that she take good care of him. However, to comply with Gawan's bidding, she says she will be hospitable, despite the possibility that, consistent with his character, Parzival may mock her. Of course, Parzival protests Orgeluse's view of him.

Then, taking Bene aside, Gawan asks her not to tell Itonje of Gramoflanz's anger toward him or of the imminent battle. Bene reminds him that Itonje loves them both and that the death of either of them could be her death as well. Itonje's grief will be inconsolable regardless of the outcome, she advises. Itonje, meanwhile, already has questions. Having noticed that Bene is here and not with Gramoflanz delivering her ring, she wonders if he still wants her love.

Arthur and Ginover now arrive at Gawan's tent to greet and welcome Parzival. Parzival recollects aloud how he was shamed by Cundrie *la ʃorcière* at their last meeting and says he trusts Arthur's assurance that he now deserves some praise. Everyone agrees that Parzival has won much well-deserved fame, and then Parzival asks the Round Table to help him return to its circle:

> Help me to win what I miss so painfully. An incomprehensible wonder banished me from the Round Table. All you who once pledged me fellowship, help me now again, as friends, to return to the Table Round.[31]

Arthur grants this request. But, when Parzival then asks that he be allowed to fight in Gawan's place the next day, Gawan declines the offer, saying he trusts in his just cause. Arthur calls for the culminating drink of the evening, and all except Parzival go to their rest. He stays up to attend to his armor, repairing and burnishing each piece.

The next day, Gramoflanz rises early and rides out, beautifully adorned in full armor to please Itonje. His irritation that Parzival interfered with the scheduled joust the day before becomes indignation when he does not find Gawan ready to meet him on the jousting field. Meanwhile Parzival rides out to the field in full armor, and Gramoflanz thinks he is Gawan. Without a word, the two charge. They fight so fiercely that Gramoflanz feels like he is fighting six men, and never again will he say that he will only fight two or more men.

Preparing at the camp, Gawan is informed that Parzival is missing. When Gawan's and Gramoflanz's armies reach the jousting field, the battle is still raging, but Gramoflanz is losing. Gramoflanz's three allies meet with Arthur and Gawan and agree the fight should end and Parzival be declared the victor. Gawan tells Gramoflanz that he will wait until the next day to meet him in combat so Gramoflanz can recover. Arthur urges Gawan not to be angry, even though Parzival has fought and won praise. Gawan quickly replies that certainly he is not angry. In fact, he would give up this joust if Gramoflanz would just release him from it.

During the rest of the day, numerous messages travel back and forth having to do with the joust, Itonje, and Gramoflanz, with Bene serving adroitly as the main go-between. Arthur also becomes involved in the intrigue when Itonje begs him to call off the battle after she discovers that her brother is the knight who is to fight her beloved. Arthur agrees to help after determining that she and Gramoflanz truly love each other and how it came to be. He invites Gramoflanz to the camp, promising him protection, and sends Beacurs, Itonje's and Gawan's brother, to be his escort.

Gramoflanz is pleased to come into the court and, because he has met Beacurs, he is able to pick Itonje out in the crowd. He goes up to her immediately and kisses her on the mouth. Meanwhile, Arthur meets with Gramoflanz's main ally, his uncle, and they decide to ask Itonje to convince Gramoflanz to give up the battle if he truly desires her love. Then Arthur goes to Gawan and together they convince Orgeluse to agree to a reconciliation with Gramoflanz. Her conditions for this agreement are that Gawan renounce the battle for her sake and that Gramoflanz stop accusing Gawan's father.

The agreements having been made, the reconciliation is accomplished, and a great marriage festival ensues. Itonje marries Gramoflanz, her sister is given to Lischois, and Sangive, Gawan's mother, marries the Turkoite. Gramoflanz's army moves near Arthur's encampment, making the grand circle complete. Amid all the festivities, Parzival, though happy for everyone else, longs for Condwiramurs and is not tempted to inconstancy. He finds his sadness ill-fitted to the joyful occasion, and, like so many times before, he puts on his armor, saddles his horse, mounts with sword and spear at the ready, and departs the camp at dawn.

Initiatory Themes

At the end of the last episode, grouchy Keie complained that Gawan seems to be "distinguishing" himself from his old friends by ostentatious display of his new wealth, his new identity. While Gawan is experiencing the pleasures of differentiation and "playing" with the new possibilities that have opened, Keie is expressing the pain of differentiation, the feeling of separation that can accompany this sorting-out process.

Sorting things out proceeds even more obviously in Book XIV, and we should not be surprised. The motif echoes the important initiatory phase of sorting found in many myths and fairy tales — particularly prominent in those with female protagonists.[32] At the beginning, Gawan and Parzival have to sort out whom they are fighting with; Arthur must try to sort out what has happened between Itonje and Gramoflanz and thereby prevent the battle between Gawan and Gramoflanz; Orgeluse must sort out her feelings about welcoming Parzival and, later, about reconciling with Gramoflanz; Gramoflanz must sort out his previously unseen beloved from among the court; and, finally, all the various brides and bridegrooms must be sorted out before the great feast can take place.

Most of this sorting activity surrounds Gramoflanz, and we might wonder why he deserves so much attention in the story. Gramoflanz possesses great pride. Favored by Clinschor — no doubt, for this very quality — he will fight with no less than two men at a time and wears the prideful peacock's plumes on his hat when he first meets Gawan. Wounded in his pride (first by the death of his father whom he thinks Gawan's father killed, and then by Orgeluse who refused his love), Gramoflanz has become indomitably dangerous. He may kill Gawan, representative of real feeling, and keep the fruitful wreath of the Tree of Life all for himself, hoarding it as Clinschor hoards his captives in the Castle of Wonders.

Yet, without ever having seen her, Gramoflanz has grown to love Itonje, who is as closely related to Gawan as blood can be. She has sent a falcon to Gramoflanz that he carries on his wrist, and we know Gawan's name closely associates this bird with him. Whenever it appears in the story, Gawan is soon to follow. Now even Gramoflanz, excessively proud servant of Clinschor, is being drawn into the hawk's circle, beginning with his uncharacteristically humble request that Gawan intercede for him with Itonje.

We might recognize Gramoflanz as that aspect of Parzival and the initiate-speaker that distinguishes itself through pride rather than service. The way he "sorts out" himself in promotion of his vanity and injured pride, is separative and, therefore, fundamentally hostile to community. There is stark contrast between the display of performance that needs community and ultimately contributes to community and the distancing that pride requires and creates.

However, with another kind of sorting out and negotiation, Gramoflanz can become related to Gawan. Once connected to Gawan, the feeling heart of the initiate-speaker, he will take pride in the considerate care he gives to the community; his prideful forces will join Arthur's world and work cooperatively within it. This task must be accomplished before Parzival can continue on his journey. No less a personage than Arthur (who rules the kingdom of one's conscious personality) is needed to conclude this tricky truce, although Gawan, Itonje and Parzival play central roles.

Before that, in a case of mistaken identity, Gawan and Parzival fight one another. This marks Parzival's third entrance into Arthur's court, and none of these has been glamorous or even conventional. First he was a starstruck kid, then, a dumbstruck lover. Now, he is a battle-weary warrior, having fought so many battles that he fights automatically and only afterward worries about whom he is fighting.

But, like Gawan, Parzival has changed, and his own words show it. When the two stop fighting, he says that he has "vanquished" himself. No longer blaming circumstances or God, Parzival acknowledges that he has been fighting with himself and takes full responsibility. This is not a happier Parzival but it is certainly a more mature one. Now he can abdicate the proud isolation of one who insists he must go it alone and do it all himself. He humbly requests help from the Round Table to return to its circle, accepting praise only because Arthur the King says he is deserving. This is a very different being from the rash young man who killed Ither.

Gawan's culpability, though not as explicitly admitted, is equally obvious. He, too, has been fighting with himself in fighting with his kinsman. Usually more careful and considered in his actions, he rode against the familiar knight in red armor simply because he saw the wreath on his helmet. He was fooled by appearances, which confirms that though Clinschor may have left this land, he certainly has not relinquished his role in the world. Gawan has been weakened from combat with Parzival — as is probably necessary. He is revived with a hat of white peacock feathers, which is to say that all the colors of that proud bird's plumage have been recombined from their boastful individuality, leaving the white that places all the colors in service of a greater radiance.

In his quest for the Grail, Parzival seeks to develop the spiritual presence to speak the healing word that restores community. He has reappeared just as Gawan and the initiate-speaker might have become stuck in prideful display. Gawan's near-defeat by Parzival weakens him just enough that he must accept the assistance of Arthur and Parzival to make peace with the other wounded, prideful one, Gramoflanz. Gawan soon evidences his more typical discernment and, after Parzival's defeat of Gramoflanz, admits readily that he has no need of this fight and will give it up if Gramoflanz will.

This intricate negotiation needs a woman's touch — or maybe more than one.

From then on, the feminine forces reweave the community. Bene, always devoted to Gawan, carries messages back and forth as ably as her father ferries boatloads of people. Both she and Itonje are closely connected to Gawan, and they are instrumental in negotiating a peaceful settlement with Gramoflanz. Finally, Orgeluse, whose rage toward Gramoflanz has diminished "while Gawan's embraces had awakened her"[33] agrees to release her vendetta — if Gawan will renounce the fight in her name. The feminine forces which Gawan has so well served now serve him, not only by preventing the battle with Gramoflanz but by actually bringing Gramoflanz into the circle of the family and the court.

The upshot for proud Gramoflanz is that he is no longer separated, demanding attention for dubious accomplishments. He has been "integrated" into the community through becoming "related" to Gawan. In his love for Orgeluse, his devotion to Itonje, then his yearning for battle with Gawan, Gramoflanz has been constantly moving toward connection with Gawan. Now the connection has been made. As we might guess from previous mirroring, a similar connection must soon be due for Parzival. A stage has been set for his meeting with the one who has sought him.

Toward Speech of the Grail

It is no coincidence that Arthur's court, and the initiate-speaker, must find a way to integrate pridefulness right after Gawan orchestrates an impressive performance. Nor is it mere coincidence that Parzival appears at that time to battle Gawan and almost defeat him.

Skillful performance can engender pride. The more skilled one becomes in shaping language and artistically expressing one's ideas through it, the more likely one is to lose the humility, the "transparency," the spontaneity which characterize truly healing speech. The prideful are always "heavy" — with themselves. They are portrayed accurately on the first cornice in Dante's *Purgatorio* bearing stone slabs so large that they themselves are almost hidden from view as they laboriously crawl around the ledge. Certainly they have little ability to leap and even less to fly.

However, as all spiritual traditions have recognized, pride is a slippery character, not easily vanquished or banished from the king-dom no matter what methods of self-abnegation or self-criticism are employed. One can become as puffed up with one's self-flagellation and self-sacrifice as with one's piousness and accomplishments. Sim-ilar temptations assail the initiate-speaker. One can become proud of one's ability to say profound or witty things, even enjoying the sound of one's own voice; and one can be equally prideful in main-taining silence or supposedly encouraging others to speak.

Wolfram told us at the beginning that the nature of human beings is black-and-white mixed, and that Parzival's journey involves com-ing to realize this in a new way. Since pride cannot be sent out per-manently from the kingdom of the self, Wolfram offers another solu-tion. He proposes to "integrate" pride into the kingdom rather than try to banish it.

First, pride is recognized for what it is — a "sorting" gone astray, an urge for distinction that has become divisive, split off, and inflated with its own importance. The degree of inflation seems directly con-tingent upon the degree to which pride feels dishonored or unloved. As Robert Bly suggests, "Every part of our personality that we do not love will become hostile to us."[34] Wolfram's approach shows Arthur and the court honoring Gramoflanz and welcoming his elaborate parade into the camp.

Secondly, however, pride must learn that something else in the personality is stronger. Gramoflanz is soundly thrashed by Parzival, who has already "vanquished himself" and now fights not for himself but for Gawan. Wolfram is no airy idealist. He knows that, at some point, the initiate-speaker who seeks to develop spiritual presence will have to do battle with pride. But the purpose is not punitive. It is so that pride's forces can be woven into the community of the self.

Finally, Wolfram connects pride to Gawan, who represents rela-tional doing, the aspect of one's character that enacts the real feeling of the heart. Disciplined action, adhering to a code that emphasizes service to the feminine forces, will curb pride and bring it into har-monious relationship with the rest of the realm. As if to underline yet again the priority of service to the feminine, Gawan and Gramoflanz renounce their battle — a seeming violation of knightly code — in the names of their ladies.

This process of integrating individualistic, often prideful, expres-sion with a greater community of purpose has a linguistic parallel.

According to Owen Barfield, "Language has two primary functions, one of which is expression and the other communication."[35] These two must work together and work simultaneously, "otherwise there is no language at all. But the extent to which either function predominates over the other will vary greatly."[36]

For Barfield, "The goal to which expression aspires, or the criterion by which it must be measured, is something like fullness or sincerity. The goal toward which communication aspires is accuracy."[37] If expression predominates, to the exclusion of accuracy, the speaker falls out of community; one may be giving voice to profound feelings and thoughts, but unless the words have some accuracy and convey shared meanings, one may as well be speaking in tongues. The speaker is enraptured but incomprehensible. If communication predominates — in the relating of a precise location on a map or a mathematical formula, for instance — then the individual human disappears. Language becomes instrumental but lacks dimension and depth. The human presence of the speaker is irrelevant, and in that case, machines speak as well or better than humans. To continue with Barfield:

> Here we get a glimpse of the true relation between the two functions. On the one hand they tend to be mutually exclusive; so that Expression could say to Communication, "The more there is of mine, the less there is of yours"; but on the other hand the relation is a dynamic rather than a quantitative one. This means that, though each of them is exclusive of, or counter to, the other, yet they are both concurrently necessary. They are, so to speak, "sweet enemies." There is a tension, or polarity between them. And it is in this polarity that the depths of language are to be found.[38]

These "sweet enemies," whether they be called expression and communication or Gramoflanz and Gawan, become working partners for the initiate-speaker through "doing" — that is speaking practices which support a wider community. The initiate-speaker may choose to practice one or more forms of "contemplative" speaking. In all such practices, one intends simultaneously to express oneself authentically, to connect with and further the community in which one is speaking, and to listen for the "still small voice" of the spiritual world so that it may also find expression in the moment.

Every exchange between human beings offers the opportunity for the practice of contemplative speaking. In addition, certain professional and private roles make it necessary. Practitioners of all helping professions, educators, and clergy, in particular, have the opportunity, when at work, to practice mindfulness in speaking. Parents can enrich a whole culture by speaking this way to each other and to their children. In addition, there are at least three other contexts in which contemplative speaking can be practiced.

Maybe the most subtly difficult is spoken prayer. Whether private or public, prayer becomes contemplative speaking when spoken aloud as one side of a dialogue. It is easiest to evaluate one's practice in private prayer of this kind. One can determine fairly easily if one feels more at peace, more insightful, during and after praying, as well as how authentically related one feels to whomever one is speaking in prayer. Public prayer, on the other hand, has the tendency to become too formalized, and it can be difficult to assess whether or not the prayer has affected the listeners. Still, in public praying, one will be quite revealed to oneself as well as others in the degree of authenticity of one's speaking — the authenticity of one's own unhiddenness and the authenticity of the connection one feels with the deity addressed.

A second context for contemplative speaking is "council process" as synthesized by educator Jack Zimmerman and others from Native American traditions, Quaker meetings and techniques of group psychotherapy.[39] Sitting in a circle around a centering symbol like a flame or flower, participants in council pass a ceremonial object, a "talking stick." Each speaks in turn upon receiving the stick and remains silent, listening, when others have the stick. The rules are simple: "Speak honestly, be brief, and listen from the heart." Graced with that quality of listening — to oneself as well as to others — everyone's ability to empathize grows, and group decisions "are made by discovery and recognition rather than argument and voting."[40] Integration of the self and of the self with the group occurs simultaneously, as Zimmerman explains:

> As in the ancient circles of elders, council members come to know they each bring a piece of the truth to the circle — a piece essential in itself, but only part of the whole. The passion of a personal vision becomes part of the larger truth of the circle. When

council is working, we all experience this truth without any threat to personal identity and without the "tyranny of the collective." Everyone recognizes what's really happening and sees the path to "right action," often more or less at the same time and usually accompanied by the special joy inherent in the co-visioning process.[41]

A third form of contemplative speaking is "Goethean conversation," so named by Marjorie Spock because of a brief dialogue Goethe includes in his "Fairy Tale of the Green Snake and the Beautiful Lily." The green snake, illuminated from within by the gold she has swallowed, finds four kings in a subterranean temple. One of them becomes her interlocutor:

> "Whence came you hither?" asked the golden king.
> "Out of the clefts where gold dwells," replied the serpent.
> "What is more glorious than gold?"
> "Light."
> "What is more quickening than light?"
> "Conversation."[42]

As outlined by Spock, Goethean conversation creates a communion among speakers who are tuning themselves within to each other, and to the spiritual world, while considering a theme. The theme has been announced in advance, and each participant has lived with it, contemplated it in meditation, researched it, and "conceived thoughts like children"[43] in regard to it. Some or none of these thoughts may be expressed during the actual conversation because this preparation is a "warming up," a "rousing the soul to maximum activity," "a brightening of consciousness to render the soul a dwelling place hospitable to the light."[44] By preparing thoroughly, by preserving silence in oneself, then joining others in acute listening, refraining from "words for words' sake," the initiate-speaker obeys Spock's injunction: "Invite the spirit by becoming spiritually active, and then hold yourself open to its visitation."[45]

It is vital to distinguish between discussions and conversations. Intellects active in discussion typically make straight for the mark of a conclusion; they penetrate fact as though with mental arrows, unaware that the fact may be a living thing that dies when so approached and becomes nothing more than a taxidermist's specimen. Whereas those who engage in conversation see their function as a group-process of inviting truth exactly as they would invite a human guest, and make the atmosphere receptive to it.[46]

With the exception of individual prayer, contemplative speaking is practiced in the presence of witnesses, but not necessarily in direct interaction with them. In such contexts, any pridefulness or leadenness in the speaking becomes readily apparent to both the speaker and the witnessing listeners. One's degree of authenticity is conspicuous — which is to say one's ability to be unhidden, to stand equanimously in the reality of the black-and-white mixedness of oneself and the world. Contemplative speaking therefore really is "speech therapy." Its consistent practice guides each initiate-speaker to become more and more present, and his or her speaking will reflect the change.

The speaking changes because as one learns to be present, one's presence can speak. Forever silent and invisible, one's "speaking presence" yet mediates all true speech.[47] In contemplative speaking, the speaking presence — rather than the desires and fears of the outer personality — serves as the tuning fork to which each initiate-speaker listens when speaking. When invited into the "performance" of speech, the delicate inspiration of the speaking presence effects transformation, both subtle and profound. Such speech, exemplified in Christ's healing dialogues, is always generative, allowing sight where there was blindness, movement where there was lameness, life where there was death.

Forms of contemplative speaking have the qualities all forms have. For Wendell Berry, the most fundamental characteristic of forms is that they are communal; they can be learned, taught, passed on through generations.[48] Therefore the forms of contemplative speaking which the initiate-speaker practices constitute a return to community.

A discernible shift now occurs in the story and in the initiation process; themes of context and community will increasingly take center stage, and the theme of individual personal development will recede into the background. The form that re-emerges at the end of Book XIV is Arthur's court, a now greatly enlarged community celebrating several marriages. Through forms, Gawan, Gramoflanz and the initiate-speaker find their way to community — a development that would not surprise Berry:

> Forms join, and this is why forms tend to be analogues of each other and to resonate with each other. Forms join the diverse things that they contain; they join their contents to their context; they join us to themselves; they join us to each other; . . . they join the generations together, the young and the old, the living and the dead. . . . Joining the form, we join all that the form has joined.[49]

Yet, with all this joyful coming together, there is one who has not yet really joined, who feels left out. This community embraces Parzival but not all that Parzival has embraced — neither his wife nor the Grail company. The festivities are only painful reminders to him of his lonely lostness. Though Gawan's task is accomplished, Parzival's is not. So, he sets forth, though no longer raging at God or men, to do the only thing he knows to do: keep going, keep battling, until he finds his way back.

NOTES

[1] Wolfram, Book XIII, 637.

[2] Wolfram, Book XIII, 643–44.

[3] Wolfram, Book XIII, 643–44.

[4] Wolfram, Book XIII, 646.

[5] Wolfram, Book XIII, 657.

[6] Wolfram, Book XIII, 659.

[7] Wolfram, Book XIII, 667.

[8] Wolfram, Book XIII, 673.

[9] Quoted in Victor Turner, *The Anthropology of Performance*, 74.

[10] Marie-Louise von Franz, *The Psychological Meaning of Redemption Motifs in Fairy Tales* (Toronto: Inner City, 1980) 19–20.

[11] Franz, 20.

[12] Turner, *The Anthropology of Performance*, 81.

[13] William Irwin Thompson, *Imaginary Landscape: Making Worlds of Myth and Science*, 128.

[14] Thompson, 74.

[15] I refer the reader to Georg Kuhlewind, *Becoming Aware of the Logos* and *The Logos-Structure of the World: Language as a Model of Reality*, and to two pamphlets by Rudolf Steiner, *The Realm of Language and the Lost Unison Between Speaking and Thinking* and *The Alphabet*, as well as to the concluding chapter in Theodor Schwenk's remarkable study, *Sensitive Chaos*, where he likens the form-creating power of words in air to the formative power of water on earth.

[16] Ginette Paris, *Pagan Grace: Dionysos, Hermes and the Goddess Memory in Daily Life*, 63.

[17] Sig Lonegren, *Labyrinths: Ancient Myths and Modern Uses*, 86.

[18] Christine Downing, *The Goddess: Mythological Images of the Feminine*, 204.

[19] Downing, 205.

[20] Aphrodite's influence is not strictly metaphoric. The physical connection between sexuality and speech is shown at adolescence when sexual hormones increase: the voices of boys "crack" and those of girls deepen. This point is made in many anthroposophical writings. Rudolf Steiner suggests further that "the human larynx appears . . . to be an organ that is entirely only at the beginning of its becoming. . . . It is the future organ of birth, the organ of reproduction. As man now brings forth the word through the larynx; so is the larynx the potential, the seed-organ that in the future will develop itself in such a way that it will be able to bring forth man, the entire human being. . ." ("The World of the Senses and the World of the Spirit," lecture, Hannover, Germany, 28 Dec. 1911, quoted in Richard Lewis, *Love, Marriage, Sex in the Light of Spiritual Science: Excerpts from the Work of Rudolf Steiner,* vol. 3, 104.

[21] James Hillman, "The Thought of the Heart," *Eranos Lectures 2*, 26.

[22] Hillman, 31.

[23] Hillman, 27–29.

[24] It requires effort, as well, to see the beauty in things, persons and events that are considered conventionally (habitually) beautiful but that are not seen "anew" or in their essence. Marilyn Monroe's tragic life comes to mind in this regard.

[25] For an artful exposition of the nature of craft, see the Introduction and Chapter XI, "The Alchemy of Craft," in D.M. Dooling's *A Way of Working: The Spiritual Dimension of Craft,* vii–xiv and 93–100.

[26] Wolfram, Book XIII, 678.

[27] Wolfram, Book XIV, 688–89.

[28] Wolfram, Book XIV, 689.

[29] Wolfram, Book XIV, 689–90.

[30] Wolfram, Book XIV, 693.

[31] Wolfram, Book XIV, 700.

[32] Psyche sorting her seeds and Cinderella separating the lentils from the ashes are two familiar examples. Finding this theme here in *Parzival* indicates that the feminine forces have indeed been freed to contribute directly to the initiation.

[33] Wolfram, Book XIV, 723.

[34] Robert Bly, *A Little Book on the Human Shadow,* 16.

[35] Owen Barfield, *Speaker's Meaning,* 35. Though they are not the only functions of language, Barfield says that these two are "both indispensable to its existence" (35).

[36] Barfield, 35.

[37] Barfield, 35.

[38] Barfield, 36–37.

[39] Jack Zimmerman and Virginia Coyle, "Council: Reviving the Art of Listening," *Utne Reader,* Mar./Apr. 1991, 80.

[40] Zimmerman and Coyle, 80.

[41] Zimmerman and Coyle, 85.

[42] Marjorie Spock, *Group Moral Artistry II: The Art of Goethean Conversation,* 1. In the 1832 translation of Goethe's story, the wording is as follows:

"Whence comest thou?"
"From the chasms where the gold dwells," said the Snake.
"What is grander than gold?"
"Light."
"What is more refreshing than light?"
"Speech."

See Johann Wolfgang Goethe, *The Fairy Tale of the Green Snake and the Beautiful Lily*, 16.

[43] Spock, 6.

[44] Spock, 6.

[45] Spock, 7.

[46] Marjorie Spock, *Group Moral Artistry I: Reflections on Community Building*, 30.

[47] Kühlewind, *Becoming Aware of the Logos*, 62.

[48] Wendell Berry, *Standing by Words*, 207.

[49] Berry, 213.

CHAPTER EIGHT

"You Shall Be Lord of the Grail"

The Grail King Speaks

Oh, Speaker,
You cannot fight the rich Stranger
To possess the gift he is
And brings.
Follow his fiery example
And you will become
Food for others:
Reading the need of each wild moment,
Improvising with ceremonial sensibility,
Accepting the dying
That leads to greater Life,
And thereby returning
To that place
Which was the Beginning
And now is again.

BOOK XV

Parzival rides out toward a great forest and in a "bright glade" meets a "rich stranger," a heathen knight whose armor and horse's trappings are so richly adorned that they "blaze with light." (Wolfram admits his inadequacy to describe them.) The many women the knight has served bestowed him with these rewards. Emblazoned on his helmet is an "ecidemon," a creature that kills poisonous snakes. The knight rides alone, although on his ships at the harbor are twenty-five armies under his command, none of whom speak the same language.

Both men charge and neither loses his seat upon contact, so they fight with swords from horseback. Then they jump to the ground and continue their sword fight. The heathen knight keeps shouting "Tabronit," the home of his wife, Queen Secundille, and with every shout he is reinvigorated. Parzival is getting the worst of it and, at one point, falls to his knees. Now even Wolfram fears for Parzival and exhorts him to think of Condwiramurs to gain fresh energy and courage or, if that is not enough, then he should think of his twin boys who, unbeknownst to him, have been growing up at Pelrapeire in his absence. Kardeiz and Loherangrin will be orphaned if he loses this fight.

Luckily, Parzival does begin to think of Condwiramurs, shouting the name of her castle, "Pelrapeire," every time the heathen knight cries "Tabronit." Parzival regains his strength quickly and is able to force the heathen to his knees, with a blow across his helmet which, at the same time, breaks the sword in Parzival's hands — the sword he had taken so unceremoniously from Ither after killing him.

The heathen knight then jumps to his feet and addresses his adversary courteously — in French, a language Parzival can understand. He admits that Parzival would definitely have won if his sword had not broken, and that he would be dishonored if he fought further with an unarmed man. He asks Parzival to introduce himself and suggests that they declare a truce for the moment, until they are rested. They sit down on the grass, and again the heathen knight asks Parzival to "tell me both your name and your race, and then I will not have made this journey for nothing."[1]

Parzival resists, however, suggesting that he is being forced "out of fear" to identify himself because the other man is armed. He says no man has a right to force him in this way. (In such a battle, the loser was obliged to reveal his name, but in this case, there is no clear loser.) The stranger quite readily accepts his reservations, responding with, "Let the odium be mine," and identifying himself as "Feirefiz the Angevin, and powerful enough to have many countries pay tribute to my hand."[2]

Astonished at this, Parzival informs the stranger that Anjou, the province that gives the name *Angevin*, belongs to him and that Feirefiz will have to choose a different name. Then, after a pause, he muses aloud that he was once told that he has a brother in heathendom who has won great knightly renown. Parzival suggests that Feirefiz take off his helmet so he can see if his face fits his brother's description. He asks Feirefiz to trust him, promising he will not attack until Feirefiz has his helmet back on again.

Feirefiz says he has little to fear, since he still has his sword and Parzival has none. With a strong, swift movement, he hurls the sword far into the woods, declaring, "This sword shall not belong to either one of us. . . . Now if there is to be any fighting done, the chances must be equal."[3] Then he asks Parzival how his brother is supposed to look, and Parzival replies that informants describe his brother's complexion to be "like a parchment with writing all over it, black and white all mixed up."[4]

"I am the one," says Feirefiz confidently, and both men immediately strip off their helmets and coifs of mail. "Parzival found a precious find and the dearest one he ever found. The heathen was recognized at once for he had the markings of a magpie."[5] The two men kiss one another, and Feirefiz praises Jupiter, Juno, and all his gods and goddesses for allowing him the happiness of meeting "noble Gahmuret's child." Parzival claims he is not "learned enough to outdo in words your noble praise,"[6] but he trusts that God knows what is in his heart, and he compliments Feirefiz for being the greatest warrior he has ever faced.

Hearing Parzival's formal mode of address, Feirefiz urges him to employ the familiar form. Parzival feels embarrassed by this, pointing out that he is not a fraction as wealthy as his brother and is the younger besides, so the polite form seems more appropriate. In quick response, Feirefiz offers to give Parzival two kingdoms — Zazamanc and Azagouc, the two won by Gahmuret when he rescued Belacane — to increase his wealth. Then, he confesses that, although he has not quite forgiven Gahmuret for leaving him orphaned, he has undertaken this costly journey to meet his father.

Parzival tells Feirefiz that he also never met their father and is acquainted with him only through his honorable reputation. He reports what he has learned about their father's death: that Gahmuret died in the East in the midst of a joust. Feirefiz mourns at hearing this news and bemoans the fact that he will never know his father. Nevertheless he realizes that

> In this hour I have both lost and found my joy. If I am to grasp the truth, my father and you and I, we were all one, but this one appeared in three parts. . . . You have fought here against yourself; against myself I rode into combat here and would gladly have killed myself; you could not help but defend my own self in fighting me.[7]

Deeply moved by this miracle of losing and finding in the same meeting, he laughs and weeps, trying all the while to conceal it.

Then he invites Parzival to come and see his great army. Amazed, Parzival asks if the army will patiently wait for Feirefiz all this time. Feirefiz replies that there is no doubt about that; the ships are well provisioned and no one needs to disembark except to get fresh water and breathe the inland air. This being the case, Parzival suggests that Feirefiz should visit Arthur's camp and see all the ladies there. The mention of ladies definitely ignites Feirefiz's interest, and his mind is made up when he hears that he will meet more of his kinsmen there as well.

After Parzival has retrieved Feirefiz's sword and returned it to him, they ride to Arthur's camp, where everyone had been saddened by Parzival's absence. The sword fight was witnessed in the pillar in the Castle of Wonders, though no one but Arthur had guessed the identity of either combatant. Arthur was sure one of them was Parzival. The two ride to Gawan's tent first, and everyone marvels at Feirefiz's rich and strange appearance. After being introduced to his kinsman, Gawan invites them in for a meal and requests Arthur and Ginover to join them.

Arthur and Feirefiz exchange acknowledgments and tell each other about themselves. Arthur also relates some of Parzival's adventures and explains his search for the Grail. He asks both Feirefiz and Parzival to give an account of all the countries they have come to know in their battles, and each, in turn, provides a long list. Gawan arranges to have Feirefiz's ornate armor and equipment brought in for the guests to see, and everyone marvels at it.

Leaving Feirefiz surrounded by admiring ladies, Arthur consults privately with Gawan, Parzival and Gramoflanz about hosting a festival to welcome Feirefiz and to invite him to join the company of the

Round Table. It is agreed that he — along with Gramoflanz, Lischois and the Turkoite — will be admitted. Gawan and Gramoflanz will bear most of the costs for this celebration, since Arthur is a guest in their land.

By moonlight, the ceremonial ground is laid out. The next day, in a flowering field, a large circular cloth is spread on the ground to represent the Round Table, and everyone gathers around for the induction. Feirefiz has been more than glad to accept the invitation to join. It is a splendidly festive occasion, the women beautifully attired and mounted, the men in burnished armor with wreaths of flowers in their hair. Contests and games on horseback precede the meal.

Suddenly, another richly dressed and heavily veiled stranger — this time a maiden — approaches the throng. It is Cundrie *la sorcière.* She rides a finely bred horse with carved trappings, and her black velvet mantle is embroidered in Arabian gold with turtledoves. Her thick veils hide her identity, but she rides directly up to Arthur and Ginover, greets them, requests their assistance, and asks them to heed her words. She then turns her horse, rides straight to Parzival, dismounts and kneels at his feet, weeping, imploring him to give her his greeting. He does so grudgingly, and only because his friends intercede, but he does not kiss her.

Then Cundrie stands, removes her headdress and veils and reveals her loathsome face once more. Her proclamation to Parzival follows the blessing she gives him and her welcome of Feirefiz:

> Show restraint now in your joy! Blessed are you in your high lot, O crown of man's salvation! — The inscription has been read: you shall be Lord of the Grail. Condwiramurs, your wife, and your son, Loherangrin, have been named therein along with you. When you departed from Brobarz the land, two sons she bore into life. Kardeiz has his sufficient share there. But even if you never again heard good tidings beyond this: that your truthful lips shall now address greeting to that noble and sweet man, and that now the question from your mouth shall make King Anfortas well again and avert from him his sighs and great misery — where would there ever be your equal in blessedness?[8]

Cundrie invokes the seven planets in heathen names well known to Feirefiz and declares that, for Parzival, "upon whatever their light is shed, that is destined as your goal to reach and achieve."[9] Parzival weeps with joy and relief at these tidings; "tears flowed from his eyes,

the fountain springs of his heart."[10] He acknowledges that this blessing could only come from God's favor and admits she was only angry
at him before because he had done wrong, that "then it was still not
time for my salvation."[11]

Then he asks her what he should do next to accomplish his task.
She advises that he must choose a man to go along as his companion, and that she will lead the way. While she goes to rest and visit
with Arnive, Parzival sits down for the feast and asks his brother to
go with him to the Grail castle. Feirefiz happily assents but decides he
wants to distribute gifts first. He challenges Gramoflanz to prove his
love for his kinswoman Itonje by helping her and Gawan to invite
all present to stay until these gifts can be brought from his ships. He
also enlists Arthur's help in assuring everyone that there is no shame
in accepting the gifts, because his wealth is so great.

Everyone agrees to wait for four days while the gifts are brought.
During this period Parzival tells the company about his meeting with
Trevrizent, who had told him that "no one could ever fight his way
to the Grail 'unless he has been summoned to it by God'."[12] Before
long, this story spreads across all the lands convincing many knights
to give up their search for the Grail. "For that reason it remains hidden still."[13]

On the third day the gifts are brought and distributed to each person according to his or her station. Parzival and Feirefiz, having vis-
ited all four quadrants of the widespread army, take their leave and
depart with Cundrie.

Initiatory Themes

In a bright forest glade at dawn, battle-weary Parzival, still burdened by the duty of keeping his seemingly futile promise to find
the Grail castle again, encounters Feirefiz, who brims with fiery zest
for life. The very sound of his name suggests the "fire" in his nature:
a fire that comes from the heights, home of the pagan gods he continually praises, and also from the earthly depths, glimmering in the
precious gemstones that stud his garments, armor and horse trappings. Every movement he makes, even the sentences he speaks, all
have the quality of swiftness, strength, sureness. He seems filled with
a great "Yes," and he shows little attachment to forms.[14] He accommodates form only so long as a form accommodates his restlessly
creative energy. This is how he helps to free Parzival from the rut of

constant, lonely battles which has seemed the only way back to the Grail castle. "The Grail cannot be won by combat — the poet expressly says so. It is a gift," W.J. Stein asserts.[15]

Feirefiz radiates "enthusiasm," which, in its original Greek root, means to be filled with the energy of god — a particular god, Dionysos, who, according to Carl Kerenyi, reigns as the "archetypal image of indestructible life."[16] The utterly strange Dionysos "arrives" or "appears" in an uproar of surging energy that is both intoxicating and terrifying. Depending on one's point of view, Dionysos brings raging madness and death *or* life-giving sacrifice and resurrection. His appearance, says Walter Otto, means "Everything that has been locked up is released."[17]

In Feirefiz's cheery, black-and-white countenance, Parzival begins to see his own face, thus incorporating the earthly-heavenly fire that will propel him, at last, back to the Grail castle. The two brothers need each other and, as Feirefiz points out, are "one" — in trinity with their father. In finding each other, they can each take the next step toward their destinies — to go to the Grail castle. Feirefiz will lend the inspirited activity of his "fire" to Parzival, and Parzival will lead Feirefiz to the cooling "water" — of baptism — through which Feirefiz will die to his old ways of seeing and begin to serve the Grail.

Bearing these two qualities — heat and coolness — Feirefiz and Parzival form a paradoxical conjunction similar to what ancient Greeks recognized in Dionysos, whose countenance they saw in both the grape vine and the ivy. "While the vine of Dionysos needs as much light and heat from the sun as it can get, the ivy of Dionysos has surprisingly little need for light and warmth, and grows green and fresh in the shade and in the cold, too," notes Walter Otto.[18] The two plants, he muses, "are like siblings who have developed in opposite directions and yet cannot deny their relationship."[19] Through the conjunction of these two qualities, the initiate-speaker now has contact with the permeating, moist energy over which Dionysos rules and through which he gives.[20] And, when moistness is present, new life patterns will surely grow.

The pattern of Arthur's court is the first to change, as Gawan, ever serving relatedness, welcomes Parzival and his brother. After the introductions, Arthur recounts Parzival's journey for Feirefiz and then asks them both to name the people and countries they have come to know in their battles. These lengthy lists, given by Wolfram in detail, represent their collective acquaintance with most of the then known world. This broad-based foundation of knowledge reflects their ability to tolerate and respect differences. Out of this experience, both Parzival and Feirefiz can welcome and learn from a stranger without feeling threatened, and now they transmit this strength to the community. They are indeed sons of Gahmuret who left the safety and honor in his own country to travel to a foreign land to serve the king who would ask the most of him as a knight.

The significance of the decision to "travel" widely — geographically, emotionally, intellectually or spiritually — is fundamentally epistemological. If one does not just visit things, as in a zoo, but really interacts with what one meets, the decision entails a fearless willingness to bring one's beliefs and assumptions into possible question in the context of new landscapes, new cultures, new systems of ideas, values and customs. Only when one has established a secure inner sovereignty through previous trials and teachings will one have the strength to be immersed repeatedly in difference and not be overwhelmed by confusion.

Given the speed of change occurring at the end of the twentieth century, there are few other viable options. People must either find a way to be open to difference or become "fundamentalist" to some degree or other. An initiatory journey, like the one described here, offers the best antidote to fundamentalism. Through the journey, one develops an artistic spirituality or a spiritually-based artistry that makes it possible not only to survive but to serve a pluralistic world. As William Irwin Thompson states: "The artist and the mystic know that you don't have to drink the ocean to swim in it; consequently, complexity does not engulf them."[21]

The Round Table, spread impromptu but decorously on the flowering field, is being augmented by this epistemological openness when, not coincidentally, Cundrie *la sorcière* reappears to announce that Parzival's name is written on the Grail. She who cursed Parzival, branding the name of the Grail on his heart, now blesses him and becomes his servant and guide. "The original stumbling block has become the final stepping stone,"[22] says Brother David Steindl-Rast regarding another initiation. The "symptom," the irritant, that ugly, unacceptable thing that does not seem to belong, is now what will lead Parzival, and the initiate-speaker, to the Grail castle.

Parzival did not realize that his first experience at the Grail

castle was a gift; certainly he could not recognize Cundrie's castiga-
tion as an extension of that gift. Furthermore, Parzival had not
learned that "A gift may be the actual agent of change, the bearer of
new life," as Lewis Hyde has written:

> In the simplest example, gifts carry an identity with them and to
> accept the gift amounts to incorporating the new identity. It is as if
> such a gift passes through the body and leaves us altered. The gift
> is not merely the witness or guardian to new life, but the creator.[23]

Parzival's quest has prepared him not only to recognize these gifts
but to return to his community the value and worth which has
accrued in him since they were given. As Hyde explains:

> with gifts that are agents of change, it is only when the gift
> has worked in us, only when we have come up to its level, as it
> were, that we can give it away again. . . . The transformation is not
> accomplished until we have the power to give the gift on our own
> terms.[24]

Given this latest gift of Feirefiz's presence, Parzival has nearly
completed his transformation. No longer rash, resentful, or preoccupied, he shows vulnerable emotion for the first time when he joyously weeps at Cundrie's proclamation. No longer the prideful,
lonely warrior upon his self-reliant high horse, he now clearly values relationship. He eagerly invites Feirefiz to Arthur's court; he
thanks Cundrie for her kind words, admitting his mistake had
deserved her anger before; he appreciates God's grace in this
moment, recognizing that he is not the one who determines the timing of his salvation. Receptive to help now, he does not hesitate to
seek Cundrie's advice for what he must do next, and, with equal
openness, asks Feirefiz to accompany him to the Grail castle.

But first, another kind of ceremony takes place. Feirefiz enlists the
aid of Gawan, Gramoflanz and even Arthur, who manage things well
on this plain — or plane — , to convince their courtiers to wait for
his gifts. He wants the recipients not to feel shamed by accepting the
gifts, because his vast wealth accommodates this giving that is really
a praising, a grateful reciprocity for the gift of meeting his brother
and other relatives and for their hospitality.

Feirefiz creates a giveaway, or "potlatch," as it was called among Native American tribes on the Pacific coast.[25] Along with those peoples who celebrate with such giveaways, Feirefiz instinctively knows that the sign of true wealth is not how much one holds onto but how much one gives away. In addition, like ancestral potlatches, Feirefiz's giveaway is rooted in the understanding that "Where we wish to preserve natural increase . . . gift exchange is the commerce of choice, for it is a commerce that harmonizes with, or participates in, the process of increase."[26]

> People with a sense of the gift not only speak of it as food to eat but also feed it. . . . The nourishment flows both ways. When we have fed the gift with our labor and generosity, it grows and feeds us in return. The gift and its bearers share a spirit which is kept alive by its motion among them, and which in turn keeps them both alive. . . . The increase is the core of the gift, the kernel.[27]

Feirefiz's give-away is an age-old ceremony of becoming "food" for others. Through that mysterious process, one actually increases one's power in the community. Dionysos, seen in his "spirit" — the intoxicating power of wine made from the crushed grape — ripens and arises again out of his dismemberment. Christ, the one who gives his body repeatedly to be eaten by his followers, is spread by them across the whole earth. As Hyde proclaims, "[T]he spirit of the gift increases because the body of the gift is consumed."[28]

One must become like the Grail to reach the Grail, and Feirefiz and Cundrie — who was herself a gift! — epitomize this for Wolfram. For her part, peripatetic Cundrie, always identified as the loyal servant of Anfortas and the Grail, serves to connect the Grail castle, Arthur's court, and Clinschor's realm. To Sigune in her forest hermitage, Cundrie takes nourishment, and, to Arnive, during her captivity at the Castle of Wonders, she brings news and healing unguents. Once we can see past her awful appearance, we can honor her as an embodiment of the Grail in her willing service to all.

Feirefiz, granting an unequivocal "yes" to whatever is asked of him, gifts others with his energy as well as his property. No proud isolationist who cannot acknowledge his interdependence, he constantly praises all the gods who have favored him with good fortune, and the name of his queen's land is on his lips from the outset of his battle with Parzival. He cooperatively tells Parzival his name when the latter refuses to tell his, and, later, offers Parzival two of his countries to equalize their wealth. His generosity, his giving to all the assembly according to their stations in life, mirrors the Grail which nourishes according to whatever each person requests.

The attributes which Feirefiz and Cundrie exemplify for Parzival, and through which they empower him to return to the Grail castle, do not resemble those of someone who spends a day helping out at a soup kitchen. Cundrie and Feirefiz embody generosity and service to such an extent that these qualities seem their most outstanding feature. In fact, they model the two virtues that Wolfram, at the beginning, promised would be present at the end: faithfulness, as seen in Cundrie, and forthrightness, as seen in Feirefiz. Shining forth, these two bright gems from the East light the path back to the Grail castle for Parzival and the initiate-speaker.

Toward Speech of the Grail

Feirefiz bears gifts for Parzival and the initiate-speaker, and the first thing he presents Parzival with is a fight. Indeed, he nearly defeats him, until Parzival remembers to call upon his imaginative soul, Condwiramurs, for strength and inspiration. Parzival and the initiate-speaker have come a long way toward the speech of the Grail, and they think they know the meaning of all this — that they are to fight on, alone, never really depending on anyone else, never really belonging anywhere, until somehow or other they reach their goal. Now, in the next-to-last episode of the story, they seem at the brink of success. Why this thrashing at the threshold?

The word "threshold" derives from a Germanic word which means to "thrash" or "thresh" — "a place where grain is beaten out from its husk, where what has been hidden is thus manifested."[29] Feirefiz "threshes" from Parzival the now useless husk of isolated self-reliance that keeps him from truly serving community. Parzival fought with Gawan to shake him out of his temptation to get stuck in prideful display. Now Feirefiz fights with Parzival to rouse him from his tendency to get stuck in one meaning, because attachment to any single meaning impoverishes oneself and one's community. Notice that Parzival still feels poor, lonely and isolated, and that the communities at Arthur's court and at the Grail castle languish for lack of his presence.

If Feirefiz can get Parzival to "stop" — to sit down on the field — and to "remember" — that he has been told about a half-brother in the East — Parzival will be able to recognize Feirefiz as fully related to him, no matter how strange he appears. That opening to the other represents the first step toward renewal of the community. Feirefiz does not serve to shame Parzival or to beat him up. His purpose is to move Parzival into relationship with community because, as Wendell Berry insists,

> if one wishes to promote the life of language, one must promote the life of the community — a discipline many times more trying, difficult, and long than linguistics, but having at least the virtue of hopefulness.[30]

So that they may promote community, Feirefiz grants Parzival and the initiate-speaker the gift of his fiery otherness. Consider three qualities of fire that characterize him. First, fire lives only in the present; unlike earth, water or air, it has no physical existence except in its moment of burning. Secondly, fire consumes itself in its own burning; like a fever, it runs its course and then is gone. Thirdly, to exist at all, fire must move. Fire is the element most often imagined in mythologies as being a "gift," probably because it reflects the "cardinal property" of gifts, as described by Lewis Hyde:

> [W]hatever we have been given is supposed to be given away again, not kept. Or, if it is kept, something of similar value should move on in its stead, the way a billiard ball may stop when it sends another scurrying across the felt, its momentum transferred. . . . The only essential is this: the gift must always move. There are other forms of property that stand still, that mark a boundary or resist momentum, but the gift keeps going.[31]

Otherness is a gift and it is a fire. Otherness will expand the initiate-speaker's world and will inevitably animate the initiate-speaker by pulling him or her into the present. (True otherness can never be adequately addressed with expectations, assumptions or unconscious habits.) The fire of otherness will also incinerate something in the initiate-speaker, ultimately burning away any cherished single meanings, any attachments to forms — of thought or speech or behavior — that impoverish or imprison the initiate-speaker and the community. To become enriched by wordless, universal meaning one has to relativize the strictly personal meanings which keep one isolated. Such relativization can initially feel threatening and painful.

The fire of otherness confronts us in people who are very different than we are and in the spirit of the divine, whose otherness cannot be circumscribed by any form. Willingness to welcome otherness insures a rich inheritance of inspiration for one's being and one's speaking. Walter Otto, while discussing Dionysos, notes that all genuine creativity testifies to the fact

> that the human mind cannot become creative by itself, even under the most favorable circumstances, but that it needs to be touched and inspired by a wonderful Otherness; that the efficacy of this Otherness forms the most important part of the total creative process, no matter how gifted men are thought to be.[32]

To be inspired by otherness, the initiate-speaker turns in two directions. One practice is to keep oneself exposed to otherness in its many earthly manifestations: differing cultures, differing personalities, differing ideas and value systems, differing landscapes and languages. The Grail serves the whole earth, and Cundrie tells Parzival that his mission now is to "reach and achieve" whatever is circumscribed by the orbits of the seven planets and receives their light. Thus the initiate-speaker will reach out for all the strangeness that the world may present. This means repeatedly letting go of one's attachment to the familiar, the safe and the comfortable.

Simultaneously, the initiate-speaker practices turning toward divine otherness. For a fully encompassing speaking presence, one opens oneself not only to human otherness but to other-worldly otherness, which, whether imagined polytheistically or monotheistically, will demand new capacities.

The first requirement is a strengthened tolerance for paradox. We have seen in limb-rendering and life-giving Dionysos the essential paradox of divine otherness. From the human vantage point, divine otherness seems to be present in both good and evil, seems to create and to destroy life. Paradox proffers no way in for the unawakened intellect. The initiate-speaker has arrived at the threshold of mystery, where purely perceptual and conceptual knowledge cannot cross, where even imaginative pictures and metaphoric thinking cannot fully serve. At this threshold, the initiate-speaker must learn to rely on intuition.

With intuition, the initiate-speaker opens to another divine otherness — the otherness-who-waits and who is so very different from Dionysos, the otherness-who-appears. The divine otherness-who-waits does so out of love, patiently allowing human individuals to arrive out of their free choice and free activity, in their own time. Free deeds, performed out of love, are engendered by intuition which is here understood differently from its common connotation as a "feeling" for how to act in a certain situation — as Gawan demonstrated in earlier episodes. Intuition, in this sense, results from long inner striving and inner struggle to strip away motivations of self-interest so that one can act for the greater good. The pioneering Dutch social psychiatrist Bernhard Lievegoed describes it as follows:

> Taking action out of intuition . . . is not something that can be mastered at the drop of a hat. For years one can struggle with the question: "If only I knew what I should really do." If one is not prepared to suffer through this and to have sleepless nights, while being tormented by this question, one cannot develop the ability to take the bull by the horns when it becomes apparent what one really has to do. . . .
>
> Only a few times in life it may happen that on awakening in the morning, intuition, appearing to come out of sleep, stands before you, worked out to the last detail. You are then shaking like a leaf, permeated by a will that far exceeds your own will, and in dismay you wonder: "Why must I do this? It interferes with all my plans and wishes, it is too much for me." The highest intuition is described in the Bible as the episode in Gethsemane when Christ becomes aware that He has to face crucifixion and exclaims in desperation: "Take this cup away from me." This cry can sound in everyone's life to a much lesser degree, but for oneself as real: "Take this cup away." If one drinks it anyway, one becomes aware that taking action out of such a situation also generates powers that far exceed one's own abilities. . . .
>
> In intuitive action, man knows himself to be the instrument for higher powers. Personal destiny has to be put aside. One makes

oneself available for that which has to be done at that particular moment in cultural history.[33]

This quality of intuition, defined originally by Rudolf Steiner — along with imagination and inspiration to which he gave equally specialized meanings — forms the foundation of "living thinking"[34] which he would probably view as antecedent to any "living speech." Living thinking grows out of imagination, by which we are able to create vivid inner images not dependent on immediate sensory data, and out of inspiration, through which we are able to listen into the world — "to hear what is going on in the heart of things."[35] Living thinking manifests when developed intuition enables one to "creep into all things"[36] and to experience them with the same reality as one's own "I."

Through intuition, one's sense of the whole[37] becomes as strong as one's sense of self, and thus one's actions sustain the whole which, for the initiate-speaker, includes the whole of language and speech. Georg Kühlewind contends,

> The Logos is not alive in contemporary languages, and has not been for a long time. These languages are word-languages, i.e., every word "means" something once and for all. They are not appropriate to express life or presence directly, but only indirectly as signals for the wordless word. True thinking, improvisation (when one does not know in advance what one is going to think — a rare achievement), *lives* beyond word-languages. Once thinking and speaking were united, as they still are today for the child. Living thinking must penetrate solidified, dead language: this is the resurrection of language.[38]

Wendell Berry maintains, "You cannot speak or act in your own best interest without espousing and serving a higher interest," and yet "It is not knowledge that enforces this realization, but the humbling awareness of the insufficiency of knowledge, of mystery."[39] In other words, the paradoxical nature of divine otherness empowers one's speaking at the same time it gives one nothing to stand on.

In his humanly divine otherness, Feirefiz resurrects Parzival and the initiate-speaker from the deadness of "single vision," where meaning lies caged in words. Multiple perspectives and multiple meanings, coming through the encounter with otherness, nourish the initiate-speaker's growing conviction that meaning is not a scarce commodity. The initiate-speaker's confidence thrives on this awareness of access to unceasing abundance. As a result, the ever more luminous spiritual presence of the initiate-speaker can be heard and felt in his or her speaking.

However, a wealth of meaning often leads to a poverty of words. Certainly the initiate-speaker will have moments when words, rhythm, presence, timeliness and beauty all harmonize, but such moments will be the exception, not the rule. The speech for which Parzival and the initiate-speaker have labored is not usually bejeweled, nor does it conceal them behind impressive articulation. Parzival admits as much when he apologetically compares his speech to Feirefiz's.[40]

Most often, the speech of the Grail reveals the initiate-speaker in naked simplicity. As poet Coleman Barks suggests: "Today the sign of devotion is the clear, plain talk of the man who's trying to be honest. . . . That is the sign of ecstasy — stammering, rather than ornate overstatement."[41] And Robert Bly emphasizes, "if you want a spiritual point to come across with full force, you need to use absolutely ordinary cat-and-dog language."[42] But James Hillman adds:

> . . . this speech cannot be uncultured and unhistorical. The grunt and slogan of an anticulture will not do, because such simplicity and rudeness do not reflect the psyche's needs. Verbal stupidities are merely the obverse of academic verbiage, a reaction against the old ego and its literalness, its lack of imagination. Although not fashioned in schools, this language will be fashioned and schooled, it will be rich and full speech, a tongue of metaphor, of poetry and myth.[43]

Ultimately, however, no rule or formula obtains for speech of the Grail, and the concern of the initiate-speaker is not so much on the simplicity or ornateness of the speech, its abundance or frugality, but, thanks to Feirefiz, on its direction and its movement. One wants to speak, of course, so that one's partner can understand; even better, says Georg Kühlewind, is to "speak in such a way that your partner is stimulated to think further."[44] The gift must always move.

The initiate-speaker has learned from Feirefiz to regard speaking as a gift, as a giveaway, as food for others. Speech-as-gift promotes community because its orientation, and primary loyalty, is toward the recipient(s), not toward the speaker or the content. Speech-as-gift partakes of an ethics that elevates "goodness" over "correctness" or even "rightness," as Rudolf Steiner elaborates:

> We must develop an ear for goodness in our speaking. . . . Today it is not a matter as to whether what is said is correct in a logical, abstract way. Much more depends on the context in which utterances are made, or are not made; one should develop a feeling for what is justified in a given context; what is good in certain relationships and not good in other relationships. We must learn an ethics of speech over and above rhetoric and logic.[45]

Departing for the Grail castle, in tandem with Feirefiz, Parzival humbly carries forth the gift of speech that will heal Anfortas. His brave heart, filled now with real feeling, beats with a new fire of faithful devotion, and, if he knew the words, he might be singing:

> O wonderful! O wonderful! O wonderful!
> I am food! I am food! I am food!
> I eat food! I eat food! I eat food!
> My name never dies, never dies, never dies!
> I was born first in the first of the worlds,
>   earlier than the gods, in the belly of what has no death.
> Whoever gives me away has helped me the most!
> I, who am food, eat the eater of food!
> I have overcome this world.
>
> He who knows this shines like the sun.
> Such are the laws of mystery![46]

BOOK XVI

The planets have returned to the conjunction when Anfortas's wound pains him most, and he screams in agony. He lies on a bed encrusted with jewels, some of which inspire high courage and others, healing. Herbs and spices are applied to ease the wound and lessen its stench, but they have little effect. Anfortas has repeatedly begged his attendants to let him die, and they might have done so if

Trevrizent had not read on the Grail that Parzival would return. Awaiting him, they continue to bring the Grail before Anfortas so he can gaze upon it, and it keeps him alive.

Parzival, Feirefiz and Cundrie arrive at the Grail castle. Templars ride out to defend the castle, then hesitate when they notice Cundrie's cloak covered with turtledoves. Feirefiz is ready to fight, but Cundrie grabs his bridle and points out that these knights are now all in Parzival's service. She introduces Parzival to the knights, who take off their helmets to honor him and his brother. Then they all enter the great hall, where they are welcomed by throngs of courtiers. Their armor is removed, and they are given identical clothes to wear and golden goblets from which to drink and refresh themselves.

They go immediately to Anfortas, who receives them with joy, though his suffering is evident. He begs Parzival to keep him from the sight of the Grail for seven nights and eight days. Then he can die and "all my lamentations will cease. I do not dare give you any further hint."[47]

Tears stream down Parzival's face as he asks where the Grail is kept. "If God's goodness triumphs in me, this throng of people shall be witness to it."[48] Facing in the direction of the Grail, he genuflects three times in honor of the Trinity, praying that he can be of help to Anfortas. Then he stands up and asks the question that he failed to ask the first time: "Uncle, what is it that troubles you?"[49] Immediately, Anfortas's grey complexion grows rosy, and his beauty surpasses everyone else's. Parzival is declared King and Lord of the castle in accordance with the writing on the Grail. Now his wealth matches that of Feirefiz.

Condwiramurs, meanwhile, has been told of the message that appeared on the Grail concerning her husband. Along with her twin boys, she is being guided toward Munsalvaesche by Sigune's father, Kyot, and others. Parzival has arranged to meet her at the place where, so long ago, he was hypnotized by the three drops of blood on the snow. In the interim, Parzival goes to see Trevrizent to tell him that Anfortas has been healed.

Trevrizent gratefully congratulates Parzival: "You have forced God by defiance to make His infinite Trinity grant your will."[50] He confesses that he lied to Parzival in one of his teachings in order to deter him from a pointless quest. After all, it had "never happened that anyone could ever fight his way to the Grail, and I would gladly have dissuaded you."[51]

Parzival asks Trevrizent's blessing to go to meet Condwiramurs. Trevrizent readily complies, commending Parzival to humility. Parzival rides through the night to Condwiramurs' camp, arriving at daybreak. Duke Kyot takes him to the tent where Condwiramurs lies sleeping, her sons naked beside her on the bed. She awakens when Kyot slaps the bed, telling her it is time to laugh merrily, and in an instant flings herself into Parzival's embrace. After they have kissed, Parzival turns to Kardeiz and Loherangrin, who are now sitting up sleepily in bed, and kisses each of them lovingly. Kyot then conducts the boys and the attendants away from the tent so that Parzival and Condwiramurs can be alone with one another until midmorning.

From here on, Wolfram refers to Parzival as "the King." After spending time with Condwiramurs and attending a Mass, Parzival confirms that one twin, Kardeiz, will become king of the lands that Parzival had inherited or won previously. Kardeiz receives his crown and, after a breakfast feast, returns homeward with his armies from those lands. Then Parzival, Condwiramurs, Loherangrin and their entourage depart for Munsalvaesche.

On the way back, Parzival recognizes the landscape and remembers a hermitage there. When he consults the templars, they say they know of it, that it houses a grieving widow who is a paragon of goodness. He asks them to lead the way there but, when they arrive, they find Sigune has died, kneeling by the coffin in the posture of prayer. At Parzival's command, the stone lid of the coffin is lifted to reveal Schianatulander still radiant in his beauty, and Sigune is placed beside him. Condwiramurs feels very sad because she was raised by Sigune's mother.

Back at Munsalvaesche, Feirefiz and Anfortas await the return of Parzival with his family. When they arrive, Condwiramurs greets Feirefiz with the accustomed kiss, but Loherangrin refuses to kiss his uncle because he is frightened of his strange appearance. Feirefiz laughs at this but is hardly at a loss for kisses since everyone is now welcoming everyone else with so many kisses that Wolfram says even he feels weary from so much kissing.

This being such a festive occasion, the Grail procession will precede the dinner. Feirefiz escorts Condwiramurs into the great hall where three huge fireplaces are blazing. Parzival, Feirefiz and Anfortas sit together on a seat more intricately adorned than the rest. No bleeding lance is brought in this time, but, otherwise, all else unfolds as it did during Parzival's first visit. The ceremony culminates with the entrance of the Grail, carried by the virtuous and beautiful Repanse de Schoye who is, following the instructions on the Grail itself, the only person allowed to carry it. The feast ensues with everyone being given whatever they request to eat or drink.

When Feirefiz asks what keeps filling the dishes, everyone realizes he cannot see the Grail. Feirefiz himself is not all that disturbed at this. What really distresses him is that his heart has been captured by Repanse de Schoye, and he now suffers great pangs of yearning for her. Anfortas suggests that, since she is Parzival's aunt, perhaps Parzival can help Feirefiz win her favor.

Meanwhile, word filters forth from Titurel, the radiant white-haired man in the inner castle, that Feirefiz cannot see the Grail because he is not baptized. Parzival and Anfortas then urge Feirefiz to receive baptism. Feirefiz responds by asking eagerly if this will help him obtain the love of Repanse de Schoye, because his longing for her causes him more pain than any he has known in battle.

Parzival, who feels comfortable addressing Feirefiz in the familiar now that their wealth is about equal, says that, if Feirefiz agrees to be baptized, he can sue for the love of Repanse de Schoye. Feirefiz is ready at once:

> If baptism can be gotten by combat, then lead me to it right away and let me serve for her reward. I have always loved the tune of splinters flying from a joust and swords ringing on helmets![52]

Parzival laughs heartily at this and gently explains that baptism cannot be gotten that way:

> I will bring her within your reach by means of *real* baptism. You will have to give up your god Jupiter for her sake, and renounce Secundille too. Tomorrow morning I will give you some advice that will serve your purposes.[53]

In the morning, Parzival and Anfortas accompany Feirefiz into the temple to stand before the Grail. Parzival reminds Feirefiz that he will have to renounce all other gods and to serve the "Highest God" steadfastly if he is to have the love of Repanse de Schoye. Tipping the baptismal font toward the Grail which then fills it with water neither too hot nor cold, an aged priest performs the rite and speaks briefly of the life-giving power of water. Feirefiz solemnly abjures both his former gods and his service to his wife Secundille. Now he is able to see the Grail, but he waits impatiently for a greater happiness, his bride Repanse de Schoye, who soon approaches him.

Upon the Grail they now find written that any Grail knight who God appoints to act as king in a foreign land can help the people there so long as no one asks his name or race. If such questions are put to him, the Grail knight will depart and no longer help the kingdoms to which he has been sent. Anfortas had to wait so long, Wolfram tells us, that now the Grail keepers want no questions asked about them: "Questioning is forever displeasing to them."[54]

As Feirefiz prepares to leave, he tries to convince Anfortas to come with him and obtain riches in the East. Anfortas declines, explaining that, through pride, he has already lost the greatest wealth, which is the crown of the Grail castle, and that from now on he intends humbly to serve the Grail as a templar. He adds that, although he bears them no ill will, he will not serve women again. Feirefiz then offers to take Loherangrin with him, but Condwiramurs objects and Parzival declares that Loherangrin is "destined for the Grail and there he must submissively devote his heart if God permits him to achieve the proper spirit."[55]

After twelve more days of festivities, Parzival sadly bids farewell to Feirefiz and Repanse de Schoye. He has sent Anfortas and many horsemen out ahead of them to make safe their path through the forests, and Cundrie *la sorcière* precedes them along the way to announce their coming and ensure they are well cared for in castles en route to the harbor. When they finally reach the harbor where Feirefiz's ships are waiting, they learn that Queen Secundille has died. Now Repanse de Schoye can feel truly glad about this journey for the first time.

She and Feirefiz go to the East, as far as India, where she gives birth to a son called Prester John. From then on, that is the name given to all kings there. Feirefiz orders writings about Christian life to be sent throughout all the lands in the East, and he continues to send messages back to Parzival through Cundrie.

Loherangrin grows up and wins honor in his service of the Grail. Brought to her shore by a swan, he wins the love of a princess of Brabant and marries her on the condition that she never ask who he is. In time, she breaks her promise and does ask him, and so he must regretfully board the swan boat and leave her to return to tending the Grail.

Wolfram ends the epic by claiming that his is the complete and true version of the Grail story and that he has remained true to telling it as it was told to him by "the master," Kyot, the Provencal.

> His children and his high race I have rightly named for you, Parzival's I mean, whom I brought to the place which, in spite of everything, his blessedness had destined for him. A life so concluded that God is not robbed of the soul through fault of the body, and which can obtain the world's favor with dignity, *that* is worthy work.
>
> To good women, if they are sensible, I am all the more worthy — in case one of them wishes me well — now that I have completed this story. If it was done for a woman's sake, she will have to speak sweet words to me.[56]

Initiatory Themes

In this final episode of the Grail epic, King Parzival shows all the signs of hard-won sovereignty and authority, incorporating the qualities of the three kings who have joined with him — Feirefiz, Gawan and Arthur. Like Feirefiz, he moves swiftly and confidently to his tasks; he heals Anfortas with the right question, visits Trevrizent, reunites with Condwiramurs, designates his son Kardeiz as ruler of his former lands. Like Gawan, he spontaneously expresses authentic feeling — weeping and laughing, joyously embracing Condwiramurs, whom he has remained loyal to and served with much suffering all this time — and then serves as mediator in helping Feirefiz marry his beloved. Like Arthur, he officiates with authority; he knows who belongs here and what the requirements of this realm are, as he demonstrates in his statements to Feirefiz about baptism and, later, about Loherangrin's apprenticeship.

Yet Parzival also differs from these other kings. Feirefiz invokes his pagan gods to accompany him, to strengthen his intention. Parzival kneels before his God and prays for the healing force of divine intercession. Gawan weeps on his own account and laughs with derision at Clinschor's castration, and his negotiations of complicated emotional claims must follow convoluted paths. Parzival weeps for another, Anfortas, then laughs with loving fondness for yet another, Feirefiz; his mediation is not so much between persons as between realms. He sends Kardeiz off to his realm, places Signune in her coffin so she may leave this realm and be with her beloved, assists Feirefiz in joining the Christian realm, arranges the wedding that takes Repanse de Schoye to Feirefiz's realm, and then receives Feirefiz's messages from the East, which, we can assume, he then communicates to Arthur. Arthur and his court defend the code of knightly conduct, making — or breaking — knights on the basis of how well they have lived in accord with its well-known mandates. Parzival, on the other hand, serves the Grail, his authority rooted in his surrender, not in his adherence to a code. The requirements of the Grail are its own and are ever changing; no one rule is written long on it. As Grail king, Parzival confers baptism instead of knighthood.

His kingship of heartful service commences when he asks the long-awaited question. There lies Anfortas. His bed sparkles with fifty-eight jewels, which gleam with all the light of the earth's depths yet cannot assuage his suffering. No earthly medicines, even the magic salves of Cundrie *la sorcière,* have eased his pain. The rhythms of his torments are enforced from above, in the movements of the planets and the stars. Since only spoken words can heal him, it can be assumed that such words belong to cosmic realms; like the human beings who speak them, they are on the earth, but they are not of the earth.

Anfortas had forgotten (or ignored) his cosmic origins and, while pursuing earthly passion, had neglected the greater love he was to serve. "He is Grail King who knows that in the human being the Cosmos is active," says W.J. Stein.[57] Anfortas betrayed his office, and now he suffers "unearthly" torment to learn what he should have known. Perhaps Anfortas failed because he inherited his position as Grail king. Parzival has earned it. The seeming paradox is that his kingship of surrender has been won by the utmost yearning, determination, and dogged perseverance. Even Trevrizent marvels that Parzival has been able to "fight his way" to the Grail, though this had been deemed impossible.

What has Parzival fought for? Remembering Wolfram's promise to tell of a hero grown "slowly wise," we might say first of all that Parzival has fought for self-knowledge: knowledge of his name, his heritage, his mistakes and failures, his task and calling, and of his human nature in all its black-and-white mixedness. Becoming aware of and responsible for that magpie nature has unveiled a swan — in the guise of his son — at the end of the story.

We could also say that Parzival has fought for the freedom to "obey." He obeys his calling, which was present from the beginning but which he could know only by becoming one with it through his journey. That calling is to serve the Grail in each moment of his life — which is to say, to serve what each moment is calling for.

Parzival and the initiate-speaker have not only fought for an introverted, reflective self-knowledge but also for an ability to see and listen which enables them to "read" the things, the people, the appearances of the world. This knowledge has a more extroverted quality, relating to the world and everything in it as "text." The "speech" of the Grail itself is silent, a commanding script that appears and disappears, that somehow conducts a dialogue with those addressed, and that must be read by those who would serve its bidding.[58]

When Parzival asks the long-awaited question, no answer is given — verbally. What changes is an appearance; Anfortas's grey, suffering countenance transforms to one of rosy, robust health and beauty. This changed appearance must be "read" as the response to the question. From now on, the Grail keepers themselves can be recognized only by this kind of "reading", since their identity may no longer be asked. They reflect the inscribed "speech" of the Grail they serve, appearing and then disappearing when their work is done or when, instead of being "read," they are questioned about their identity. Anyone who serves the Grail will be recognized, if at all, by who they are — which is to say, how perceptively they "read" and serve what they "read" — more than by what they say.

That Parzival has developed this more extroverted knowledge is evident in his surer sense of orientation now, as compared with his wanderings when he let loose the reins of his horse and knew neither where he was going nor where he had arrived. At the beginning of the episode, he knows his destination is the Grail castle. He knows where he has been because he can find his way back to meet Condwiramurs at the place where the three drops of blood on the snow held him hypnotized long ago. He knows where he is, as shown by his recognition — for the first time in four encounters — of Sigune's place in the forest.

Significantly — and this represents a great change in him — his "reading" of things does not result in his going off alone to respond to what calls to him in each of these instances. Instead, he follows Cundrie to the Grail castle and accepts her advice when the templars come out to meet them. He seeks Trevrizent's blessing to go to reunite with Condwiramurs. He asks assistance from his knights to lead him to Sigune's hermitage. Service of the Grail takes place in community and always facilitates union; it is not a matter of individual heroics such as service of the Round Table inspires. Servants of the Grail foster connections in the world and with each other, as we see in Cundrie. Parzival's first act as Grail king is to help Feirefiz win Repanse de Schoye through baptism.

The fiery "yes" of restless Feirefiz unites with the gentle, plantlike assent of Repanse de Schoye, whose skin has the "luster of flowers"[59] and who, in her dark green cloak, is the only person permitted to carry the Grail. The water of baptism makes this marriage possible, and when fire meets water, the force of steam erupts. If harnessed, this force can move even iron locomotives; the powers of fire and water are both augmented. Feirefiz, who teaches Parzival how to be food for others, instinctively knows that his "yield" will increase in verdant partnership with Repanse de Schoye. When fire of the sun unites with moisture of the earth in the plant, the flower blooms. Flowers, as we remember each spring, always announce new life — on the earth and in the seeds within them, which are the secret of the next year's new life. Thus, the marriage of Feirefiz and Repanse de Schoye represents a flowering, facilitated by Parzival's service of the Grail, which bears all life toward the future.

The activity of the Grail revives the ailing, relieves stagnation, reunites people and kingdoms, *and* sets them in motion toward their destinies. It is noteworthy that all Parzival's actions in this episode portend something for the future. His work here differs from the delicate sorting out and matching up that Gawan achieved prior to the great wedding ceremony. That had the feeling of "they all lived happily ever after" — a fairy tale kind of completion. In contrast, each of Parzival's deeds accomplishes or will beget change.

His question heals Anfortas, yet changes the requirements of those who serve the Grail; they are now not to be questioned about their identity. Anfortas himself will now have quite a changed life. The armies returning home with their young king Kardeiz will, no doubt, have a long period of transition while their king grows up. Condwiramurs is now queen of the Grail castle. We are not told what change she will bring, but certainly her and Parzival's reign will be very different from that of the headstrong, then wounded Anfortas.

We are given a glimpse into the future of their other son, who, having grown up under the tutelage of the Grail, becomes the mysterious Swan Knight for the princess of Brabant. Feirefiz and Repanse de Schoye's future is also described, along with their future son's importance in spreading Christianity in the East.

Finally, there is Sigune placed gently in the coffin, reunited in death with Schianatulander. His body has not decomposed, which implies that he is not subject to the laws of time and decay. Now she, the ever-sorrowing widow, has been returned to him, outside of time as we know it. Something has ended here: Sigune's mourning. But most certainly something else has begun — in Parzival. This has been true every time he met Sigune. She has appeared "like clockwork" at important moments in the story: first when she told him his name and some of his past; then when she announced his failure at the Grail castle, thus informing him of his present; then when she sent him after Cundrie, which led to his encounter with Trevrizent and his future. In this last meeting, she offers him a glimpse of timelessness, a realm extending beyond past, present and future.

The journey toward speech of the Grail does not proceed in a linear manner, starting and ending all at once. It is an unfolding in the field of what we call time, enfolded, all the while, in what we call the timeless. The speech of the Grail, Wolfram seems to be saying, keeps these two realms in touch, in a proper marriage to one another. Through that conjunction, new life — change and transformation — appears. Thus Wolfram's weaving concludes with "loose ends" — some mysteries, some previews, but no tidy knots.

We have come full cycle in the spiral, and a new cycle has already begun. Gahmuret's high yearning, which he sought to satisfy in the East, has returned with Feirefiz coming to the West, marrying Repanse de Schoye and returning to the East with a higher king to serve, Christ. Herzeloyde's tears at being abandoned are transmuted in the waters of baptism over which Parzival officiates and by which he reconnects the realms: East and West, horizontal and vertical. When the highest aspirations of East and West are married through baptism, Christ's nourishment — that feast of brotherly love, so different from the feisty comradeship of the Round Table — can be shared throughout the far reaches of the earth.

Toward Speech of the Grail

The end of the story does not signal the end of the journey for the initiate-speaker either. Certainly an increasing confidence underlies one's speaking, but, since the speech of the Grail ever requires attunement, an ability to "read" the moment and recognize what it calls for, there is never a sense of having "arrived" once and for all. For the speech of the Grail to engender liveliness and healing in the world, each moment must be met as new, as a wondrous wildness to which one seeks to relate, not to control.

How to relate creatively to wildness, how to leave things intact, free, still breathing in all their beauty and mystery, while simultaneously building an understanding of them, is a definitive late twentieth-century concern in fields as diverse as science, ecology, archetypal psychology, poetry and literary criticism — and the question concerns the initiate-speaker no less. The challenge is to claim a place for oneself, for one's imagination and intellect, in this world without having to kill the world to do it. The wildness in the world, in other people and in ourselves will, now and then, confound us, betray our expectations and ideals, challenge our need to feel in control and therefore terrify us.[60] To maintain respectful relatedness under such conditions can only be accomplished by a courageous commitment to stay open, to keep learning, to live out of ever-changing questions rather than hardened definitions.

Improvisation is the key. The initiate-speaker emulates the jazz musician who makes no claim for any final answer or all-encompassing knowledge of the right way. Rather, holding onto a basic "line" of intention, the musician improvises out of what arises within and appears without, constantly accepting new impulses and ideas and working them into a pattern that somehow "fits," expresses some truth or coherency for that moment.[61] Wise fools portrayed in old stories and spiritual masters have always known that the harmonies of the wild world are two intricate for ordinary consciousness to comprehend fully. These teachers point beyond modes of ordinary understanding — to presence, to play, to improvisational artistry. But they do not say this is easy. Those who embody the presence to relate playfully to wildness have undergone rigorous initiation.

From here on, the initiate-speaker's practice is to be simultaneously "conscious" and "spontaneous" in relating to each moment.

This could be called "performance" of relationship, the performance essential for human beings to feel at home in this world. When we do not perform relationship, then we tend to perpetuate violence, overtly or subtly, toward others or ourselves. The word "performance" seems appropriate because it suggests the "as if" quality in this making, this claiming, of relationship. Relationship must always be created, then re-created; it is never given and cannot be taken for granted.

In traditional human communities, the time-honored form for performing relationship was ceremony. Ceremonies marked all life transitions, re-establishing the community's (and therefore the individual's) connections, social and spiritual, when birth, puberty, marriage, illness, death, hunting, planting, war, startling natural phenomena and other wild occurrences required the community to re-organize in relationship to something new. From these ancestors, as well as Gawan and Feirefiz, Parzival and the initiate-speaker have learned the value of ceremony, and a ceremonial sensibility will infuse their improvisational relatedness with each wild moment.

A closer look at the moment when Parzival asks the long-awaited question, and at the question itself, should disclose how all this actually works in the speech of the Grail. First, though, let us remember who leads Parzival to the Grail castle and helps him to recognize that the templars riding out to meet them have not come to attack but are in his service. Cundrie, the dark and loathly one, she who shames and scourges him and then announces his call to the Grail, rides in front. To approach the Grail castle, Parzival and the initiate-speaker must follow her guidance. She represents forthright self-honesty, not confined by appearances, and she will not be mocked or ignored. When the initiate-speaker becomes inflated, or attempts to "look good" or "sound good," she will be there to shame the sham. When the initiate-speaker is authentic — as Cundrie herself is — and not attached to appearances, she offers her willing service as connecting messenger, keeping all the personages within in contact with one another. As we gaze with Wolfram into the future, we see that she is still carrying messages between Feirefiz in far-off India and Parzival at the Grail castle.

When Parzival arrives in the great hall, he goes straight to Anfortas. No longer in the thrall of what he has been told to do and say, Parzival "reads" Anfortas's suffering, and his own spontaneous tears flow from his eyes. In other words, he is now able both to *see* and *bear the pain of seeing* the suffering around him. But the spontaneous emotions do not deflect him from his calling. Nor is he unaware of timing and ceremony. He does not awkwardly blurt out the question. Instead, he asks where the Grail is kept and, facing in its direction, genuflects three times and prays for God's goodness to "triumph in me." Then he asks the question: "Uncle what is it that troubles you?"

A subtle alchemy operates here. What Parzival says is not entirely his own, and yet it is. Certainly, Trevrizent told him the content of the question. And certainly, he is deeply pained by Anfortas's suffering and wants to be of help. Yet, finally, the question he asks is neither only what he has been *"taught"* to ask nor only what he *"wants"* to ask but also what he *"must"* ask, in freely chosen service of the Grail. Just as the dishes fill when placed in front of the Grail, just as the baptismal font fills when tipped toward the Grail, so Parzival is filled with the speech of the Grail when he points himself in its direction. And what the Grail fills him with is speech that serves all its recipients and the wider world. Although the content of what the initiate-speaker says may be very personal,[62] if the speaking is not first placed in service of the whole community, then it is not speech of the Grail. It will not heal the ailing king nor accomplish the marriage between the realms.

In its many possible expressions, speech of the Grail transmits meaning and inspires change or movement by opening a space in which its recipients experience the freedom to choose, the freedom to create. And, it must be remembered, one of these recipients is always the speaker. Wolfram's story portrays the change such speaking produces in the initiate-speaker by crowning Parzival king of the Grail castle, after he has spoken the question. The crowning experience for the initiate-speaker is the increasingly strong contact with his or her speaking presence, the unconditioned "I-being" that lives in any truly free activity of each human being. When united with that speaking presence, the initiate-speaker becomes spiritually sovereign: like Parzival and Christ, free to follow and obey his or her highest calling.

The actual question Parzival asks, however, is utterly unremarkable. Certainly it is a loving inquiry, which commentators have noted. And, as we have seen, any serious question simultaneously reveals something about the speaker, makes contact with another person, and, if followed far enough beyond physical appearances, can lead both inquirer and respondent to profoundly connective philosophical and metaphysical insights. But, still, we might expect some more noteworthy rendering of Parzival's first speech of the Grail at this dramatic moment toward which the whole story has been directed. Wolfram's version of the Grail hero's question seems so ordinary, so obvious in its meaning that it has received little attention.

And right there is the clue: attention. Our attention is so ordinary, so taken-for-granted, that we rarely notice it. Only when something "grabs" it — like a frightening, horrific, or sexually stimulating image — or when someone "wants" it — like our teachers or our children — do we become aware of our attention. Otherwise, our attention seems as unexceptional as Parzival's question, as inconspicuous as a pebble on the road. Yet the source for Parzival's question is the Grail, a "stone of the purest kind," says Trevrizent, with such power that "flesh and bones are at once made young again" and the whole world can be healed. Surely the question Parzival asks must somehow partake of this power.

Within Parzival's question resides his human attention, his genuine interest, and this is what has the power to heal Anfortas, to transform the world suffering for its lack. The power of focused human attention is mighty, and can be used, and manipulated, for good or ill as long as a person remains unconscious of it. Parzival's whole journey has awakened him to the power of his attention and has trained him in obedience to its highest expression: faithful and active love. Unconsciously directed attention is not the same as love, though it can be loving. But making a totally free choice to give our attention *is* the same as love, producing all the results we associate with love. And that is why no response to Parzival's question is necessary; the result is the response.

We should notice that Parzival does not merely think about the Grail nor simply imagine its nearby presence before he speaks. He turns his body toward the Grail and then genuflects for the Trinity whose goodness flows toward him through the Grail. "If you want to enroll in the mystery school of incarnate love, the form you have to fill out is a human body," affirms William Irwin Thompson.[63]

Heart, mind, and imagination all work together in the speech of the Grail, and also the body.

Like all words,[64] "body" can be read with more resonances than "just" a physical corpus. Given recent insights of ecological and immunological sciences and even Biblical scholarship,[65] it has become increasingly difficult to define just what the body is, distinct from its total environment. Yes, the body, as we sense and experience it, appears to be that aspect of us which is most time-bound and particular — down to its individual voiceprint and fingerprint. At the same time, the body is a mysterious manifestation, or incarnation, through which some not-so-physical soul-spirit experiences the world. So, speech that comes from the body is speech born of this manifest union of the time-bound and particular with the timeless and universal.

Part of what the body manifests is its relationship to time, thereby giving us the experience of the "passage" of time, of aging and death. The body, from the moment of birth, is giving itself to death, even as it works very hard to live. Thus the speech of the Grail, embodied as it must be, is speech fully imbued with a sense of transience, of death.[66] In the time of purely oral transmission, before printed texts, when words were said, they were truly gone, "dead" except for whatever movements they inspired in their speakers and hearers. A poignant sense of aesthetic immediacy, though not necessarily urgency, permeates speech infused with one's awareness of one's own death and the impermanence of what one is saying. One must have an acceptance and trust, like that sometimes witnessed in dying humans and animals, that, though something dies, it is not lost.

Like the great river of life itself, the speech of the Grail flows from all that has gone before and all that has yet to come in all the realms. Reposing serenely upon that current, Parzival and the initiate-speaker bring to mind the swan, the last bird Wolfram associates with his hero, who — in the person of his son, the Swan Knight — glides on into the future. The silent presence of the swan floats alluringly on the reflective surface of the water, gazing into depths beyond its own reflection. Through the ages, poets have maintained that swans can see into the future and will only open their throats — to sing! — at their death.[67]

What vision causes the swan to sing when it dies? Will it share this secret with the initiate-speaker so that the silent faithfulness of his or her speaking presence can take wing in the speech of the Grail? We leave Wolfram's story carrying these questions, as articulated by Mary Oliver in her poem "The Swan."[68]

> Across the wide waters
>   something comes
>   floating — a slim
>   and delicate
>
> ship, filled
>   with white flowers —
>   and it moves
>   on its miraculous muscles
>
> as though time didn't exist,
>   as though bringing such gifts
>   to the dry shore
>   was a happiness
>
> almost beyond bearing.
>   And now it turns its dark eyes,
>   it rearranges
>   the clouds of its wings,
>
> it trails
>   an elaborate webbed foot,
>   the color of charcoal.
>   Soon it will be here.
>
> Oh, what shall I do
>   when that poppy-colored beak
>   rests in my hand?
>   Said Mrs. Blake of the poet:
>
> I miss my husband's company —
>   he is so often
>   in paradise.
>   Of course! the path to heaven

doesn't lie down in flat miles.
    It's in the imagination
        with which you perceive
           this world,

and the gestures
    with which you honor it.
        Oh, what will I do, what will I say, when those
        white wings
           touch the shore?

NOTES

[1] Wolfram, Book XV, 745.

[2] Wolfram, Book XV, 745.

[3] Wolfram, Book XV, 747.

[4] Wolfram, Book XV, 747.

[5] Wolfram, Book XV, 748.

[6] Wolfram, Book XV, 749.

[7] Wolfram, Book XV, 752.

[8] Wolfram, Book XV, 781.

[9] Wolfram, Book XV, 782.

[10] Wolfram, Book XV, 783.

[11] Wolfram, Book XV, 783.

[12] Wolfram, Book XV, 786.

[13] Wolfram, Book XV, 786.

[14] Feirefiz's loose attachment to form is shown by his willingness to introduce himself first, when Parzival refuses; by his throwing his sword away; and, in the last episode, by his laughing when Loherangrin is too afraid to kiss him, and his renunciation of his gods and his wife so that he can be baptized and marry Repanse de Schoye.

[15] Walter Johannes Stein, *The Death of Merlin: Arthurian Myth and Alchemy*, 195.

[16] Carl Kerenyi, *Dionysos: Archetypal Image of Indestructible Life.*

[17] Walter F. Otto, *Dionysus: Myth and Cult,* 95.

[18] Otto, 154.

[19] Otto, 153.

[20] Otto, 156.

[21] William Irwin Thompson, *Imaginary Landscape: Making Worlds of Myth and Science,* 69.

[22] Brother David Steindl-Rast, "Paths of Obedience: Fairy Tales and the Monk's Way," *Parabola,* Aug. 1980, 43.

[23] Lewis Hyde, *The Gift: Imagination and the Erotic Life of Property,* 45.

[24] Hyde, 47.

[25] Hyde: ". . . Like the Maori or the Jews of the Old Testament, the North Pacific tribes developed a relationship to the natural abundance of their environment based upon a cycle of gifts" (26).

[26] Hyde, 27.

[27] Hyde, 36.

[28] Hyde, 33.

[29] Victor Turner, *The Anthropology of Performance,* 92.

[30] Wendell Berry, *Standing by Words,* 34.

[31] Hyde, 4.

[32] Otto, 25.

[33] Bernhard Lievegoed, *Man on the Threshold,* 71–72.

[34] "Living thinking" is a central concept within Steiner's spiritual science and would take many pages for an adequate account. I refer the interested reader to three of Steiner's major works: *The Philosophy of Freedom* (now entitled *Intuitive Thinking As a Spiritual Path*) is Steiner's treatise on freedom in thinking; *How To Know Higher Worlds* describes the processes by which organs of spiritual perception, prerequisite for living thinking, can be developed; *An Outline of Occult Science,* especially chapter 5, "Cognition of the Higher Worlds: Initiation," discusses "sense-free" thinking, which is a synonym for "living thinking."

[35] Rudolf Steiner quoted in publisher's note in Bernhard Lievegoed's *Towards the 21st Century,* v–vi.

36 Ibid., vi.

37 Steiner, in *The Philosophy of Freedom*, states: ". . . What appears to us in observation as separate parts becomes combined, bit by bit, through the coherent unified world of our intuitions. By thinking we fit together again into one piece all that we have taken apart through perceiving" (72–73).

38 Georg Kühlewind, *Becoming Aware of the Logos*, 21–22.

39 Wendell Berry, 50.

40 Wolfram, Book XV, 749. "I would speak better still if I could and without malice. Unfortunately, I am not learned enough to outdo in words your noble praise. But God knows my intention. All the skill of my heart and eyes will never fail to follow what your renown prescribes."

41 Katy Butler, quoting Coleman Barks, "Poetry as Path," *Common Boundary* Nov./Dec. 1991, 16.

42 Butler, 19.

43 James Hillman, *The Myth of Analysis*, 207.

44 Georg Kühlewind, *From Normal to Healthy*, 104.

45 Werner Glas, *An Analytical Study of the Rhetorical Thought of Rudolf Steiner with Some Implications for the Teaching of Speech*, 107. Georg Kühlewind, in *From Normal to Healthy*, concurs: "Speaking is always speaking to and with someone, so that the content and the manner is determined by the partner with whom we are speaking. . . . `I have something to tell you' — and the `something' and the `you' form a unity, neither of which can be right by itself" (104–105).

46 Hyde, xviii, quoting the Taittirya Upanishad.

47 Wolfram, Book XVI, 795.

48 Wolfram, Book XVI, 795.

49 Wolfram, Book XVI, 795. In Chrétien's version (rendered by translators Mustard and Passage on p. 415), there are two questions: "Why does the lance bleed?" and "Whom does one serve with this Grail?" In Robert de Boron's version, the questions are "what the Grail is and who is served from it?" (Jung and Franz, *The Grail Legend*, 290).

50 Wolfram, Book XVI, 798.

51 Wolfram, Book XVI, 798.

52 Wolfram, Book XVI, 814.

[53] Wolfram, Book XVI, 815.

[54] Wolfram, Book XVI, 819.

[55] Wolfram, Book XVI, 820.

[56] Wolfram, Book XVI, 827.

[57] Stein, *The Ninth Century and the Holy Grail*, 209.

[58] Wolfram, Book IX, 483–84.

[59] Wolfram, Book XVI, 809.

[60] Wildness *per se,* by the way, cannot be destroyed: only its forms. Humans may decimate the wild landscape, but then, for instance, the garbage goes wild. Wildness is alive, if not well, in new diseases, economic crises, irrational violence. Just what connection exists between the destruction of nature's wildness and the appearance of wildness in these other forms gives much food for thought.

[61] Georg Kühlewind, in *From Normal to Healthy* suggests: "If one tries to organize one's soul with an orientation to health, that is, to form it consciously, then one thing is of great importance. All exercises seek to dismantle the finished human being, habits and well-worn tracks of the life of the soul, and to call into life an unfinished human being capable of improvisation. . ."(110–111).

[62] Hillman gives us a sense of what is called for in speech that is psychologically alive: "It is speech that leads to participation, in the Platonic sense, in and with the thing spoken of, a speech of stories and insights which evoke, in the other who listens, new stories and new insights, the way one poem and one tune ignite another verse and another song. It is conversations, letters, tales, in which we reveal our dreams and fantasies — and our psychopathology. It evokes, calls forth, and creates psyche as it speaks. It speaks of mood: of 'sadness' and 'despair' before 'depression'; of 'rage' before 'aggression'; of 'fear,' 'panic,' and 'anguish' before 'anxiety attacks'. . . . It must be speech that works as an 'imaginative agent,' stirring fantasy. Such speech has impact because it carries body in it; it is speech alive, the word itself alive, . . . not carefully defined, but freely imagined" (*The Myth of Analysis*, 206).

[63] David Spangler and William Irwin Thompson, *Reimagination of the World: A Critique of the New Age, Science and Popular Culture*, 200.

[64] Georg Kühlewind, "The Pedagogy of the Word: A *Towards* Interview with Georg Kühlewind," *Towards*, Summer/Fall 1984: "Every word has a cloud of meaning. It is not very exact, of course, but all the same each word has a

different cloud. But each word has also another cloud, a cloud of feeling, and this is very often used in poetry. And in meditative language there is a third cloud, an even greater cloud of will. This is used in meditative language and can direct the reader or hearer to find the meaning which is not informative of a meditative sentence. It can direct the movement of the understanding to its source. . . . [T]he appearing part of a language is only a fraction of the real event, of the real process, because this appearing part is integrated by an immense hidden part by which we understand words, connect them, read them together, read the paragraphs together, even chapters together" (8–9).

[65] Robert Mcafee Brown, in *A Handbook of Christian Theology:* "In Pauline thought, for example, the body (*soma*) is an inclusive word for the psychophysical unity of the flesh (*sarx*) and soul (*psyche*). No hard and fast distinction between the two can be established. The body is the whole man, and not a detachable part of man which is distinguished in dualistic fashion from the soul" (355).

[66] Otto: "Death is not to be sought first at the end of life but at its beginning, and . . . it attends all of life's creations" (139).

[67] Beryl Rowland, *Birds with Human Souls: A Guide to Bird Symbolism,* 170.

[68] Mary Oliver, *House of Light,* 16.

The Cloak of Bird-Feathers

Literature is a technique of meditation, in the widest and most flexible sense. We journey through a narrative; then we stop and confront what we have read as though it were objective. It is not objective, because it is already a part of ourselves. There is a further stage of response, however, where something like a journeying movement is resumed, a movement that may well take us far beyond the world's end, and yet is still no journey.[1]

Mazes are in relation to directions what betwixts-and-betweens are in relation to opposites. In passing through a maze one reaches a destination which cannot be located by reference to the points of the compass.[2]

Even through the heavy doors, the silvery jingling of tiny bells could be heard as the Celtic bard strode toward the great hall for the evening festivities. The bard carried a branch of gold, silver or bronze, depending on the degree of training that had been completed, and the branch sported bells that chimed, announcing the entrance of the welcome guest.[3] The bard's ceremonial garment was, typically, a mantle of bird feathers, the *tuigen*, which, as Caitlin Matthews reports, was made of "the skins of birds white and many-colored. . .from the girdle downwards and of mallards' necks and of their crests from the girdle upwards to the neck." Other sources say that the *tuigen* was predominantly of small songbirds' feathers, but that the neck was made of the skin and feathers of the swan, with the swan's neck hanging down behind like the tippet on a modern university gown.[4]

No doubt the bard's footsteps sounded confident on the stones. After all, the initiatory training, much of it conducted in darkness, had lasted at least twelve years,[5] and the status of the bard in society was on a par with that of the king.[6] Such were earthly sources of the bard's confidence. More substantially, through personal aptitudes and then initiation, the Celtic bard — like shamans elsewhere, some of whom also wore bird feathers — had learned to "fly." Carried on the soft winds of the breath, the bard spread wings of words, wondrously lifting self and listeners to worlds far and near in songs, stories, and praise of heroes, ancestors, and beings beyond the mist. In the rich silence that followed, each person and the community as a whole felt restored in the confidence first heard in the bard's step across the threshold.

Some years ago, the inspiration of images such as these spawned a question in my mind: "Is it possible, today, to learn to speak in a way that heals and transforms?" I realized from previous studies and experiences that any answer must come in the form of an initiatory journey that would entail the classical phases: separation, metamorphosis, and return. But where was I to find an initiated master to guide the process? Lacking a druidic bard, I turned to an old story told by a master teller that had, at its heart, an act of healing, transformative speech. This story became a launching point for a "meditation in the widest and most flexible sense" which has included readings, seminars, workshops and numerous inter- and intra-personal events. Now, as I complete the book that resulted from that meditational journey, I think back to those original images of the Celtic bard and wonder if there is any decisive moment when the initiate-speaker "returns" and can authentically claim the cloak of bird-feathers?[7]

Nowadays there is a tendency to make what we imagine into "things," thereby deadening the images. A more demanding practice is to think imaginatively without freezing images into symbols[8] and to embody what we think without hardening our thoughts into "techniques" and "processes," which we then "apply" to others. I use the quotation marks to emphasize that, very often, the noun-forms into which we crystallize experiences and thoughts are not "things" at all but abstractions which have none of the sensual qualities of a thing. (This is not to say that sensual qualities belong only to material things; a mathematical formula can be beautiful, a thought can be penetrating, an emotion can be soft or heavy, and so on.)

Thus my intention was to write an imaginative document that would inspire further imagining about speech of the Grail, that would display scholarly support of the ideas presented, but would not portray either the initiation process or the speech of the Grail as "things" that can be marketed in "how-to" manuals. I hoped to avoid any suggestion that the journey toward speech of the Grail can be taught in some conventional fashion. Werner Glas believes that, if Rudolf Steiner had established a school for the spiritual training of speakers, he would have required apprentices to be at least in their mid-thirties. I agree with Glas that, in most cases, considerable life experience is prerequisite for speech of the Grail.[9]

The initiatory labyrinth that leads to the speech of the Grail does not exist in physical space, as did, purportedly, the labyrinths in ancient Crete and other places. The labyrinth imagined here is a spiraling movement through one's life as one practices attentive relatedness to oneself, other people, the world, and language itself. Ripening through that labyrinthine journey, the contact with one's speaking presence gradually empowers one's speech to further others in like movement in their own lives.

Such furtherance, whenever it occurs in private or professional milieus, is experienced as "meaning." The recipient of the speech of the Grail feels a sense of "coming home" and of new possibilities opening. At one and the same moment, one feels both more known (and knowing) and more cognizant of the vast unknown. Mystery and familiarity dance together, as they do in all good marriages. Journeying with Parzival, we have seen that the speech of the Grail creates, manifests within, and is sustained by such marriages.

Four marriages in particular structure the labyrinthine pattern of the journey. Each of the characters of these marriages, I propose, lives within the initiate-speaker and, as the initiate-speaker comes to know and unite these pairs within — as Wolfram does in his story —

the speech of the Grail becomes possible. Each pair contributes to an aspect of the labyrinth. The labyrinth itself represents a movement which we apprehend in three ways: as the speech of the Grail, as the path toward it, and as the speaker.

Arthur and Ginover mark the place where the labyrinth appears. They rule the whole of the everyday, conscious personality of the initiate-speaker, and they are noble, if not observably powerful, in Wolfram's depiction. They seem to reign as enlightened older "parents." Though sometimes "in the dark," not really knowing what is happening, they are able not only to adapt to, but even to go out of their way — by moving the whole court — to welcome newness and change as it enters their realm through Parzival, Gawan, and Feirefiz. At the same time, they maintain the integrity of the whole. They serve the community of the initiate-speaker's personality as patient, enlightened elders, who fit the characterization Jungian analyst Allan Chinen derives from fairy tales about persons at midlife and after: "If the virtues of youth are courage, perseverance and confidence, those of the elder are alertness, openness and curiosity."[10]

Gawan and Orgeluse, as it were, compose the line demarcating the labyrinth. Manifestation in the realm of appearance is fraught with peril. One can easily be misled and become captive to magic in the Castle of Wonders. Thus, this union takes the longest to accomplish and comes about only through Gawan's courageous humility[11] as he seeks to develop the real feeling of the heart able to see and listen past appearances. Through Gawan and Orgeluse, the initiate-speaker learns to stop and discipline impulsiveness, to make imaginative leaps between worlds through metaphor, and to discriminate and sort things out (particularly pride). He or she learns to bring gesture into speech, to practice poetic expression in praise, storytelling and playful performance, and to practice forms of contemplative speaking. Orgeluse and Gawan are "doers;" they make things appear by doing.

Parzival and Condwiramurs, so invisible or inscrutable much of the time in the story, are very different. They constitute the space between the lines in the labyrinth, representing the meaning drawn from the invisible, inaudible dimension of language. As the silent, speaking presence in the initiate-speaker, they teach about the source that is silence, about imagination and memory, about timing, timelessness and transience, about faith and faithfulness. They transmit the quality of understanding that bestows depth and significance on speaking and makes speech more than mere talk. They are the "being" within the speaking (and the speaker's awareness of being speaker).

Finally, Feirefiz and Repanse de Schoye are married. Feirefiz's arrival facilitates Parzival's movement to the Grail castle. Repanse de Schoye's appointed task of carrying the Grail moves it first toward Parzival and then toward Feirefiz. Feirefiz and Repanse de Schoye, who immediately leave the Grail castle to spread Christ's message in the East, animate the movement through the labyrinth. Their gifts of improvisation, ceremonial sensibility, generosity and service, move the initiate-speaker toward becoming food for an ever-widening community of others. They keep the initiate-speaker moving through the labyrinth, and, we can assume, keep the labyrinth itself moving, spiraling like the great galaxy that holds the whirling earth.

In coming to know and marry all of these characters within, we discover that we are, each one of us, a labyrinth and, at the same time, we learn to dance the labyrinth. Probably no moment arrives when the initiate-speaker can claim the cloak of bird-feathers once and for all. Increasingly, however, the initiate-speaker will develop a sense of dancing in the labyrinth rather than laboring fearfully through it. After sufficient circling and cycling through the labyrinth (wandering like Parzival with the reins loose on his horse), the initiate-speaker will discover that, as Kerenyi says, the labyrinth and

the spiral . . . are to be taken as paths on which one involuntarily goes back to the beginning. Thus the present-day notion of a labyrinth as a place where one can lose one's way must be set aside. It is a confusing path, hard to follow without a thread, but, provided one is not devoured at the mid-point, it leads surely, despite twists and turns, back to the beginning.[12]

When the initiate-speaker awakens to the vision of the speech of the Grail, meandering becomes journeying, and a subtle but definitive sense of personal "purpose" or even cosmic "destiny" begins to infuse the initiate-speaker's awareness of human life. As Kerenyi further recalls from ancient Crete: "The labyrinth suggested by meanders and spirals was a place of processions and not of hopelessness, even though it was a place of death."[13]

> There resulted a classical picture of this procession, which originally
> led by way of concentric circles and surprising turns to the decisive
> turn in the center, where one was obliged to rotate on one's own axis
> in order to continue the circuit.[14]

The initiate-speaker will eventually realize, at one of those decisive turns, that the labyrinth is mysteriously "a passage to the
light."[15] Medieval architects encoded this insight in stone and glass,
as Sig Lonegren recollects:

> Perhaps you're familiar with the magnificent stained glass rose win-
> dow that is directly above the main door of the nave at Chartres. It
> is the same distance above the floor as the labyrinth is down the
> nave from the front door. The circular rose window and the Chartres
> Labyrinth are the same size. If you could imagine there being a
> hinge at the end of the nave where the main doors are, and if you
> could fold the front facade down toward the altar, the rose window
> could lie directly on top of, and would be congruent with, the
> labyrinth. The light of that famous window, and the darkness of the
> pilgrimage are one.[16]

With that realization, the initiate-speaker will share the sense of
victory that Theseus celebrated — after *his* adventure in the Cretan
labyrinth — by teaching youths and maidens to dance the
labyrinthine movements of cranes at mating time. The ancients associated this ring-dance with the sun,[17] and thus, in East and West
alike, cranes are associated with longevity, for they are apparently
able — by dancing perhaps? — to prevail in all the sun's seasons. The
cranes' dancing, of course, always preceded flight — nine steps, and
then a leap to flight.[18] And, in flying, wonder of wonders, according
to Beryl Rowland's sources, the cranes inscribe the sky with the
alphabet:

> The cranes' flight was said to have inspired the invention of letters.
> The birds fly in v-formation and the characters of all early alpha-
> bets nicked with a knife on bark or on clay tablets were naturally
> angular. . . . According to the fables of Hyginus, the curator of the
> Palatine Library under Augustus, Mercury invented certain letters of
> the alphabet after watching the flight of cranes "which make letters
> as they fly." Mercury's counterpart in Egypt was Thoth, the god

whose symbol was the crane-like white ibis, and he too was credited with inventing hieroglyphs.[19]

Learning to dance the labyrinth, as the cranes teach, enables the initiate-speaker to leap toward that flight in which the alphabet is inscribed in the air — words soaring, fluttering, diving, flapping, hovering, floating, circling on the currents of the breath. In those moments of flight, the initiate-speaker wears the cloak of bird-feathers, and, somewhere in the nest of memory, high, sweet bells peal their approval.

The Movement

There are two ways to dance a labyrinth. Either the path between the lines or the lines themselves can be the way. The two produce slightly different experiences. If the path is between the lines, one arrives at an inner sanctum where one can stay or, "turning on one's own axis" and backtracking, can return to the entrance and the beginning. But, if the lines are the path, then the movement is continuous, in and out, back and forth. Here, the path from innermost to outermost is direct; no backtracking, just spiraling.

NOTES

[1] Northrop Frye, *Words with Power: Being a Second Study of the Bible and Literature,* 96.

[2] Alwyn Rees and Brinley Rees, *Celtic Heritage: Ancient Tradition in Ireland and Wales,* 346.

[3] Caitlin Matthews, *Elements of the Celtic Tradition,* 49. On page 36 of the same study, Matthews mentions that both men and women were druids.

[4] Matthews, 50, quoting *Sanas Chormaic* (Cormac's Glossary). Alwyn and Brinley Rees also refer to the cloak of bird-feathers which, they suggest, was similar to garments worn by Siberian shamans. Matthews notes the similarity of feathery garb worn ceremonially by Maori tribespeople in New Zealand (also page 50).

[5] Matthews, 45.

[6] Matthews, 37, states: "The distinctions between king and druid are sometimes blurred in Celtic tradition. For though the king is assumed the leader of his people it is the druid who really rules, for his or her word is law."

[7] The "return" phase of any initiatory experience in our times (whether it be an illness, death or loss of someone or something significant in one's life, birth of a child, change of vocation, etc.) is problematical. The transformation resulting from the initiatory journey is not often easy to display or even talk about, and the community — if there is one at all for the initiate — often fails to recognize that the person has undergone an initiatory experience and therefore offers no acknowledgment.

[8] I am grateful to James Hillman for the distinction between image and symbol that he often makes in his writings. For example, in *Re-visioning Psychology*, he warns that "we sin against the imagination whenever we ask an image for its meaning, requiring that images be translated into concepts," 39.

[9] Werner Glas, *An Analytical Study of the Rhetorical Thought of Rudolf Steiner with Some Implications for the Teaching of Speech,* 225.

[10] Allan B. Chinen, *In the Ever After: Fairy Tales and the Second Half of Life,* 149.

[11] Anna Morduch points out, "in German the word *Demut* (humility) is connected with the word *Mut* (courage)." (*The Sovereign Adventure: The Grail of Mankind,* 86).

[12] C. Kerenyi, *Dionysos: Archetypal Image of Indestructible Life,* 92–93.

[13] Kerenyi, 94.

[14] Kerenyi, 96.

[15] Kerenyi, 94.

[16] Sig Lonegren, *Labyrinths: Ancient Myths and Modern Uses,* 43.

[17] Beryl Rowland, *Birds with Human Souls: A Guide to Bird Symbolism,* 31.

[18] Rowland quotes a statement from Polwart in 1605: "The crane must aye/Take nine steps ere shee flie." (32).

[19] Rowland, 34.

APPENDIX A

Parzival's Lineage

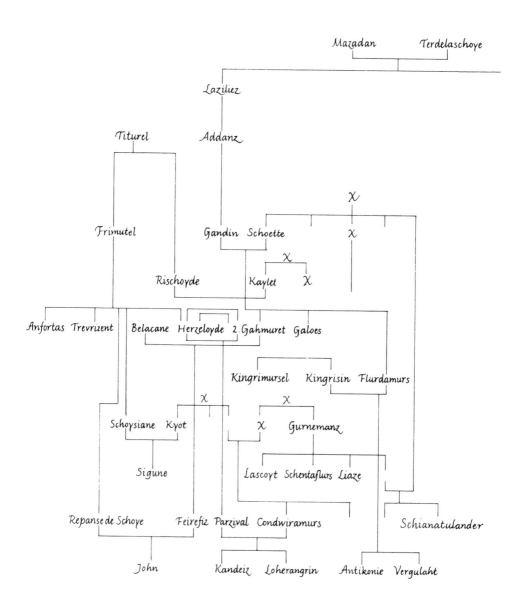

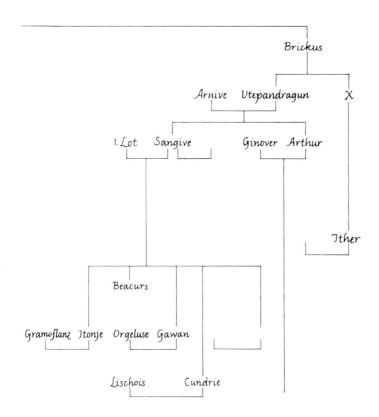

APPENDIX B

Major Characters in Parzival

ANFORTAS: The wounded Grail king

ANTANOR: Previously silent jester at Arthur's court who speaks when Parzival arrives

ANTIKONIE: King Vergulaht's sister whom Gawan tries to seduce

ARNIVE: Mother of Arthur

ARTHUR: King of the Knights of the Round Table; Gawan's uncle

BELACANE: Queen of Zazamanc; Gahmuret's first wife; mother of Feirefiz

BENE: Daughter of the ferryman Plippalinot

CLAMIDE: Undesired suitor of Condwiramurs; later, husband of Cunneware

CLINSCHOR: Magician; original lord of the Castle of Wonders

CONDWIRAMURS: Queen of Pelrapeire; wife of Parzival

CUNDRIE *LA SORCIÈRE*: Loathly messenger of the Grail; sister of Malcreatiure

CUNDRIE: Gawan's sister; Sangive's daughter

CUNNEWARE: Maiden who laughs when Parzival appears; sister of Orilus; later, wife of Clamide

FEIREFIZ: Parzival's half-brother; son of Gahmuret and Belacane

GAHMURET: Father of Feirefiz and Parzival; husband of Belacane and, later, Herzeloyde

GAWAN: Cousin of Parzival; nephew of Arthur

GINOVER: Wife of Arthur; Queen of the Round Table

GRAMOFLANZ: Undesired suitor of Orgeluse; later, husband of Itonje

GURNEMANZ: Aged knight; mentor of Parzival

HERZELOYDE: Mother of Parzival; Gahmuret's second wife

ITHER: The Red Knight; Arthur's cousin whom Parzival kills

ITONJE: Gawan's sister; beloved of Gramoflanz

JESCHUTE: Orilus's wife from whom young Parzival steals kiss, ring and brooch

KARDEIZ: One of Parzival and Condwiramur's twin sons

KEIE: Arthur's steward

LIAZE: Daughter of Gurnemanz

LIPPAUT: A prince; father of Obie and Obilot

LISCHOIS GWELLJUS: A knight of Orgeluse; later, husband of Cundrie

LOHERANGRIN: Twin son of Parzival and Condwiramurs who becomes the Swan Knight

MALCREATIURE: Dwarf brother of Cundrie *la sorcière*

MELJANZ: Suitor of Obie

OBIE: Older daughter of Lippaut; beloved of Meljanz

OBILOT: Lippaut's younger daughter who chooses Gawan as her knight

ORGELUSE: Duchess of Logrois; beloved, eventually wife, of Gawan

ORILUS: Husband of Jeschute; brother of Cunneware

PARZIVAL: Son of Gahmuret and Herzeloyde; destined to be Grail king

PLIPPALINOT: A ferryman; father of Bene

REPANSE DE SCHOYE: Carrier of the Grail; Parzival's aunt; later, wife of Feirefiz

SANGIVE: Mother of Gawan

SCHIANATULANDER: Dead knight; beloved of Sigune

SECUNDILLE: Queen in the East; first wife of Feirefiz

SIGUNE: Mourning widow of Schianatulander

TREVRIZENT: A hermit; brother of Anfortas; uncle of Parzival

VERGULAHT: King of Ascalan; brother of Antikonie; Gawan's accuser

References

Applebaum, David. *Voice*. Albany: State U of NY, 1990.

—. *Everyday Spirits*. Albany: State U of NY, 1993.

Barfield, Owen. *Speaker's Meaning*. Middletown, CT: Wesleyan UP, 1967.

Bateson, Mary Catherine. *Composing a Life*. New York: Penguin, 1990.

Baur, Alfred. *Healing Sounds: Fundamentals of Chirophonetics*. Fair Oaks, CA: Rudolf Steiner College Press, 1993.

Baynes, H.G. *Mythology of the Soul*. London: Methuen, 1949.

Beane, Wendell C., and William G. Doty. *Myths, Rites, Symbols: A Mircea Eliade Reader,* Vols. 1 and 2. New York: Harper, 1975.

Berendt, Joachim-Ernst. *The Third Ear: On Listening to the World*. New York: Henry Holt & Co., 1988.

Berman, Morris. *The Reenchantment of the World*. New York: Bantam, 1981.

Berry, Patricia. *Echo's Subtle Body: Contributions to Archetypal Psychology*. Dallas, TX: Spring, 1982.

Berry, Wendell. *Standing by Words: Essays by Wendell Berry*. San Francisco: North Point, 1983.

Bly, Robert. *Leaping Poetry: An Idea with Poems and Translations*. Boston: Beacon, 1972.

—. *News of the Universe: Poems of Twofold Consciousness*. San Francisco: Sierra Club Books, 1980.

—. *Selected Poems of Rainer Maria Rilke: A Translation from the German and Commentary by Robert Bly*. New York: Harper, 1981.

—. *A Little Book on the Human Shadow*. Memphis: TN: Raccoon, 1986.

Boer, Charles, trans. *The Homeric Hymns*. Dallas, TX: Spring, 1970.

Briggs, John, and F. David Peat. *Turbulent Mirror: An Illustrated Guide to Chaos Theory and the Science of Wholeness*. New York: Harper, 1989.

Brown, Norman O. *Love's Body*. New York: Vintage, 1966.

—. *Hermes the Thief*. Great Barrington, MA: Lindisfarne, 1990.

Buber, Martin. *I and Thou.* New York: Scribner's, 1958.

Burckhardt, Titus. *Alchemy: Science of the Cosmos, Science of the Soul.* Baltimore, MD: Penguin, 1960.

Butler, Katy. "Poetry as a Path." *Common Boundary* Nov./Dec. 1991: 16–23.

Campbell, Joseph. *The Masks of God: Creative Mythology.* New York: Viking, 1968.

Casey, Edward. *Spirit and Soul: Essays in Philosophical Psychology.* Dallas, TX: Spring, 1991.

Chernin, Kim. *Reinventing Eve: Modern Woman in Search of Herself.* New York: Harper, 1987.

Chinen, Allan B. *In the Ever After: Fairy Tales and the Second Half of Life.* Wilmette, IL: Chiron, 1989.

—. *Once Upon a Midlife: Classic Stories and Mythic Tales to Illuminate the Middle Years.* Los Angeles: Jeremy P. Tarcher, 1992.

Dicenso, James Joseph. *Hermeneutics and the Disclosure of Truth: A Study in the Thought of Heidegger, Gadamer and Ricoer.* Diss. Syracuse U, 1988. Ann Arbor: UMI, 1989.

Dooling, D.M. *A Way of Working: The Spiritual Dimension of Craft.* New York: Parabola Books, 1979.

Downing, Christine. *The Goddess: Mythological Images of the Feminine.* New York: Crossroad, 1981.

Duerr, Hans Peter. *Dreamtime: Concerning the Boundary Between Wilderness and Civilization.* Trans. Felicitas Goodman. Oxford, Eng.: Basil Blackwell, 1985.

Elbow, Peter. Appendix essay. "The Doubting Game and the Believing Game — An Analysis of the Intellectual Enterprise." *Writing Without Teachers.* New York: Oxford UP, 1973. 147–91.

Eliade, Mircea. *Rites and Symbols of Initiation.* New York: Harper, 1958.

—. *The Forge and the Crucible: The Origins and Structures of Alchemy.* Chicago: U of Chicago P, 1962.

Eliot, T.S. *Collected Poems, 1909–1962.* New York: Harcourt, 1963.

Ewing, Lee B. "Exploring the Near at Hand: An Interview with Richard Nelson." *Parabola* Summer 1991: 35–43.

Fideler, David R. "The Path Toward the Grail: The Hermetic Sources of Wolfram von Eschenbach's *Parzival.*" *Alexandria* 1991. Grand Rapids, MI: Phanes Press, 1991: 187–227.

Fierz-David, Linda. *Women's Dionysian Initiation: The Villa of Mysteries in Pompeii.* Dallas, TX: Spring, 1988.

Franz, Marie-Louise von. *An Introduction to the Interpretation of Fairytales.* Dallas, TX: Spring, 1970.

—. *The Feminine in Fairy Tales.* Dallas, TX: Spring, 1972.

—. *The Psychological Meaning of Redemption Motifs in Fairy Tales.* Toronto: Inner City, 1980.

Frye, Northrop. *The Great Code: The Bible and Literature.* San Diego: Harcourt, 1982.

—. *Words with Power: Being a Second Study of the Bible and Literature.* San Diego: Harcourt, 1990.

Glas, Werner. *An Analytical Study of the Rhetorical Thought of Rudolf Steiner with Some Implications for the Teaching of Speech.* Diss. Wayne State U, 1977. Ann Arbor: UMI, 1991. 48106.

Goethe, Johann Wolfgang von. *The Fairy Tale of the Green Snake and the Beautiful Lily.* Trans. Thomas Carlyle. New York: Steinerbooks, 1979.

Goodrich-Dunn, Barbara. Interview. "Walking the Critical Path." By Morris Berman. *Common Boundary* July/Aug. 1991: 12–21.

Grahl, Ursula. *The Wisdom in Fairy Tales.* London: New Knowledge, 1955.

Hall, Nor. *The Moon and the Virgin: Reflections on the Archetypal Feminine.* New York: Harper, 1980.

A Handbook of Christian Theology. New York: Meridian, 1958.

Harrell, John. *Origins and Early Traditions of Storytelling.* Kensington, CA: York, 1983.

Havelock, Eric A. *The Muse Learns to Write: Reflections on Orality and Literacy from Antiquity to the Present.* New Haven, CT: Yale UP, 1986.

Heidegger, Martin. *On the Way to Language.* Trans. Peter D. Hertz. New York: Harper, 1971.

—. *Poetry, Language, Thought.* Trans. Albert Hofstadter. New York: Harper, 1971.

Hillman, James. *The Myth of Analysis: Three Essays in Archetypal Psychology.* New York: Harper, 1972.

—. *Re-Visioning Psychology.* New York: Harper, 1975.

—. "Further Notes on Images." *Spring* 1978. Dallas, TX: Spring, 1978: 152–82.

—. "Peaks and Vales: The Soul/Spirit Distinction as Basis for the Differences Between Psychotherapy and Spiritual Discipline." *Puer Papers*. Dallas, TX: Spring, 1979. 54–74.

—. "The Thought of the Heart." *Eranos Lectures 2*. Dallas, TX: Spring, 1981.

—. *Healing Fiction*. Barrytown, NY: Station Hill, 1983.

Huizinga, Johan. *Homo Ludens: A Study of the Play Element in Culture.* Boston: Beacon, 1950.

Hycner, Richard H. *Between Person and Person: Toward a Dialogical Psychotherapy.* Highland, NY: The Gestalt Journal, 1988.

Hyde, Lewis. *The Gift: Imagination and the Erotic Life of Property.* New York: Vintage, 1979.

Illich, Ivan, and Barry Sanders. *ABC: The Alphabetization of the Popular Mind.* New York: Vintage, 1988.

Johnston, Charles. *The Creative Imperative.* Berkeley: Celestial Arts, 1984/86.

Jung, C.G. *Memories, Dreams, Reflections.* New York: Random, 1961.

—. *Analytical Psychology: Its Theory and Practice.* New York: Vintage, 1968.

Jung, Emma, and Marie-Louise von Franz. *The Grail Legend.* Boston: Sigo, 1980.

Kahane, Henry and Renee. *The Krater and the Grail: Hermetic Sources of the Parzival.* Urbana: U of Illinois P, 1965.

Kahn, Judith. *The Hebrew Bible as a Journey Through Consciousness.* Project Demonstrating Excellence. Graduate School of the Union Institute, 1991.

Kerenyi, C. *Dionysos: Archetypal Image of Indestructible Life.* Princeton, NJ: Princeton UP, 1976.

King, Nancy. "Myth, Metaphor, Memory: Archaeology of the Self." *Journal of Humanistic Psychology* Spring 1990: 55–72.

Kühlewind, Georg. "The Pedagogy of the Word: A *Towards* Interview with Georg Kühlewind." *Towards* Summer/Fall 1984: 8–13.

—. *Becoming Aware of the Logos: The Way of St. John the Evangelist.* West Stockbridge, MA: Lindisfarne, 1985.

—. *Forgiving.* Ghent, NY: Adonis, 1986.

—. *The Logos-Structure of the World: Language as a Model of Reality.* Hudson, NY: Lindisfarne, 1986.

—. Interview. "Thinking and Higher Consciousness." *Towards* Fall 1987: 36–40.

—. *From Normal to Healthy: Paths to the Liberation of Consciousness.* Great Barrington, MA: Lindisfarne, 1988.

Lain Entralgo, Pedro. *The Therapy of the Word in Classical Antiquity.* Trans. L.J. Rather and John M. Sharp. New Haven, CT: Yale UP, 1970.

Layard, John. *A Celtic Quest: Sexuality and Soul in Individuation.* Dallas, TX: Spring, 1975.

Levertov, Denise. *The Poet in the World.* New York: New Directions, 1960.

Lewis, Richard, ed. and trans. *Love, Marriage, Sex in the Light of Spiritual Science: Excerpts from the Work of Rudolph Steiner.* Sacramento, CA: By the Author, 3506 Eisenhower Drive, n.d.

Lewis, Richard. "The First Question of All." *Parabola* Fall 1988: 22.

Lievegoed, Bernhard J. *Towards the 21st Century.* Vancouver, Canada: Steiner Book Centre, 1972.

—. *Man on the Threshold: The Challenge of Inner Development.* Stroud, UK: Hawthorn Press, 1985.

Lockhart, Russell A. *Words as Eggs: Psyche in Language and Clinic.* Dallas, TX: Spring, 1983.

—. *Psyche Speaks: A Jungian Approach to Self and World.* Wilmette, IL: Chiron, 1987.

Lonegren, Sig. *Labyrinths: Ancient Myths and Modern Uses.* Glastonbury, Eng.: Gothic Images, 1991.

Loomis, Roger Sherman. *The Grail: From Celtic Myth to Christian Symbol.* Princeton: Princeton UP, 1963.

Lopez-Pedraza, Rafael. *Hermes and His Children.* Zurich: Spring, 1977.

Luthi, Max. *Once Upon a Time: On the Nature of Fairy Tales.* Bloomington: U of Indiana P, 1970.

Matthews, Caitlin. *Elements of the Celtic Tradition.* Longmead, Shaftesbury, Dorset: Element, 1989.

—. *Arthur and the Sovereignty of Britain.* London: Arkana, 1989.

Matthews, John. *The Elements of the Grail Tradition.* Longmead, Shaftesbury, Dorset: Element, 1990.

—. *Gawain: Knight of the Goddess.* Wellingborough, Northamptonshire, Eng.: Aquarian, 1990.

Maturana, Humberto R., and Francisco J. Varela. *The Tree of Knowledge: The Biological Roots of Human Understanding.* Boston: Shambhala, 1988.

Merry, Eleanor C. *The Flaming Door: The Mission of the Celtic Folk-Soul.* 1936. Edinburgh: Floris, 1962.

Miller, David. *Gods and Games: Toward a Theology of Play.* New York: World, 1970.

—. "Through a Looking Glass: The World as Enigma." *Eranos Yearbook, 1986* vol. 55, 1987: 349–402. (Eranos Foundation, Ascona, Switzerland)

Monaghan, Patricia. *The Book of Goddesses and Heroines.* New York: Dutton, 1981.

Morduch, Anna. *The Sovereign Adventure: The Grail of Mankind.* Cambridge, Eng.: James Clarke, 1970.

Moyne, John, and Coleman Barks. *Open Secret: Versions of Rumi.* Putney, VT: Threshold, 1984.

Munro, Eleanor. *On Glory Roads: A Pilgrim's Book About Pilgrimage.* New York: Thames and Hudson, 1987.

Nelson, Richard. *The Island Within.* New York: Random House, 1991.

Oliver, Mary. *House of Light.* Boston: Beacon, 1990.

Ong, Walter. *Orality and Literacy: The Technologizing of the Word.* London: Methuen, 1982.

Otto, Walter F. *Dionysos: Myth and Cult.* Dallas, TX: Spring, 1965.

Palmer, Parker. *To Know as We Are Known: A Spirituality of Education.* New York: Harper, 1983.

Paris, Ginette. *Pagan Grace: Dionysos, Hermes and the Goddess Memory in Daily Life.* Dallas, TX: Spring, 1990.

Picard, Max. *The World of Silence.* 1948. Trans. Stanley Goodman. Washington, DC: Regnery Gateway, 1988.

Querido, Rene. *The Mystery of the Holy Grail: A Modern Path of Initiation.* Fair Oaks, CA: Rudolf Steiner College, 1991.

Rees, Alwyn and Brinley Rees. *Celtic Heritage: Ancient Tradition in Ireland and Wales.* London: Thames and Hudson, 1961.

Renault, Mary. *The Praise Singer.* London: Book Club Associates, 1978.

Rowland, Beryl. *Birds with Human Souls: A Guide to Bird Symbolism.* Knoxville: U of Tennessee P, 1978.

Sardello, Robert. *Facing the World with Soul: The Reimagination of Modern Life*. Hudson, NY: Lindisfarne, 1992.

—. *Introduction to Psychoanalysis and Spiritual Psychology by Rudolf Steiner,* Hudson, NY: Anthroposophic Press, 1990.

Schoen, Stephen. "Psychotherapy as Sacred Ground." *Journal of Humanistic Psychology* Winter 1991: 51–55.

Schwenk, Theodor. *Sensitive Chaos*. London: Rudolf Steiner Press, 1965.

Spangler, David, and William Irwin Thompson. *Reimagination of the World: A Critique of the New Age, Science and Popular Culture*. Santa Fe, NM: Bear, 1991.

Spock, Marjorie. *Group Moral Artistry I: Reflections on Community Building*. Spring Valley, NY: St. George, 1983.

—. *Group Moral Artistry II: The Art of Goethean Conversation*. Spring Valley, NY: St. George, 1983.

Stafford, William. *An Oregon Message*. New York: Harper, 1987.

Stein, Walter Johannes. *The Death of Merlin: Arthurian Myth and Alchemy*. Edinburgh: Floris, 1984.

—. *The Ninth Century and the Holy Grail*. London: Temple Lodge, 1988.

Steindl-Rast, Brother David. "Paths of Obedience: Fairy Tales and the Monk's Way." *Parabola* Aug. 1980, 33–43.

Steiner, Rudolf. *An Outline of Occult Science*. Spring Valley, NY: Anthroposophic Press, 1950.

—. *The Alphabet*. Spring Valley, NY: Mercury, 1982.

—. *The Realm of Language and the Lost Unison Between Speaking and Thinking*. Spring Valley, NY: Mercury, 1984.

—. *How To Know Higher Worlds*. Hudson, NY: Anthroposophic Press, 1994.

—. *Intuitive Thinking As a Spiritual Path*. Hudson, NY: Anthroposophic Press, 1995. [formerly entitled *The Philosophy of Freedom*]

Sussman, Linda. "Creating Personal Myth." Master's thesis. U of Redlands, 1981.

Thompson, William Irwin. *The Time Falling Bodies Take to Light: Mythology, Sexuality and the Origins of Culture*. New York: St. Martin's, 1981.

—. *Imaginary Landscape: Making Worlds of Myth and Science*. New York: St. Martin's, 1989.

Tomatis, Alfred A. *The Conscious Ear.* Barrytown, NY: Station Hill, 1991.

Turner, Victor. *Dramas, Fields and Metaphors: Symbolic Action in Human Society.* Ithaca, NY: Cornell UP, 1974.

—. *The Anthropology of Performance.* New York: PAJ, 1986.

van der Post, Laurens. "The Creative Pattern in Primitive Africa." *Eranos Lectures 5.* Dallas, TX: Spring, 1957.

—. *About Blady — A Pattern Out of Time.* New York: William Morrow & Co., 1991.

Vanstone, W.H. *The Stature of Waiting.* London: Darton, Longman and Todd, 1982.

Weston, Jessie. *From Ritual to Romance.* Gloucester, MA: Peter Smith, by arrangement with Cambridge UP, 1957.

Wheelwright, Philip. *Metaphor and Reality.* Bloomington, IN: U of Indiana P, 1962.

Whitmont, Edward C. *Return of the Goddess.* New York: Crossroad, 1982.

Wiggins, James B., ed. *Religion as Story.* New York: UP of America, 1975.

Wilkinson, Roy. *The Origin and Development of Language.* Stroud, Eng.: Hawthorn Press, 1992.

Wolfram von Eschenbach. *Parzival.* Trans. Helen M. Mustard and Charles E. Passage. New York: Vintage, 1961.

Wolkstein, Diane. *The First Love Stories.* New York: Harper Collins, 1991.

Wolkstein, Diane, and Samuel Noah Kramer. *Inanna: Queen of Heaven and Earth.* New York: Harper, 1983.

Zimmer, Heinrich. *The King and the Corpse: Tales of the Soul's Conquest of Evil.* Princeton, NJ: Princeton UP, 1948.

Zimmerman, Jack, and Virginia Coyle. "Council: Reviving the Art of Listening." *Utne Reader* Mar./Apr. 1991: 79–85.

Acknowledgements

The success of any Grail quest depends on the seeker's community, and I have many people to thank for their contributions to my journey. I can mention here only those who have been most fundamentally and recently of help, but my gratitude extends to all those who have been teachers, friends and fellow travelers. Among these, first thanks goes to my parents, Robert and Opal Sussman, who provided the foundation.

This book began as a doctoral dissertation in spiritual psychology and oral tradition at The Union Institute, and I am deeply grateful to my doctoral committee, Doctors David Miller, Hugh Redmond, Penny MacElveen-Hoehn, Robert McAndrew, Terrell Beck and Nina Ross, who were part of the company of my Round Table for almost five years. Along with them, offering encouragement and compassionate listening, were friends Dee Packard and Deborah Ham and my sister Marjorie Iburg. In addition, the company has included several teachers who became friends and whose work, so important for my own, was developed largely outside academic or institutional settings, sometimes with considerable personal sacrifice. I acknowledge educator Dr. Jack Zimmerman, storyteller Laura Simms and voice teacher Richard Armstrong for the long years they have devoted to their respective crafts. Deserving special mention is storyteller Susan Strauss, a friend and colleague, whose passion to serve the environmental movement with her art prompted my awareness that the renewal of speaking is vital for the wider ecology.

My son, Ram, growing from child to young man during these years of study and writing, has kept my life from becoming stagnant. Being his parent presents me daily the most challenging opportunities for brave improvisation, and his wit and playfulness invited lovely laughter, a precious gift after long days alone with books and typewriter.

I thank publisher Christopher Bamford of Lindisfarne Press for his supportive interest in this book and for selecting Susan Roberts and Andy Cooper as editors. Their insightful comments and questions during the revising stimulated me to think ideas through more completely, to sing them more clearly. Finally, I am grateful to Dr. Robert Sardello, whose long-time involvement with the Grail story, archetypal psychology and anthroposophy parallels my shorter engagement with all three, for writing the inspiring foreword for this volume.